T0339680

OF HERDS AND HERMITS

OF HERDS AND HERMITS

AMERICA'S LONE WOLVES AND SUBMISSIVE SHEEP
OR
THE AMERICAN INTELLECTUAL AS LONER AND OUTCAST

Terry Reed

Algora Publishing
New York

Library of Congress Cataloging-in-Publication Data —

Reed, Terry, 1937-
  Of herds and hermits : America's lone wolves and submissive sheep / Terry Reed.
     p. cm.
  Includes bibliographical references and index.
  ISBN 978-0-87586-684-0 (pbk.: alk. paper) — ISBN 978-0-87586-685-7 (alk. paper)
— ISBN 978-0-87586-686-4 (e-book) 1. Individualism—United States. 2. Social role—
United States. 3. Group identity—United States. 4. Interpersonal relations—United
States. I. Title.

  HM1276.R44 2008
  302.5'40973—dc22
                        2008048536

Front Cover: Priest on Meadow with Sheep, © Christine Schneider/zefa/Corbis

Printed in the United States

In memory of my father
who opened the doors of possibility

TABLE OF CONTENTS

CHAPTER 1. THE BIKE AND THE BENCH

> Avoid as far as thou canst the tumult of men.... Many a time I wish that I had held my
> peace and had not gone amongst men.
> — Thomas à Kempis, *The Imitation of Christ* (1418)

The crucial decision to cultivate a life removed as possible from human contact is also a decision to reach for direction and meaning from within instead of without. It is a choice not to be taken lightly. The eminent sociologist David Riesman, whose *The Lonely Crowd* (1950) Richard Posner praised as "one of the all-time public-intellectual classics," raises the hypothetical question of whether, given a choice between two gifts, a boy might prefer a bicycle or a workbench. To select the bicycle is to opt for something more social, more outgoing and more public. To elect the bench is to favor a more private, contemplative, inward option. The selection is a critical one, inasmuch as it forecasts the sort of life one may anticipate. The stakes are high. To select the bicycle suggests a way of life that reaches out to others, invites their friendship, cultivates their company, nurtures their acceptance, relies upon them for support, guidance and direction in a variety of ways, among them educational, occupational, cultural, spiritual, political, financial and so forth. The theory is that to get along, one goes along. To rise in the world virtually demands that one work in concerted harmony with others who are in a position to advise and direct one's life because one cannot ably expect to do so unassisted. Such a person hangs, as they say, upon his peers' *every word*, always ferreting out counsel, always keeping his antennae activated for the purpose of inferring more precise signals on any of several fronts, among them which candidate to support, which shade of geraniums to plant, which brand of vodka to consume, which motion pictures to view, which charities to support, which tennis racket to brandish, which outfitter to patronize, which preparatory school to send his children. Moreover, such a person thrives upon approval and social acceptance. He walks a psychological tightrope, taking the utmost care never to place himself in any sort of social peril. All this is no laughing matter. He was graduated from the proper university where he elected the proper major in business administration, joined the proper fraternity, found the proper girl who had properly majored in elementary education and properly joined the proper sorority, properly married her, and joined the proper corporation. Make no mistake: if others approve of him, then he approves of himself.

The kid who requested a workbench, in front of which there is space for only one worker, is of a considerably different mentality. Such a person views himself and his destiny in ways quite different from our corporate friend. He has seen quite a bit of the world, and quite a bit of himself, concluding that he will administrate only himself, and not be burdened by other people, almost all of whom he candidly takes to be fools and dunces. He has learned not to solicit advice, except from professionals, and not to curry the friendship of people for whom he has no interest and quite possibly no respect. He has received the generous education he wants. He tells himself when to rise in the morning, what tasks to complete that day, and in what order. He sets his own goals and meets them. He has no wife, because he has too often seen the misery that marriage brings. He knows his best friend and most reliable counselor is himself. He reads what he wants, drinks what he wants, wears what he wants, views what he wants, eats what he wants, goes to bed when he wants, answers the telephone when he wants, wants what he wants — and gets it. He ignores invitations, solicitations, entreaties, and social obligations. Because he has managed to slough off a goodly proportion of life's detritus, he lives a better, happier, more prosperous life, enjoying good health and antisocial contentment. People refer to him disapprovingly as a loner.

Riesman is perhaps best remembered for distinguishing between those who are "inner" directed (thanks to the internalization of what he calls "adult authority accepted early in life") and those who are "other" directed. In other words he marked a line between those who take direction from inside as opposed to those who are guided by outside influences such as prevailing public opinion, peer pressure, and by what might be construed by the more naive as "common sense," something that the *Oxford English Dictionary* deprecatingly calls "the endowment of natural intelligence possessed by rational beings [of] normal or average understanding." Ralph Barton Perry, in his amusing introduction to philosophy published in the 1914 edition of Charles William Eliot's ambitious fifty volumes known as *The Harvard Classics*, argues that the discipline of philosophy begins by summarily dismissing common sense. He reminds us that "the absurdities of yesterday are the common sense of to-day, whereas the common sense of yesterday is now obsolete and quaint," adding that "the crank of the sixteenth century was the man who said that the earth moved; the crank of the twentieth century is the man who says it does not." Accordingly, this study argues that direction taken within is overwhelmingly to be preferred over messages that originate from without. It is obviously preferential, for example, to accept orders from the inside rather than to have the same orders barked from the outside by some confrontational drill sergeant or other swaggering buffoon.

The world has always celebrated individualism over collectivism. Homer's Achilles and Odysseus are classicism's hallmarks of inner direction. "Each individual, being complete in himself," Aristotle jotted down in his *Politics*, " will be in the same position as the others with respect to the whole." It was Cicero, that part actor, part courtroom orator, who opined, *Id maxime quemque decet, quod ist cujusque suum maxime* (that becomes anyone best which is most his own). In the opinion of classical historian H.D.F. Kitto, "The ancient Greeks, although they understandably preferred to be viewed as individuals, nevertheless yielded to participation communal activities. We must remember," Kitto averred, "how the Greek, individualist though he was, liked to work in groups, partly because he wanted to take part in what was going on, partly because he loved rivalry. This was to evolve, at least in Greek literature. In the fourth century," he reminds us, "there is more individualism. We can see it wherever we look in art, in philosophy, in life. Sculpture for instance becomes more introspective, to concern itself with individual traits, with passing moods, instead of trying to express the ideal or universal. In fact, it begins to portray men, not Man."[1] In his *On Liberty* (1859), John Stuart Mill, in defense of the supremely independent intellect, tells us that "Mankind can hardly be too often reminded, that there was once a man named Socrates, between whom and the legal authorities and public opinion

---

1 H.D.F. Kitto, *The Greeks* (New York: Penguin Books, 1951) 159.

of his time, there took place a memorable collision," referring, of course, to the death of Socrates as a martyr, represented at the conclusion of Plato's *Phaedo* where a mob converges upon and attempts to destroy an individual of transcendent genius.

English humanists such as John Colet, Desiderius Erasmus and Sir Philip Sidney attempted in English to reproduce the definitive elegance of Cicero's Latin prose which they assumed to have come from within Cicero's singular genius. Roughly a hundred years before the time of Colet, Erasmus and Sidney, the Italian Renaissance had given rise to its extraordinary Renaissance Man: the ideal and multifaceted gentleman, a privately contemplative titan of multiple if not universal intellect and talent, such as Michelangelo, Raphael and Leonardo, himself the artist (sculptor, painter, musician) and scientist (engineer, anatomist, geologist, botanist, architect, mathematician). To be sure, the *Pietà*, the *Deliverance of St. Peter*, and the *Mona Lisa* are not the collective blossoming of some team-playing committee. John Milton, in his *Of Christian Doctrine* (1656–60), has with full Miltonic force and authority defended the primacy of the individual by asserting that "Man is a living being, intrinsically and properly one and individual." He continued by insisting that "He is not double or separable: not, as is commonly thought, produced from and composed of two distinct and different elements, soul and body. On the contrary, the whole man is soul, and the soul man: a body, in other words, or individual substance: animated, sensitive and rational." The Swiss-born arch romantic Jean Jacques Rousseau (1712–1778) argued that men are essentially benevolent, provided that societal pressures do not corrupt them. In his *Confessions*, published in his 69th year, he asserted his sublime independence. "I alone," he wrote, "I know my heart, and I know men. I am not made like any of those I have seen; I dare to believe that I am not made like any of those who are in existence. If I am not better," he concluded, "at least I am different." Charles Darwin, of all people, felt the same way, but for altogether different reasons. "No one," he wrote in his chapter on variation in *The Origin of Species* (1859), "supposes that all the individuals of the same species are cast in the same actual mould."

Independence and individuality have generally been cherished, if eroding, aspects of the American character. American historian Carl Degler has rightly argued, "Try as the rulers of Massachusetts might make men to conform to their dogmas, their own rebellious example always stood as a guide to those who felt the truth was being denied. Such individualism, as we would call it today, was flesh and bone of the religion which the Puritans passed on."[1] Horace Greeley, the up-from-poverty American newspaper editor and 1872 presidential candidate who coined the phrase, "Go West, young man; Go West," said of Benjamin Franklin, the quintessential American renaissance figure, "Of the men whom the world currently terms Self-Made, that is, who severally fought their life-battles without the aid of inherited wealth, or family honors, or educational advantages, perhaps our American Franklin stands highest in the civilized world's regard.... I must place Franklin above [Washington] as the consummate type and flowering of human nature under the skies of colonial America.... [He] was great enough to write...after he had achieved power and world-wide fame, a frank, ingenuous confession of the youthful follies and sins [he had fathered two children out of wedlock] for the instruction and admonition of others." Referred to elsewhere as "a witty and benign backwoods sage [and] a sort of Rousseauistic Socrates," Franklin was enough the team player to assist in crafting the *Declaration of Independence*; nevertheless, he insisted in his celebrated *Autobiography* that "one man of tolerable abilities may work great changes, and accomplish great affairs among mankind."

After his celebrated ten-month American sojourn, 1831–1832, during which he was on assignment from the French government to evaluate American penitentiaries, Alexis de Tocqueville noted with approval that "Individualism is a calm and considered feeling which disposes each citizen to isolate himself from the mass of his fellows and withdraw into the circle of family and friends." Three years later Ralph Waldo Emerson (1803–1882) in his Harvard "Divinity School Address" (1838) asserted, "Let me admonish you, first of all, to go it alone." Harvard was more than happy to allow Emerson to go it alone and did not invite him back for 30 more years. In 1840, Emerson declared that in all his lectures he had taught one doctrine: "the infinitude of the private man." Among the first series of his essays, published in 1841, was "Self-Reliance," wherein Emerson, given to hammering the same points with relentless fervor, advised that one should "trust thyself: every heart vibrates to that iron string." William Ellery Channing (1780–1842), a leading New England intellectual remembered for his anti-Calvinism and his Unitarianism, argued in his essay "On the Elevation of the Laboring Classes" (1840) that rather than being "a mere part of a machine," the American laborer recognized his "importance as an individual" who "exists for his own sake, for the unfolding of his nature, for his own virtue and happiness."

---

1 Carl N. Degler, *Out of Our Past: The Forces That Shaped Modern America* (New York: Harper Colophon Books, 1959) 16.

It was in about 1835 that Emerson encountered Henry David Thoreau (1817–1862), 14 years his junior. Emerson later commented that Thoreau was a difficult man to know and remarked that he might be dismissed as a mere "captain of a huckleberry party." Others had similar reservations about Thoreau's authenticity. In 1842, Nathaniel Hawthorne (1804–1864), the American literary romanticist, observed, "Mr. Thorow [sic] dined with us yesterday. He is as ugly as sin, long-nosed, queer-mouthed and uncouth and somewhat rustic, although courteous in manner.... He had repudiated all regular forms of getting a living, and seems inclined to lead a sort of Indian life among civilized men." A classic proponent of American individualism and self-reliance, Henry's amazing independence of thought traces well beyond Franklin. "I am very familiar with all his thoughts," said Emerson defensively. "They are my own quite originally drest." Thoreau's *Walden* (1854), the product of eight years during which he, through an organic, inside-out process of manuscript development, prepared seven drafts and doubled its original length, made the results of his meditation known, and worked out his relatedness to his rustic environment. Walden Pond became the symbol of himself while his rhetoric became precise, speculative, colorful, sensuous, learned, scientific and humorous. *Walden* is record of a self-reliant man who wishes to "front only the essential facts of life." At the outset he explains that, "when I wrote the following pages, or rather the bulk of them, I lived alone, in the woods, a mile from any neighbor, in a house that I had built myself, on the shore of Walden Pond, in Concord, Massachusetts, and earned my living by the labor of my hands only. I lived there two years and two months. At present I am a sojourner in civilized life again." Henry had discovered and explored his solitary environment. Speaking as one solitary soul about another, abstruse literary scholar Guy Davenport speculated that had the opportunity availed itself, "Thoreau [being the naturalist that he was] would have married a woodchuck."[1]

Indeed, as long as there have been romanticists, there has been absorption with stand-alone men and women who comprise a higher, contemplative edge of society. "Romanticism," as Jacques Barzun explains, "places a higher value on the individual. According to some, it exaggerates the worth and powers of the individual man." Additionally, as he later comments, it "implies also creation, diversity and individual genius." Romanticism's primary tendencies have always centered upon psychology, sensibility (meaning that one allows one's feelings to become a conduit to truth, rather than

---

1 Guy Davenport, *The Geography of the Imagination* (San Francisco: North Point Press, 1981) 71.

relying upon reason as a guide), primitivism, love of nature, absorption with the past, mysticism, revolt against established restriction (as for instance how poetry should be written, how pictures should be painted, how music should be composed), and devotion to liberty, such as a passing fascination with the 1789 French Revolution with its short lived idealistic notion of disseminating liberty, equality and fraternity the world over. International romanticism tended to assert that God operates in ways more mystical than better-known rationalists such as John Locke and Isaac Newton could possibly explain. As a rule, romanticists embrace a tone of high seriousness, and view themselves with the straightest of faces, leaving little margin for levity. They prefer dark, legendary, anti-intellectual ("I loathe books," Rousseau wrote in his 1762 narrative *Emile*. "They only teach you how to speak about things of which you know nothing"), melancholic, forlorn, tragic, imaginative, indistinct, retrospective, long ago, away, remote, old, ruined, rustic, primitive, pastoral, wild, desolate, and emotional, especially when that emotion originated *straight-from-the-heart*. "Feeling is all," Goethe proclaimed in *Faust*, as if in three-word summary of what romanticism means. A more cheapened subspecies of romanticism is the gothic mode, characterized by its macabre preoccupation with terror associated with graveyards, funerals, corpses, ghouls, burials, crypts and coffins. Edgar Poe, a distinctive romanticist but not a cheap one, wrote in "The Premature Burial" (1844) about the "stifling of the hundred and twenty-three prisoners in the Black Hole at Calcutta," the "body-snatchers with which London abounds," and of his narrator's own live burial. He relied upon the Gothic mode and managed to get away with it without falling prey to escapism, wish fulfillment, daydreaming, fantasizing, lachrymose sentimentalism and nostalgia. Davenport remarked that "Poe's imagination was perfectly at home in geographics he had no knowledge of except what his imagination appropriated from other writers." Be the romanticism high brow or low, it always centered upon individualism, often in the form of supposedly salt-of the-earth common man and his common rustic language. Richard Hofstadter has characterized individualism less as "a high tolerance for deviance, eccentricity, non-conformity, privacy and dissent," but more something that afforded "favorable conditions for the development of personal assertiveness and ambition...material aspiration, self-confidence...aggressive morale [as well as] multiple opportunities for advancement and encourages the will to seize them." Individualism also, he continued, "may indicate the absence of mutuality or of common or collective effort in a society that supposedly functions almost as a conglomerate of individual atoms." In addition to designating "a more or less formal creed in which private action is at a premium and governmental action is condemned," he felt, it also served "as a synonym in short, for laissez-faire." Indeed, some sociological commentators have dismissed "society" as little more than an army of individuals.

American literature, like American life, trots out an astonishing gallery of romantic loners especially in the form of self-styled eccentrics. Major American writers and poets have to a person been subversively inclined, partly as a result of their being marginalized outside the American middle class main stream. A carpenter's son, Walt Whitman (1819–1891), for example, was the second of nine kids in the family farmhouse in West Hills, near Huntington, Long Island. The Whitmans were not an especially attractive bunch. Walt's brother Andy became a professional drunk; his brother Jesse contracted syphilis from a prostitute and died in a mental hospital. His brother Eddie was a crippled epileptic imbecile; his sister Hannah became a squalid, eccentric painter. Walt himself developed a preoccupation cleanliness and health, although in his last days he enjoyed neither. Moreover, he seemed to regard himself as backward: "I am a slow arriver," he remarked later in life. "I get there, but I always come in last." One of his landladies described him as slovenly, morose and withdrawn. By 1842 he had written a temperance novel called *Franklin Evans, or the Inebriate*, a piece of hackwork that he claimed to have cobbled together in three days while drunk. "It was damned rot," Whitman later conceded. "Not insincere, perhaps, but rot." At about this time he altered his image, transforming himself from slovenly, morose, and withdrawn into a dandy, a Brooklyn boulevardier. One observer caught a glimpse of Whitman decked out in a "frock coat and a high hat, [sporting] a small cane." At other stages in life he became what one commentator called "the full-bearded, sunburned, clean-limbed, vigorously sexed, burley common man." Emerson, in his 1844 essay entitled "The Poet," called for a native American poet, one who could synthesize the national experience, as partly illustrated by the various poses Whitman had attempted to carry off. It has even been suggested that homosexuals are availed to a more comprehensive view of humanity. "We have yet had no genius in America, with tyrannous eye, which knew the value of our incomparable materials," Emerson lamented. "Yet America is a poem in our eyes; its ample geography dazzles the imagination, and it will not wait long for metres." Whitman seemed then, and seems now, the fulfillment of Emerson's comprehensive all-encompassing American national poet — as if any common Joe on the street cared a good goddamn. In the meantime, however, he had apprenticed as a printer, worked for a lawyer and a doctor, tried his hand at teaching (although he had not been enrolled in any school since the age of 11), edited newspapers, campaigned for Martin Van Buren, carpentered, dabbled in real estate, become a battlefield nurse, pushed a pencil in the Army Paymaster's office and eventually morphed into a trademark identity as "the good gray poet," as his friend William Douglas O'Connor publicized him. O'Connor glorified Whitman as "massive and handsome with firm blue eyes; the eyebrows and eyelids especially showing that fullness of arch seldom seen save in the antique busts," drawing attention to the poet's "flowing hair and fleecy beard, both very gray, and tempering with a look of age the youthful aspect of one who is but forty-five." Bronson Alcott wrote with wonderment in his journal that Whitman "has never been sick, he says, nor taken medicine, nor sinned... a bachelor, he professes great respect for women." Indeed, although some criticized him for his homoeroticism, others found fault with his womanizing. He identified and introduced himself in "Song of Myself" when he wrote, "I am the man, I suffered, I was there." In a letter dated 21 July 1855, however, Emerson wrote him, "I greet you at the beginning of a great career." It was indeed a great career, beyond anything that Emerson might have imagined. In his last days, however, Whitman contracted pneumonia. A nurse assigned to provide his care reported, "It would be impossible to properly clean up the room he is in without removing him to another. The walls are too dusty to touch near his bed. The bed is infested with bugs and the carpet with moths.... I am now at a loss how to proceed." Whitman died after uttering his less than famous last words: "Help me up, Horace; I've got to shit." He may never have had the opportunity. We do know, however, that he was buried at Harleigh Cemetery in Camden, New Jersey.

Whitman adopted the expression "personalism" that Gay Wilson Allen has interpreted as "the term which [he] uses to cover his whole program, an all-round development of the self and the individual, including health, eugenics, education, cultivation of moral and social conscience, etc." Among his passions was a clarion call for "the great individual, fluid as Nature, chaste, affectionate, compassionate, fully armed." Allen also noted that Whitman's personalism "rejects institutionalized religion [whereas] a genuine, personal religious life is of paramount importance." Personalism fuses all these developments, including participation in politics and removing the inequality of women," Allen continued. "Since the future American democracy depends upon the development of great persons (or personalities) such as the world has known before, literature and art must not be imitative or derivative of other times or nations, for none of them possessed or attempted to achieve the great American dream of a transcendent democracy."[1] Whitman was bent upon establishing himself as a singular figure, proclaiming, "I celebrate myself, and sing myself, / for every atom belonging to me as good belongs to you." He invited criticism, as one commentator remarked, because of his playing the "inveterate poseur, androgynous, bisexual, elusive, power-seeking, libidinous — who set out naively to introduce poetry to the common man by absorbing the length and breadth of America." Like Emerson and Thoreau, Whitman considered his soul to be but a fragment of the world soul. Thoreau saw in Whitman "something a little more than human." Whitman, in the meantime, preferred to view himself as some innocent, primitive genius whose "barbaric yawp" emanated organically from the inside out.

His fierce independence of mind cost him dearly, however. The Providence *Journal* opined blatantly in 1897, "We struggle with those critics who have called him the greatest poet America has yet produced.... If everything else [other than 'O Captain! My Captain!' in remembrance of Lincoln] that Whitman wrote could be buried at the bottom of the sea the world would be better off.... But no sane and reasonably clean-minded person can possibly read the lines scattered with disgusting indecency through this foul volume [*Leaves of Grass*] and escape a violent attack of mental nausea.... Nothing was ever put to paper more deliberately vile and atrociously nasty than this stuff, which some critics profess to admire. And where there is no dirt there is plenty of drivel." Nevertheless, Walter Whitman elbowed a place for himself in the pantheon of world literature. Allen has duly noted that O. E. Lessing, who had published a piece called "The Walt Whitman Cult in Germany" in 1910, declared him "the center, summit, and fountain-head of the first great epoch in the intellectual life of the new world," and commenced to call Whitman "the greatest poet since Goethe," adding that "he is the embodiment, the representative, and the illuminator of American Literature in the same sense that Dante is of the Italian, Shakespeare of the English, and Goethe of the German."

Herman Melville, who like Whitman lived between 1819–1891, was a man of solitary habits, who went to sea at 20 as a ship's boy on the St. Lawrence to Liverpool, then two years later shipped as a common seaman aboard the whaling vessel *Acushnet* from New Bedford Harbor in Fairhaven to a four year sojourn in the South Seas, famously referring to his ship as "my Yale College & my Harvard," meaning that what he lacked in formal learning, he acquired by ambitious adventuring. Melville jumped ship in the Marquesas

---

1 Gay Wilson Allen, *Walt Whitman Handbook* (Chicago: Packard and Company, 1946) 191.

Islands and survived for a month as a guest of the cannibalistic Typees. Following his escape, he joined the crew of another whaler, this one called the *Lucy Ann*, from which he went ashore and managed to be detained in a state of "light confinement" as a mutineer. Escaped again, he passed the summer of 1842 in Maui and Honolulu, setting pins in a bowling alley. "From my 25th year I date my life," Melville wrote in 1843. Within five years, Melville set upon an extraordinary literary voyage that embraced such a range of literary forms as travel books, romances, allegories, satires, comedies, fantasies and realities. He spent all but six of his last discouraging years as a customs inspector (calling that assignment "an asylum for nonentities") at New York Harbor, and in a letter to Hawthorne declared in desperation, "all my books are botches."

Melvillian characters are isolates. His titanic one-legged Captain Ahab, whose name derives from one of the great and wicked kings of Israel cited in *I Kings* 16-22, looms large in *Moby Dick* (1851) where the narrator Ishmael remarks that after the sailing of the *Pequod*, Ahab "had hidden himself away with ... Grand-Lama-like exclusiveness." Melville biographer Newton Arvin saw in Ahab "the very rapture of ideal individualism: neither Carlyle nor Emerson nor Nietzsche ever uttered it more loftily," commenting later that "there is something of Prometheus, of Agamemnon, of Oedipus in Ahab: he is guilty of an inflated arrogance similar to theirs, a similar conviction of his superiority to the mass of ordinary men."[1] Similarly, in his seriocomic *Bartleby the Scrivener* (1853), Melville explicitly addresses the plight of the chronically detached individual pinned in the cross currents between individuality and conformity. Supporting characters Turkey, Nippers and Ginger Nut, eccentrics all, have, like Bartleby, no certain identities but respond only to nicknames. The best the narrator, an anonymous Wall Street lawyer, can say about himself and Bartleby is that they are "sons of Adam." It gradually becomes evident that the narrator and Bartleby, a 20-year-old (whose onerous task is to copy monotonous legal documents), are in every respect opposites. Bartleby is "one of those beings of whom nothing is ascertainable," and that he is "pallidly neat, pitiably respectable, incurably forlorn." He labors at a bench that offers no prospect of the outside world. At the outset he accomplishes an extraordinary amount of work, but thereafter develops a resistance to taking orders, announcing that he has "permanently given up copying." As one who applies what might be called "passive resistance," his response to directives is to say "I prefer not to." Through it all, he adamantly refuses to surrender

---

1 Newton Arvin, *Herman Melville* (New York: Viking, 1950) 175.

any personal information. Having in the end been confined to an actual New York lockup known as the Tombs, where he turns down an offer of preferential treatment, death carries him to his eternal destiny "with kings and counselors," a phrase borrowed from *Job*: 3:13–15. We learn afterward that Bartleby had supposedly "been a subordinate clerk in the Dead Letter Office at Washington." He is a misfit, a dropout, a prototypical dissenter who follows his own leadership but moves from one prison to another long enough to know that he cannot possibly march in step with the human race. While he settles for less and less, the narrator ever yearns for more and holds pecuniary interests above all, and yet develops a sense of responsibility toward his enigmatic ward whom he cannot find it in him to dismiss.

In the opening pages of *Benito Cereno* (1855) we encounter a ship christened the *San Dominick*, upon which the ironic inscription "Seguid vuestro jefe" (follow your leader) appears. Whereas the lawyer-narrator of *Bartleby* undergoes a gradual revelation about his enigmatic employee, here we encounter Captain Amasa Delano of the *Bachelor's Delight* who, vaguely perceiving that the *San Dominick* is in some sort of distress off the coast of Chile near an uninhabited island called St. Maria, boards her to render some sort of unspecified assistance. He too is by stages made aware that, as in *Bartleby*, amid apparent order there is disorder. It develops that the *San Dominick* en route to Lima from Buenos Aires carries a cargo of some 300 unfettered black slaves who, though their numbers have diminished, have staged a mutinous insurrection, unwittingly abetted by a crew of 50, many of whom were lost to storm and disease. The leader of the uprising is the cunning Babo, whose name suggests "babble," and "baboon," which is to say not much of a leader at all. "Sequid vuestro jeffe," therefore, carries an ambiguous message, inasmuch as the "negro slaves, amongst other valuable freight," have on the surface of it found a leader in Babo, not Amasa Delano with his propensity for fainting spells. The *San Dominick*, therefore, is bereft of any authority until the naive Delano assumes control and resumes the voyage to Lima, whereupon Babo is hanged. Cereno, having first repaired to a monastery, soon dies also and "did, indeed," we are told, "follow his leader." But there are, alas, no leaders to follow. Delano gradually sees Babo as the imposter he is: "some low-born adventurer, masquerading as an oceanic grandee; yet so ignorant of the first requisites of mere gentlemanhood as to be betrayed into the present remarkable indecorum." However, Delano is himself less able to lead, hopelessly misreading the nature of the slaves who fall under his command. "Most negroes," he muses, "are natural valets and hair-dressers; taking to the comb and brush congenially as to the castanets." Melville, who in *Moby Dick, Bartleby,* and *Billy Budd* seemed to recommend authority and order, at the same time undermines it by casting doubt on those who appear to represent it. The solitary Bartleby himself will never accede to authority. Neither, as we shall see, will the equally solitary Billy Budd.

Accordingly, *The Confidence-Man* (1857) reworks the basic pattern of a stranger's entering the company of a group, in the same manner that Ishmael boarded the *Pequod,* Bartleby hired into a Wall Street law firm, and Delano invited himself onboard the *San Dominick.* They illustrate the intrusion of a lone figure into an uncongenial, not to say treacherous, environment. This time Melville turned the tables and presented a professional fraud's intruding upon the company of a veritable ship (ironically christened the *Fidele*) of fools — on April Fools' Day. The confidence man is, in all eight of his guises, the devil, and his prey is the common herd comprised of a microcosmic cross section of humanity comparable to "Chaucer's Canterbury pilgrims or those oriental ones crossing the Red Sea towards Mecca in the festival month." In the 26th chapter the subject turns to Indian-hating and introduces an American backwoodsman, described as "a lonely man" who, regardless of external circumstances, "must continually look to himself. Hence self-reliance, "to the degree of standing by his own judgment, though it stand alone." In *Billy Budd,* the novella Melville began in 1888 (when he was 70), revised in 1889 and completed in 1891, five months before his death, but which was not published until 1924, finds its title character inclined again to civil disobedience. Melville likens him both to Christ and to the archetypal American Innocent, who has been impressed (read "drafted") from a ship called the *Indomitable,* and delivered, against his will, to serve on the *Atheist* where he has been assigned, appropriately enough, to the foretop as befits his divine, if illiterate, nature. As was true with Bartleby, Budd leaves an indelible mark after having been hanged for striking and killing an evil superior officer who accused him of conspiring to foment mutiny. The circumstances of his death are particularly telling. "At sea in the old time," we are informed, "the execution by halter of a military sailor was generally from the fore-yard. In the present instance, for special reasons the main-yard was assigned," signifying that, since this is a three-masted vessel, the condemned martyr is to be hanged from the center of three crosses. At the moment of his death, it chances that "the vapory fleece hanging low in the East was shot thro with a soft glory as of the fleece of the Lamb of God seen in mystical vision." For Melville, Budd was one more singular man, civilly disobedient to the end, a miraculous figure among the rabblement that has falsely accused him and ultimately failed.

Melville and Nathaniel Hawthorne, two constitutionally reclusive giants of American literature, met in 1850 when Hawthorne was 46, Melville 31, and when Hawthorne and his quietly ambitious wife, the former Sophia Peabody, occupied a residence known as the Red House at Lenox in the Berkshires. Referring to Melville, he wrote, "He is a little heterodox in the matter of clean linen." Hawthorne himself long developed unconventional, solitary habits, bowing neither to civic nor social pressures. In 1836 he jotted fragments of thought in his journal, among them that "In this dismal chamber fame was won," and then mused upon "a recluse, like myself, or prisoner, to measure time by the progress of sunshine through his chamber." In an 1837 letter to his Bowdoin classmate Henry Longfellow, he remarked that "You had me pictured as dwelling in an owl's nest; for mine is about as dismal; and, like the owl I seldom venture abroad until after dark." In isolation, partly inherited from his mother, Elizabeth Manning Hathorne (as it was then spelled), Hawthorne lived a solitary life. She took her meals alone, apart from Nathaniel and his sisters Elizabeth and Louisa. His father, a sea captain, presumably died from yellow fever in Surinam in South America when Hawthorne was four. Later, Nathaniel referred to their Salem, Massachusetts home on Herbert Street as "Castle Dismal," and commented to another Bowdoin classmate, Horatio Bridge, about "the gloom and chill of [his] early life." At Bowdoin his fellow undergraduates referred to him as "Oberon," a reference to the outermost of Uranus' larger satellites, but also to the fairy king and husband to Titania in Shakespeare's *Midsummer-Night's Dream*. In Hawthorne's all-but-forgotten "Journal of a Solitary Man" (1837), he refers in the third person to "my poor friend Oberon who 'sleeps with the silent ages.'" Oberon, he continues, "was a solitary man" who "never came up to the city except once in three months for the purpose of looking into a book-store." The "shrinking sensitiveness of his nature rendered him not misanthropic, but singularly averse to social intercourse." Oberon himself entertains the notion that he is to die "unwept, unhonored, and unsung." In 1841 Hawthorne, unlikely though it seems, attempted to join George Ripley's utopian socialist community called Brook Farm in West Roxbury, south of Boston. He stuck it out between April and November, then departed, dismissing the experiment as "a polar paradise." His sister Elizabeth, well understanding her brother's reclusive ways, counseled him against marrying Sophia on grounds that "the mingling of another mind" would "spoil the flower of his genius." Fortunately, nothing of the sort happened. To the contrary, it was she who encouraged him to compose *The Scarlet Letter* and who protected him from their three children and from the public at large until at least mid-afternoon when he completed his work. Henry James Sr. commented that Hawthorne "buried his eyes in a plate, and ate with such voracity that no person should dare to ask him a question." Hawthorne himself wrote in 1855, nine years prior to his death, "I have fewer friends than most men." Even so, he formed lifelong friendships with Bowdoin mates Bridge, Longfellow, and Franklin Pierce, the 14th president of the United States, in whose company Hawthorne died in Plymouth, New Hampshire on the night of May 18–19 in 1860.

If Hawthorne were the recluse he claimed to be, it seems inconsistent that he was not only married but contentedly so. In his published work, paradoxically, Hawthorne had ironically little use for loners, and yet the best known of his fictional characters is Hester Prynne, the courageous, independently-minded single mother in *The Scarlet Letter* (1850) who, in the opinion of some, is America's first literary heroine, representing as she does such virtues as strength, individuality, fortitude and transcendent goodness, despite having violated the Seventh Commandment. Like some of Melville's characters, she becomes a victimized protagonist likened at one point in this romance to a "Sister of Mercy," marginalized, to be sure, but not in the manner of Hawthorne's ugly outcasts, the template for which is the ill proportioned Roger Chillingworth, described as "a man of thought, the book-worm of great libraries, a man already in decay, having given [his] best years to feed the hungry dream of knowledge." What establishes Chillingworth as villain of *The Scarlet Letter* is his intellectuality coupled with his repudiation of heart, itself a major symbol of warmth, compassion, and community in Hawthorne's work. He is a kind of psychiatrist gone haywire and another of Hawthorne's dehumanized experimenters whose assumed name befits his frigid constitution. Like rapacious Professor Rappaccini in *Rappaccini's Daughter* (1844), Chillingworth is a cold-blooded intellectual who makes the emotional harassment of neurotic Arthur Dimmesdale his all consuming psychological experiment, using his knowledge as a physician to keep the moody cleric alive for the purpose of tormenting him emotionally for seven years. Why Hester married him remains unexplained, since it was neither for love nor money. There is a description of Chillingworth at the end of Chapter 2, depicting him as "a man well stricken in years, pale, thin, scholar-like visage, with eyes dim and bleared by the lamp-light that had served them to pore over many ponderous books," described as "the misshapen scholar" so absorbed in himself and the objects of his obsessions that he commits what Hawthorne later called the Unpardonable Sin of isolation from the community of human kind.

The Unpardonable Sin, first cited in "Ethan Brand," published a year after *The Scarlet Letter*, courses throughout Hawthorne's work and underscores his ironic disapproval of intellectual loners. Such a person is young Goodman Brown in Hawthorne's 1835 story of the same name. Brown, three months married, feels compelled to make a nocturnal errand into the wilderness for the general purpose of learning the degree to which evil motivates the human heart, and becomes consumed and debilitated by his own quest. "Silly fellow" that he is, he returns after a nightmarish, even orgiastic, interlude convinced that "evil is the nature of mankind." It divides him from the companionship of his wife and transforms him into "a stern, a sad, a darkly meditative, a distrustful, if not a desperate man" so obsessed with what he believed he learned that, when he "was borne to his grave a hoary corpse," those who followed his funeral procession "carved no hopeful verse upon his tombstone, for his dying hour was gloom." Similarly, in "Wakefield," also published in 1835, the title character (being an "intellectual, but not actively so") takes a 20-year furlough from his wife, as a "little joke." By contrast, however, "The Gray Champion," another 1835 sketch, highlights a messianic title character, heralded as "New England's hereditary spirit," a single-minded, benevolent authority figure.

There are not many gray champions in Hawthorne, however. John Endicott, sometimes spelled *Endecott* (1589? –1665), who was in real life the Calvinist governor of Massachusetts Bay Colony, is the villainous "Puritan of Puritans" in "The Maypole of Merry Mount" (1836). There we encounter Edgar and Edith, also known as the Lord and Lady of May, who are "to join in holy matrimony," after which Endicott and his "dark Puritans" do in the name of religious intolerance transform a blissful affair into a scene of "moral gloom" when, among other outrages, they destroy the Maypole, itself a fertility symbol, phallic and erotic. Endicott emerges alone in the center of a circle surrounded by "evil spirits in the presence of a dread magician." Hawthorne in "Endicott and the Red Cross" depicted Endicott's tearing the cross from a British flag to demonstrate his discontent with what he viewed as popery. Continuing with his gallery of abstracted loners, "The Birthmark" (1843) has its "man of science" in the person of Aylmer, whose name suggests "ailment" and who "had devoted himself, however, too unreservedly to scientific studies ever to be weaned from them by any second passion," that second passion being his wife Georgiana whom he manages inadvertently to kill after performing a little amateur dermatology to remove her facial birthmark in the form of a crimson hand-shaped spot, "the visible mark of earthly imperfection." Accordingly, to read "The Artist of the Beautiful" (1844) is to meet Owen Warland at war with the Philistines who surround him, and with his own fatal preoccupation with perfection. His plight is similar to Aylmer's, except that Aylmer is an admixture of scientist (i.e., watchmaker) and artist (jeweler). But his passionate absorption is every bit the equal of Aylmer's, and the rest of Hawthorne's loners bitten by a certain fatal proclivities that inexorably lead them into intellectual abstractedness and (in Aylmer's case) butterfly-chasing. Women involved with such men invariably drift away. Chillingworth loses Hester Prynne, his wife; Goodman Brown loses touch with his wife Faith, Aylmer disposes of his Georgiana and Owen Warland lets his Annie Hovenden float off. Similarly, the saturnine Parson Hooper, morbid loner and Dutch Calvinist in "The Minister's Black Veil" (1836), becomes so convinced of his innate evil that he spurns his Elizabeth. At the end we learn that this intellectualized lost soul molders in his grave. In "Ethan Brand" we find in essence a man of "solitary and meditative life" who has passed 18 years searching for the Unpardonable Sin, returned home, and committed suicide. It is a sin of the intellect "that triumphed over the sense of brotherhood with man and reverence for God," we are told, "and sacrificed everything to its own mighty claims!" Later, and still more to the point, is the "essence of that sin: that Brand "had lost his hold of the magnetic chain of humanity" that Hawthorne so emphasized. Of particular interest — as it involves herds and hermits — is his "Feathertop" (1852), which he characterized as "a moralized legend," a sort of didactic adult fairy tale wherein the title character is himself a satire upon social automatons who utter the right clichés, embrace the proper opinions, don the right clothes and, as Hawthorne wrote, "playest [their] part to perfection." Feathertop is another laboratory monster, a "simulacrum" fiendishly created from castoff anatomical parts and reconstituted, like the Tin Man in *The Wizard of Oz*, without a heart. Lest anyone misperceive the message, it is articulated directly: that "There are thousands upon thousands of coxcombs and charlatans in the world, made up of just a jumble of wornout, forgotten and good-for-nothing trash as [Feathertop] was. Yet they live in fair repute, and never see themselves for that they are."

The freakish loners who skulk and lurk in the pages of Edgar Allan Poe (1809–1849) are every bit worthy of their creator, a tortured man who as a youth "kept to himself," as one observer understated it. Poe's personal history is amply documented. Born to Elizabeth "Eliza" Arnold Hopkins Poe, a

British-born woman who became one of America's better known actresses, having played over 300 roles on American stages. Her husband was David Poe, an alcoholic actor, dancer and sometime law student who abandoned her in July of 1810. She died in a shabby Richmond, Virginia (where she was reduced to working as a milliner) boarding house on December 8, 1811, leaving three children. The first, William Henry, found a home with David Poe's Baltimore family. The third, a mentally handicapped girl named Rosalie, became the ward of Jane MacKenzie of Richmond. Edgar was adopted, but never legally so, by Frances "Fanny" Allan, who was interested in theater, who had brought aid and comfort to Eliza Poe in her last days, and who had answered a newspaper advertisement appealing for someone to take charge of Edgar. Fanny Allan's dapper husband was the Scottish-born philandering tobacco merchant John (aka "Jack," "Jock," or "Scotch") Allan. Importing Poe into the boozy Allan household was her idea. In 1815, the Allans and their new son, whom they called "Ned," visited Scotland and then England, where Poe enrolled at the Reverend John Bransby's Manor House School at Stoke Newington, four miles from London. He was made to understand that he was never a part of the Allan family that afforded him the pocket money to do as he wished until the London tobacco market declined, and with it John Allan's business fortune. When they returned to Richmond in 1820 he became known as Edgar Poe, whereas in England he'd been known as Edgar Allan. By the age of 13 he demonstrated promise in reading French and Latin, although John Allan was to say of him, "he does nothing & seems quite miserable, sulky & ill-tempered to all the family. How we could have acted to produce this is beyond my conception — why I have put up with his conduct is a little less wonderful."

Rebel to the end, Poe at 15 served as "lieutenant" among a group of Richmond boys who called themselves the "Junior Morgan Riflemen," and a year later he drew attention to himself by swimming six miles across the James River. As a teenager, he showed other promising athletic traits that enabled him to run, fence and box. At 17 he enrolled at the rowdy University of Virginia, although history tells us that the institution did not yet confer academic degrees. There he affixed a portrait of Lord Byron to his ceiling, cultivated a talent for singing, tried his hand at broad jumping and debate without sufficient encouragement, and took to drinking and gambling — without insufficient money. A classmate referred to him as "very excitable and restless, and at times wayward, melancholic and morose." He began borrowing money — a lifelong habit — until December of 1826 when, after Poe amassed somewhere between $2,000 and $2,500 in debt, Allan removed him from school, whereupon Poe, always the gothic jokester, later turned up in the guise of a ghost at one of Allan's card parties. In May of 1827, he enlisted as a private in the U.S., Army in Boston using *the nom de guerre* of Edgar A. Perry, and later in life developed other identities ("Henri le Rennet" and "Edward S. T. Grey," for instance), as do his literary characters. Having attained the rank of sergeant major, he arranged his discharge in 1829, on condition that the he find a substitute to take his place. He secured an appointment to West Point where he studied French and mathematics and amused his classmates as a prankster. As a way of exiting West Point, he managed to secure an 1831 court-martial on the pretext of his failure to appear at chapel services and parades. When *Al Aaraaf, Tamerlane, and Minor Poems* appeared, Poe dedicated the 124-page volume "To the U.S. Corps of Cadets," 232 of whom were said to have chipped in a dollar apiece to see it through press.

In the meantime Fanny Allan died, in 1829; John Allan soon remarried at age 51 to a woman 20 years his junior, who lost no time writing to Poe to say, "I'm not particularly anxious to see you." Poe wrote to Allan in 1833, saying, "For God's sake, pity me, and save me from destruction." Allan died the following year, leaving his estate to his many children born in and out of wedlock, but to Edgar he bequeathed nothing. Poe visited him shortly before his death and was greeted by Allan's brandishing his cane as if to attack him. In 1836, Edgar formally married his 14-year-old (her age was listed as 21 on marriage records) cousin Virginia Eliza Clemm, whom he had likely married the previous year. By 1840 Poe had developed an interest in cryptograms and had attracted the attention of George Bernard Shaw, who called him "the greatest journalistic critic of his time." On April Fools' Day of the following year he wrote to his physician and editorial friend J. E. Snodgrass, saying, "I presume no physician can have difficulty in detecting the drunkard at a glance," adding, "Nothing stronger than water ever passed my lips." In January of 1842, Virginia broke a blood vessel (or so he preferred to think) in her throat while singing. She had probably contracted tuberculosis and been coughing blood. "I took leave of her forever and underwent the agonies of her death," he recorded. "She recovered partially and again I hoped. At the end of the year the vessel broke again...Then again — again — again and even once again." In the meantime his drinking problem worsened to the point that by the end of the year he was written about in a temperance magazine. By 1845, Thomas Holley Chivers, the mystic southern American poet of somewhat unstable disposition, encountered Poe on New York's Nassau Street, "tottering from side to side" in alcoholic excess. Even so, Poe was temporarily something of a fixture in New York drawing rooms, despite that he and

Virginia were living in destitution and without heat on what is now 192nd Street. A visitor reported that Virginia "lay on a straw bed, wrapped in her husband's greatcoat, with a large tortoise shell cat on her bosom." Newspapers in New York and Philadelphia, one of them averring that Poe was "without money and without friends," solicited donations. She died on January 30, 1847, at 24, the same age at which Poe's mother and brother had passed. A year later Poe wrote to Maine friend George Eveleth, "I am constitutionally sensitive — nervous in a very unusual degree. I became insane, with long intervals of horrible sanity. During these fits of absolute unconsciousness I drank — God only knows how often or how much." About seven weeks later wrote to Eveleth, "The fact is thus: — my habits are rigorously abstemious...I rise early, eat moderately, drink nothing but water, and take abundant exercise in the open air...The desire for society comes upon me only when I have become excited by drink...the causes which madden me to the drinking point are no more, and I am done with drinking forever." That was dated February 29, 1848. July 17 found him in Richmond "horribly drunk and discoursing [upon his pseudo-metaphysical treatise] *Eureka* on the audience of Bar Rooms." November found him in Boston, where he ingested laudanum, an alcoholic tincture of opium. Instead of killing him, it made him deathly ill. At age 40 in 1849, the year of his death, he appeared in a delirious state at the doorstep of his friend John Sartain in Philadelphia, explaining that some men he had encountered on a train were conspiring to kill him. Shortly after, he claimed to have been held in prison while being compelled to observe torturers sawing off his mother's legs. Shortly after, Poe proclaimed, "I am resolved to get rich. I must get rich — rich." While in Lowell, Massachusetts, however, he wrote a bad check.

Edgar Allan Poe's history has been retold endlessly, but never in such a way as to resolve all the questions it raised. On July 14, he wrote, "My clothes are so horrible, and I am so ill." On October 3, 1849, an election day, passersby discovered Poe unconscious in Baltimore, wearing clothes not his own, at a polling place in a run down tavern called Gunner's on Lombard Street. He was transported to Washington College Hospital but never fully regained consciousness. When he seemed to awaken, he spoke vacantly to images on the hospital walls. Dr. Snodgrass, in the meantime, received a note reading, "There is a gentleman, rather the worse for wear, at Ryan's 4th ward polls, who goes under the cognomen of Edgar A. Poe, and who appears to be in great distress, and who says he is acquainted with you, and I assure you he is in need of immediate attention." Poe died on Sunday, April 7, at five in the morning when he is alleged to have cried, "Lord, help my poor soul." History records that the wife of Dr. John Moran, a physician at Washington College Hospital, fashioned a shroud for the deceased and prepared his body for burial, placing one of his hands upon the other, and ordering his black hair. Poe's friends buried him under early morning darkness at the Westminster churchyard on October 8 (his brother purchased a grave marker that was broken on delivery and never replaced), only to have him reburied 35 years later at the same cemetery, next to Maria Clemm, in 1875. Two days following Poe's death, *The New York Times* carried a purported Poe memorial entitled "Ludwig" but authored by Poe's thoroughly unscrupulous literary executor, Rufus Wilmot Griswold, a Baptist minister who published three of Poe's verses and paid him nothing and who presumed to write a biography of the dead author laced with falsehood and innuendo, portraying his subject as debauched, arrogant, friendless, unprincipled and mentally ill — that thereafter colored Poe's reputation. Griswold wrote in *The New York Tribune* that Poe's death "will startle many, but few will be grieved by it," adding that "he had few or no friends."

Fertile ground that Poe is for psychoanalytic speculation, Poe seemed to view himself as a lonely, misunderstood, ignored, isolated, despised and spurned Byronic figure. He was quite likely all of those things. His readers, however, have tended to attach their literary interpretations to his biographical record. They might naively assume, for example, that his criminally insane narrators indirectly reveal his own personality, presuming that Poe too was criminally insane. His work, however, carries a comedic aspect that eludes most readers. Literary scholars, as a rule, refrain from drawing parallels between a writer's life and his work, preferring instead to let the work speak for itself. It is not unusual for purported friend or close relative to claim, in effect, that to know the person is to understand his work. It is easy to draw biographic assumptions from Poe's 1880 lyric poem entitled "Alone" that reads, in part:

> From childhood's hour I have not been
> As others were — I have not seen
> As others saw — I could not bring
> My passions from a common spring — "

Adding four lines later,

> "And all I lov'd — I lov'd alone."

We know, however, that his work trades ostensibly with the strangest of the strange, a memorable rogue's gallery of daft, if compellingly bizarre raving loners, that assuages the illusion among Poe's popular readers that they are all, as one might say, "perfectly normal" and therefore socially acceptable in an other-driven society. One might review, for means of comparison, Thomas Mann's *The Magic Mountain* (1924) where we are introduced to one Hans Casdorp, "life's delicate child," an intellectually curious and newly-minted naval engineer who visits a sanatorium on a mountain at Davos in Switzerland where at dinner he assures a robust physician named Krokowsky that "he was, thank God, perfectly healthy," to which Krokowsky smiles broadly and replies, "then you are a phenomenon worthy of study. I, for one, have never in my life come across a perfectly healthy human being." No one in Poe, we may be assured, is perfectly anything, either, excepting perhaps perfectly mad. The increasingly frenzied narrator of "MS Found in a Bottle" (1833) claims to have been driven from home and family and to have taken "great delight" in the "eloquent madness" of the German moralists, albeit he suffers from a certain "nervous restlessness which haunted me as a fiend." It is "with a long and bitter laugh" that the dangerously deranged narrator of "Morella" (1835) bears the second Morella to her mother's tomb. When he remarks upon the former's "rapid increase in body size," we are assured that he is decidedly beyond the pale, if we did not know it before. In her mother had he found the perfect mate, namely "one who shunned society, and, attaching herself to me alone, rendered me happy." So too, "Berenice" (1835) introduces a criminal-crackpot, this one calling himself "Egaeus" who, emboldened by his "excited imagination," claims to have been descended from "a race of visionaries." The narrator was born in a library that he calls a "wild [dominion] of monastic thought and erudition." He has developed a disease characterized by terminal monomania, what with his fixation upon, of all things, Berenice's teeth. In the end, it appears that she has bitten his hand, after which he has retaliated by extracting all 32 of them that "scattered to and fro about the floor." Likewise, the narrator of "Ligeia" (1838), "feeble through much suffering," is an emotionally compromised psychopathic killer. He is fixated upon eyes: "Those eyes! Those large, those shining, those divine orbs!" He is yet another unstable, disturbed, and above all unreliable voice with a message a rendered as a confessional. He is also muddled about where he first met his low-voiced Ligeia, and about the identity of her maiden name. He confuses his first wife with his second, whom he has poisoned. In the amusing tale — albeit all of Poe's tales are in some sense or another comic — entitled "The Man that was Used Up" (1839), the speaker admits to being forgetful and "constitutionally nervous," leaving him in "a pitiable state of agitation." What commences is a broad satire taking aim at such communal sacred cows as military arrogance, societal progress, overbearing ministers, overblown theatrics, drawing room foibles, social pretension and campaign hype. Poe's General John A. B. C. Smith is an artificial man who is the grotesque product of American technological ingenuity that has provided him with artificial limbs, artificial shoulders, an artificial chest, artificial hair, eyes, teeth and palate. "I left General Smith," the narrator says, "with a heightened interest in the man, with an exalted opinion of his controversial powers, and a deep sense of the valuable privileges we enjoy in living in this age of mechanical invention." In "William Wilson" (1839), one of the earlier instances of Poe's doppelgängers that assume the form of two persons sharing one body, the narrator refers to himself as "outcast of all outcasts most abandoned" and then launches into his "family character," the cause of his being "self-willed, addicted to the wildest caprices, and a prey to the most ungovernable passions." Emerson counseled in "Self-Reliance" that "to be great is to be misunderstood." If Wilson (which is not his name) is the latter, he is anything but the former, although he does remind us "of the passionate energy of mind which enabled me to excel." But when he peers into a mirror (a favorite prop in both Hawthorne and Poe) the glass hands back what he always was and promises to remain: an egotistical, overbearing self-satirizing crackpot.

All good writers are ironists; and Poe, albeit it he was writing sensational literature for popular consumption, tailored to popular audiences, provided them what the wanted to hear while at the same time handing them a canard, beneath which they could neither isolate nor discover a lightly veiled comic amusement. David S. Reynolds in his *Beneath the American Renaissance: The Subversive Imagination in the age of Emerson and Melville* observes that "nowhere is the dual process of enthusiastic absorption and studied redirection of the sensational so visible as in Poe's writings," adding later that "Poe was clearly trying to tap the new market for sensational literature,"[1] but not, we might add, without pulling the reader's tail. Ben Franklin, that self-made, self-sufficient, self-reliant, self-starting American genius, remarked in his autobiography that although he had not attained perfection, "I was," he said with obvious satisfaction, "a better and happier man than I otherwise should have been." Poe (never at a loss for one-liners) leads Wilson (having acknowledged his "disordered imagination") to speculate that, had circumstances not developed as they had, "I might, to-day, have been a better, and

---

1 David S. Reynolds, *Beneath the American Renaissance: The Subversive Imagination in the Age of Emerson and Melville* (Cambridge: Harvard University Press, 1989) 226.

thus happier man." The same is not so in "The Fall of the House of Usher" (1839), where we encounter the ghoulish Roderick Usher, one of Poe's better neurasthenic screwballs given to "nervous agitation," and an appearance handicapped by a "cadaverousness of complexion." His intention of preserving his sister Madeline's corpse runs afoul when she kicks the lid off of her coffin. All of this good literary fun is aimed squarely at normal, average folks, exercising good common sense, who would rather not admit Poe's maniacs into their secret fraternities and knitting groups. The basic message is to leave loners — alone.

That message surfaces in "The Man of the Crowd" (1840) where the speaker is at the outset in an excited state, and is recovering from some undisclosed illness, quite possibly psychiatric in nature. He, like the 65-70-year-old man he observes in a crowd, has a few secrets of his own concealed in the story's subtext. If the narrator fears him, it is an expression of self-fear, suggesting that the narrator and this man of the crowd are the same. Both wander in romantic isolation, separated from the rest of the miserable human race by some undefined and inexorable urge for solitude. In "Leonora" (1841) we are greeted by a defensive narrator who prefatorily and eccentrically explains that he is unusually passionate, that he his been thought mad, but that madness may, after all, be evidence of "the loftiest intelligence." His remarks suggest that for all his supposed intellect, he remains mentally off-stride. With "The Murders in the Rue Morgue" (1841) Poe introduces the super sleuth Monsieur C. August Dupin who, though having been reduced to poverty, embraces books as his "sole luxuries" and is to be counted among those unique personalities who derive "pleasure from even the most trivial occupations," being as he is "fond of enigmas, of conundrums, of hieroglyphics." Dupin solves the mystery because he enlists his heightened imagination to the assistance of reason. Similarly, in "The Pit and the Pendulum" (1843), the narrator seems to move "down" from despair to insanity to insight — another laughable example of inspired romantic creativity. Mad or not, he is able to calculate the degree to which the bladed pendulum might be expected to descend upon its victim. Similarly, in "A Descent Into the Maelstrom" (1841) the fisherman (if we are willing to believe him or any other unreliable narrator in Poe) saves himself in the same manner as the speaker in "The Pit and the Pendulum": by means of an uncanny sense of intuition, although that brilliant intuition hovers on the rim of madness. Within the pages of "The Masque of the Red Death" (1842) one encounters some inexorable pestilence that selects its victim and "shut[s] him out from the aid and from the sympathy of his fellow-man." Its protagonist is the more than usually eccentric

Prince Prospero within whose castellated abbey he foolishly attempts to wall out the inevitable. "There [were] some who would have thought him mad," obviously, and on the story's final page the prince falls prostrate in death, itself an ironic mockery of the lone holdout against institutionalized tyranny. He is precisely the crackpot loner toward whom readers of his day evidently harbored curiosity. One finds something of that same sort of lunatic in "The Black Cat" (1843) where, from his felon's cell, the narrator (a wife beater, an animal abuser and a murderer) has understandably a pressing psychological urge to unburden himself through a monolog that begins placidly, then with seeming rationality admits to criminally frenzied, bizarre atrocities. Ostensibly an alcohol abstinence tale illustrating that drink begets uncontrollable violence, it begins by claiming that he began life as an average, benevolent man-on-the-street, "noted for the docility and humanity of [his] disposition," explaining too that he was once "especially fond of animals, and pets." Similar to it is "The Tell-Tale Heart" (1843) that is a maniac's ever amplified and talkative confession of a flawlessly good murder he all but committed, had he not mistaken the imagined sound of his victim's heartbeat for his own. The narrative implies that while the reader is safely within the boundaries of conventionally acceptable, law-loving and profoundly good normal and profoundly sane middle class deportment, while the narrator is obviously, outrageously the opposite. If there is a satiric joke, something for which Poe's readers must be forever on guard, albeit concealed beneath the carpet, it is aimed at bourgeois notions of healthy, church-going neighborly conduct. This rhetorical practice established Poe as the satiric enemy of his own readership.

For "The Gold Bug" (1843) Poe drew loosely upon the career of a real life outlaw and maverick, that being William "Captain" Kidd (1645?–1701) the English pirate who was originally commissioned as an English Privateer in 1645 to safeguard the British fleet from buccaneers in the Red Sea and Indian Ocean, only to become one of the most celebrated of abjectly cruel pirates of his day. Kidd was reportedly taken prisoner in Boston, and then remanded to London where he was found guilty and hanged (twice, since the hangman's rope broke on the first try) for his misdeeds. Legend has it that some of Kidd's loot remains buried and undiscovered. William LeGrand, who appears in that story, mirrors not only Kidd's life experience but also Poe's. Ostensibly well-educated, he lives on Sullivan's Island near Charleston, South Carolina where, as an eccentric recluse with an intellect that is somewhat unsettled, struggling with misanthropy and manic depressiveness. By his own admission, Poe's "The Premature Burial" is a hoax that he passed off as one of his "bugaboo tales." The speaker's ludicrous instructions for his own entombment that begin with the words, "I exacted the most sacred oaths," develop into a *reductio ad absurdum*, what with his request for a coffin replete with light and fresh air, a spring cushion and a rope leading to an overhead alarm bell. He ends that narration by arguing in favor of a mentally healthy attitude, for breathing "the free air of Heaven," and for eschewing gothic books with their "charnel apprehensions" that apparently encouraged his "cataleptic disorder" that has now vanished, leaving him a "new man" prepared to live a "man's life." Poe's Augustus Bedloe in "A Tale of the Ragged Mountains" (1844) is yet another eccentric loner "in the highest degree, sensitive, excitable, enthusiastic," three characteristics that may well have been occasioned by his "habitual use of morphine, which he swallowed in great quantity, and without which he would have found it impossible to exist." Such are colorful chaps to read about, perhaps, but not invite to a Rotary luncheon. For Poe, it was merely another literary freak show rendered as popular literature and, for a chosen few, a field mined with good comedy, as for example Bedloe's narcotic sojourn into Charlottesville's Ragged Mountains. "The solitude seemed absolutely virgin," he says enthusiastically, adding, "It is by no means impossible that I was indeed the first adventurer — the very first and sole adventurer who had ever penetrated its recesses."

The spurious Senecan epigraph in "The Purloined Letter" (1845) reads: nil sapientiae odiosius acumine nimio (nothing is more repugnant to learning than too much insight). The story accordingly pivots on the absurdly simple notion that hiding an object in plain sight is to place it where one would least expect to uncover it. As the tale winds to its conclusion, C. August Dupin says, "Il y a parier que toute idée publique, toute convention reçue, est une sottise, car elle a convenu au plus grand nombre" (chances are that any popular idea, any accepted notion, is foolishness, since it has proved agreeable to the mass of mankind). The reader cops his first glimpse of Dupin, deep in Sherlockian cogitation, ensconced in the darkness of his library with "curling eddies of smoke" rising from his meerschaum, hardly in a disposition to embrace popular opinion. The injured narrator of "The Oval Portrait" (1845) is another neurasthenic loner-eccentric who claims to be "unwell," being as he is in a "desperately wounded" condition that brings the "incipient delirium" of one suffering in near isolation. Poe, in a letter to Eveleth, admitted the obvious when he conceded, "The Facts in the Case of M. Valdemar" (1845) "was a hoax, of course." When he writes that Valdemar is the compiler of "Bibliotheca Forensica" and that he is the author "under the *nom de plume* of Issachar Marx of the Polish versions of "Wallenstein" and

"Gargantua," and that life has rendered his lower limbs similar to those of John Randolph (a liberal political pundit of the day), it is all satire calculated to amuse the independently intelligent while blindsiding the common reader with egregious poppycock. There was more to follow in "The Cask of Amontillado" (1846), a murder tale recounted 50 years after the crime. It is a comic piece, one calculated again to amuse the few and horrify the many. The narrator, until he reveals his secrets at the conclusion, executed the perfect crime against an idiotic oenophile ironically named "Prospero," to whom the narrator says hilarious things like "you are a man to be missed." When Prospero says, "I shall not die of a cough," his soon-to be killer replies, "True — true," and then toasts his life that hasn't many hours left on its meter. He then hands poor Prospero "a flagon of De Grave." When Prospero asks his killer whether he is "of the brotherhood," he clarifies by saying, "You are not of the mason," to which his killer, mindful that he is about to brick a wall around him, responds to the contrary.

"Hop-Frog, or The Eight Chained Orang-Outangs" surfaced in *The Flag of Our Nation* on March 17, 1849. Poe, who died the following October 7, left this cynical piece as his final *coup de grâce*. Viewed symbolically, the story addresses the role of the despised, alienated artist depicted as Hop-Frog, a humiliated, misshapen figure "expected to be always ready with sharp witticisms" and forced to come to terms with his public, represented by an arrogant king who demands "characters, man — something novel — out of the way," and finds himself rewarded by surviving upon table scraps. The artist's third adversaries are his critics, described as "seven wise men." He further represents himself as a "lean joker" that he jestingly calls a *rara avis in terris*, a rare bird upon the earth, in the words of the Roman satirist Juvenal. Hop-Frog and Trippeta (possibly a depiction of the similarly disadvantaged Virginia Clemm), in whose face the king tosses a goblet of wine, are but captives. When the king commands Hop-Frog to drink himself into a stupor ("Here, drink this!"), it cannot but recall some of Poe's companions who, well knowing that Poe could not hold his liquor, encouraged him to swill alcohol. This, like "The Cask of Amontillado," is a revenge tale wherein Hop-Frog's vengeance comes through psychological cunning. At the conclusion we see "eight corpses swung in their chains, fetid, blackened, indistinguishable mass." In the end, the lone wolf enjoys the last modicum of satisfaction. "As for myself," he concludes, "I am simply Hop-Frog the jester — and *this is my last jest*."

America's primary, but not last, literary jester was the independent-minded Samuel Langhorne Clemens, was born and died beneath Halley's

Comet (1835–1910). At least as early as 1863 he signed off as "Mark Twain," an expression meaning "two fathoms" (i.e., twelve feet) deep, employed in Mississippi riverboat navigation to signify safe sailing. Reading Twain is never what one would call safe sailing, primarily because of his perplexing ambiguities, among them his conviction that anything not American was somehow comical, despite his having taken up residence in London, Vienna, Paris, Berlin, Munich and Florence — and visited Europe about 30 times. Another was his conflicting optimistic–pessimistic conviction that technology could ameliorate the human condition, versus his contrary opinion that the human race (being as it is variously greedy, lying, cheating, hypocritical, self-serving, foolish, vain, easily tempted, racist, duplicitous and jealous) is damned and therefore ineligible for redemption. The setting for *The Mysterious Stranger* (1916) is Eseldorf, "village of asses," and the time is 1590, "The Age of Belief." Satan, in true Twainian form, vents his misanthropy by proclaiming that "man is a museum of diseases, a home of impurities; he comes today and is gone tomorrow; he begins as dirt and departs as stench." Other questions, such as whether Twain was by nature tough-minded or tender-minded, whether he was inclined to believe more in determinism or in free will, whether he was more the realist or the romantic — still perplex and challenge his readers. "Adam was but human," he said in *Pudd'nhead Wilson* (1894). "This explains it all. He did not want the apple for the apple's sake; he only wanted it because it was forbidden. The mistake was in not forbidding the serpent; then he would have eaten the serpent." Some aspects of his literary apprenticeship are similar to other American writers such as Franklin, Whitman and Ernest Hemingway, notably his days as a printer's devil and his reportorial apprenticeship at newspapers in St. Louis, Keokuk, Carson City, Virginia City and San Francisco. "I was born," he recorded in his autobiography, "on the 30th of November, 18, 1835, in the most invisible village of Florida, Monroe County, Missouri. The village contained a hundred people and I increased the population by 1 per cent. It is more than many of the best men in history could have done for a town. It may not be modest in me to refer to this but it is true. There is no record of a person doing as much — not even Shakespeare. But I did it for Florida and it shows that I could have done it for any place — even London, I suppose."

Twain's signature voice, however, is best remembered as a boy's, as in *The Adventures of Tom Sawyer* (1876) and *The Adventures of Huckleberry Finn* (1884). "In *Huckleberry Finn*," Twain recalled, "I have drawn Tom Blankenship [son of a chap Twain identified as "the town drunkard"] exactly as he was. He was ignorant, unwashed, insufficiently fed; but he had as good a heart as ever any body had. His liberties were entirely unrestricted. He was the only really independent person — boy or man — in the community, and by consequence he was tranquilly and continuously happy and envied by all the rest of us." The notion of an idyllic boyhood characterized by freedom and delicious self-reliance was something he too had known. "When I was a boy," Twain recorded in *Life on the Mississippi* (1883), there was but one permanent ambition among my comrades in our village on the west bank of the Mississippi. That was, to be a steamboatman." This he accomplished, regarding it as a memorable exercise in discipline. "Piloting on the Mississippi River was not work for me," he said nevertheless. "It was play — delightful play, vigorous play, adventurous play — and I loved it." At maturity, however, Twain was one of the great, original, mid-continent voices and superb raconteurs in American literature, with an original but greater than mid-continent American package of messages attached, most notably his devotion to social equality. His mastery of backwater American English as experimented upon by native American humorists, introduced a new literary voice, but it was not all comedy. "I vividly remember," he wrote, "seeing a dozen black men and women chained to one another, once, and lying in a group on the pavement awaiting shipment to the Southern slave market. Those were the saddest faces I have ever seen." Strong too were his misgivings about the problem of unbridled Gilded Age excesses in American wealth. In the opinion of some, his literary career was under the control of his mother and his wife Olivia "Livy" who combed his manuscripts and insisted upon politic emendations where she believed appropriate. "She edited everything I wrote," Twain said. "And what is more — she not only edited my works, she edited me." She did not edit his preoccupation with nudity and pornography, however. His authorial masks — be it Huck Finn, Captain Ben Stormfield, Adam, Sam Clemens, Eve, Thomas Jefferson Snodgrass, Mark Twain, Hank Morgan, Sergeant Fathom, Sieur Louis de Conte, a horse and a dog — continue to invite speculation about the voices in his writing. Twain wrote profusely throughout his long career, all the while bedeviled with the perception that he was hardly more than a popular sub-literary writer influenced by southwestern American humorists, as well as a standup comedian who had not seen the inside of a school since the age of 12, and therefore quite unworthy of being taken seriously among straight laced *litterateurs.*

Twain was defensively jocular about conventional education, for example in "The Celebrated Jumping Frog of Calaveras County" (1865) where he asserted, "all a frog wanted was education, and he could do most anything." In his autobiography he acknowledged that "it pleased me beyond measure when Yale made me a Master of Arts, because I didn't know anything about art; I had another convulsion of pleasure when Yale made me a Doctor of Literature, because I was not competent to doctor anybody's literature but my own. After Missouri University proclaimed him Doctor of Laws, he replied that he "knew nothing about laws except how to evade them." When Oxford University proposed to christen him Doctor of Letters, he said, "what I don't know about letters would make me a multi-millionaire if I could turn it into cash." Later he wrote, "a cauliflower is nothing but a cabbage with a college education." Sitting through an entire opera, he said in a similar tone, was "the next thing to suicide." Summarized Bernard Devoto in *Mark Twain's America* (1932), "He was a humorist. He had no formal education. His life has been spent in activity, away from what are known as artistic pursuits. The society that formed him was mobile, not static. His mind flashed, sometimes, with brilliance, a penetrating illumination that is unmistakable genius."[1] Twain traded in misspelling, dialect, malaprop, picaresque, sketch, fable, travel record, epistolary narrative, comic tale, mystery, memoir, polemic and epigram. However, he remained in voice and on subversive message. "I believe that our Heavenly Father invented man because he was disappointed in the monkey," he opined like the literary rebel he was, firing salvos directly at canonical American "littery" personalities such as Henry Longfellow, Oliver Wendell Holmes, Ralph Waldo Emerson, and Fenimore Cooper — whose wooden rhetoric he satirized in an essay entitled "Fenimore Cooper's Literary Offenses" written sometime between 1894 and 1895. But Twain's sum and substance came from within. "I know the look of an apple that is roasting and sizzling on a hearth on a winter's evening, and I know the comfort that comes of eating it hot, along with some sugar and a drench of cream," he remembered from his youth John S. Tuckey of Purdue University articulated it perfectly in 1970 when he posited that "the central issue of Clemens's dialogue was one that is still before humanity: whether man is essentially an automated or an autonomous being; whether he is a slavish and perishable mechanism or a free and immortal spirit."[2]

Such are representative snippets from the lives and works of five major American writers of what were in their time independent, usually subversive opinions. Sociologist John J. Macaionis has more or less defined public opinion as "widespread attitudes about controversial issues," cautioning that "exactly who is or is not included in any 'public' depends on the issue

---

1 Bernard DeVoto, *Mark Twain's America* (Boston: Little, Brown, and Company, 1932) 207.
2 John S. Tuckey, "Mark Twain's Later Dialogue: the 'Me and the Machine.'" *American Literature*, January 1970: 533.

involved," and adding that "'publics' have formed over numerous controversial issues, ranging from water fluoridation, air pollution, and the social standing of women to handguns and health care," and cautioning that "on any given issue, anywhere from 2 to 10 percent of people offer no opinion at all because of ignorance or indifference."[1] Bernard Burleson, another sociologist, somewhat clumsily remarked that as a field of inquiry, public opinion studies have "become technical, and quantitative, a-theoretical, segmentalized, and particularized, specialized and institutionalized, 'modernized,' and 'groupized' — in short, as a characteristic behavioral science, Americanized." Even so, as Russell Jacoby has written, today's public may be gone tomorrow. "A public that once snapped up pamphlets by Thomas Paine or stood for hours listening to Abraham Lincoln debate Stephen Douglas hardly exists; its span of attention shrinks as its fondness for television increases."[2]

Emerson, Thoreau, Franklin, Emerson, Thoreau, Whitman, Hawthorne and Poe and Twain are still objects of scrutiny in American universities, and possibly in a few American high schools that have not collapsed beneath the anti-intellectual heel of teachers led fatally astray by colleges of "education." If one can be assured that their collective views were worthy of acceptance in their time, then they may yet survive in ours. Substantial ideas, however, never utterly wear thin. From ancient Greece one still reads Homer, Aeschylus, Sophocles, Eurypides, Aristophanes, Aristotle, Plato and Epicurus. From ancient Rome, Plautus, Terence, Plutarch, Cicero, Virgil, Epictetus, Horace and Ovid still survive. From the Middle Ages there is yet Dante and Chaucer; from the Renaissance one still peruses Goethe, More, Machiavelli and Cervantes, Rabelais and Cellini. In this sense, today's public, or at least today's reading class, is still with us. There are people who, well outside of Sunday school, still read the old and new testaments. Such it is also for American authors and their preoccupations that may still represent our national culture.

In a jocular, but none-the-less earnest letter to John Taylor on August 24, 1819, the brilliantly free spirited English romantic poet and theorist Samuel Taylor Coleridge (1772–1834) declared that "I equally dislike the favour of the public with the love of a woman — they are both a cloying treacle to the wings of independence." When Coleridge died, his schoolmate Charles Lamb claimed the he "was the proof and touchstone of all my cognitions." Coleridge's marital cognition, however, fouled his wings of independence with the tackiness of treacle. On October 4, 1795 he married Sara Fricker, the

1 John J. Macionis, *Sociology: Ninth Editon* (Upper Saddle River: Prentice Hall, 2003) 608.
2 Russell Jacoby, *The Last Intellectuals: American Culture in the Age of Academe* (New York: Noonday Press, 1987) 6.

woman, said Coleridge, "whom I love best of all created Beings." His marital bliss lasted for less than two years when she dumped boiling milk on his foot, taking him out of service for a few days. Like Coleridge, other people of independent ways may encounter difficulty reconciling themselves with the opposite gender. Independence and matrimony do not ordinarily cohabit with one another. Marriage among our independently inclined American literary friends either did not happen, or if it did happen, succeeded only tentatively. Ben Franklin had his ups and downs with women, noting in his *Autobiography* "that hard-to-be-govern'd Passion of Youth, had hurried me frequently into Intrigues with low Women that fell in my Way, which were attended with some Expense and great Inconvenience, besides a continual Risque to my Health by a Distemper which of all things I dreaded, tho' by great good Luck I escaped it." Ben did not entirely escape being snared by women, however. Indeed he seemed to enjoy every erotic minute of it. He was hardly what one would call a hermit, except in the sense that he was extremely much the independent figure, predictably motivated from within. Franklin had generally an ambivalent attraction-aversion to women, as is made clear early on when the sloop upon which he had booked passage took on passengers in Newport, Rhode Island, among them two young women to whom the flirtatious Franklin made himself known, only to have "a grave, sensible Matron-like Quaker-Woman" intercede, saying "Young Man, I am concern'd for thee, as thou has no Friend with thee, and seems not to know much of the World, or of the Snares Youth is expos'd to; depend upon it those are very bad Women, I can see it in their actions...I advise thee in a friendly Concern for they Welfare, to have no Acquaintance with them."

At age 21, Franklin wrote to his 14 year old sister Jane, advising her that "modesty makes the most homely virgin amiable and charming," and sending her a spinning wheel rather than the tea table he had first contemplated, commenting that "a good housewife [is] far preferable to that of being only a pretty gentlewoman." Always with a mind to cutting a deal, Franklin turned down an arranged marriage on grounds that her father might erase Franklin's printing business. Having turn'd my Thoughts to Marriage," he recalled, "I look'd round me, and made Overtures of Acquaintance in other Places. But soon found that the Business of a Printer being generally thought a poor one, I was not to expect Money with a Wife unless with such a one, as I should not otherwise think agreeable." He did take Deborah Read to wife, albeit common law wife, on the chance that her previous marriage to a chap named Rogers might still, in the opinion of Pennsylvania courts, have been in force. At the age of nearly 50 Franklin dashed off a note to 23-year-old Catherine

"Katy" Ray, a Rhode Islander with whom he carried on a 30 year flirtation, imploring her to "be a good girl and don't forget your Catechism. — Go constantly to Meeting — or church — till you get a good Husband, — then stay at home, & nurse the Children, and live like a Christian." Professor William H. Shurr of the University of Tennessee observed in 1922 that Franklin's children, consisting of two sons and one daughter, "were technically illegitimate," and that his son William Temple Franklin sired three more illegitimate children (if any child may justifiably be labeled "illegitimate") without the encumbrance of a wife."[1] By 1768 Franklin was happily situated in England with other female company and obviously unconcerned about Deborah, who was both ailing and lonely back in Philadelphia. She died in December of 1774. William Franklin assured his father that "a very respectable number of... inhabitants were at her funeral." Five years later Franklin wrote from France that "Somebody, it seems, gave it out that I lov'd Ladies; and then every body presented me their ladies (or the ladies presented themselves) to be *embrac'd*, that is to have their Necks kiss'd. For as kissing of Lips or Cheeks it is not the Mode here. The French ladies have however 1000 other ways of rendering themselves agreeable." In 1782 he composed a felicitous treaty rendered in the third person for an ongoing extramarital arrangement between himself with a certain Madame Brillon who was married to someone 24 years her elder, stipulating in Article 9 "That when he [Franklin] is with her, he will do what he pleases." Indeed, as an independent operator, he seemed always to do as he pleased. Before returning to Philadelphia, Franklin took up with canine fancier Madame Helevetius, who was apparently the subject of a letter from Abigail Adams to Lucy Cranch, reading, in part, "She had a little lap-dog, who was next to the Doctor [Franklin], her favorite. This she kissed, and when he [the dog] wet the floor she wiped it up with her chemise. This is one of the Doctor's most intimate friends, with whom he dines once every week, and she with him...."

Waldo Emerson, who preached vigorously and often with secular ardency about the glories of independent bliss, was nevertheless twice under the yoke of matrimony. Was it not Emerson who advised his disciples to "go it alone"? Whether he regarded this as a contradiction we may never know, although he did let it be known that he was a person of ideas and not of practical action, meaning that he did not always follow his own advice. He must therefore be accorded the freedom to advocate one thing and then do the opposite. He first married attractive 17-year-old Ellen Louisa Tucker (1811–

1 William H. Shurr, "'Now, Gods, Stand Up for Bastards': Reinterpreting Benjamin Franklin's Autobiography," *American Literature*, September 1992: 444.

1831), heiress to at least part of her Bostonian family's mercantile fortune, such as it was, since the family had fallen on difficult times. Nevertheless, Emerson's brother William, after assessing Ellen, ambiguously pronounced her "the fairest & best of her kind." After a trip to Florida, Waldo wedded her in 1828, and thereafter, perhaps out of a feeling of inadequacy, prudently invested in a set of barbells. She died 17 months later, February 8, 1831, from what may have been tuberculosis. "Farewell blessed Spirit who hast made me happy in thy life & in thy death make me yet happy in thy disembodied state," he wrote five days after her death. The following March 29 after having repeatedly visited her grave site, he visited her tomb, lifted the lid of her coffin and had a peek at its contents, something he did after his son Waldo died of scarlatina in 1842. Seven years after his marriage to Ellen, he married Lydia Jackson, about eight months older than himself, whom he insisted upon calling "my noble Lidian," sometimes "Asia," and in lighter moments, "Queenie." She, in turn, called him "Mr. Emerson." Unlike Ellen, Queenie was no beauty, if that matters. Emerson's brother Charles put it quite bluntly: "She is not beautiful anywise that I know." Waldo once called her a "miserable Dyspeptic." There is evidence, too, that the American transcendentalist Margaret Fuller (1810-50) developed a sexual and marital interest in Emerson, speculating, as she said, that "nothing could be nobler, nor more consoling than to be his wife." He was put off by what he called her "extreme plainness" and by what scholar Marie Urbanski called "the incessant movement of her eyelids, and her nasal voice."[1] The ironical, if not outright impolitic lecture that Emerson presented before a Boston women's rights convention in September of 1855 put on the table his none-too-veiled policy toward women. "They are more delicate than men," he told the assembled ladies, "and thus more impressionable." Continuing in his usual sententiously sermonesque manner, he observed, "man is the will, and woman the sentiment. In this ship of humanity Will is the rudder, and Sentiment the sail. When woman affects to steer, the rudder is only a marked sail. When woman engages in any art or trade, it is usually as a resource, not as a primary object." It was women's appropriate place, he said, to "lose themselves eagerly in the glory of their husbands and children." On another occasion, he conceded, "A man's wife has more power over him than the state has." Turning to politics, he told the ladies, "We may ask, to be sure," he said, "why need you vote?" Women ought not to vote, he continued, for three reasons, "first: a want of practical wisdom; second, a too purely ideal point of view; and third, danger of con-

---

1 Marie Urbanski, "An Ambivalence of Ralph Waldo Emerson Toward Margaret Fuller," *Thoreau Journal Quarterly*, July, 1978: 34.

tamination." He did, however, liberally endorse equal educational opportunity for the weaker sex.

On the surface of it, the primary 19th century American literati did not much broach questions of sexuality, wishing instead to divert attention elsewhere so not to rattle anyone's refined sense of decorousness and decency. Henry Thoreau, the independent thinking (or so it appeared), very prototypical American isolate (or so *he* appeared) nevertheless, as an acquaintance of ours rightly pointed out, "had some good-sized parties out in his shack." He was far more socially inclined than one might presume, although he had an annoying tendency to quarrel about anything that came his way and did not present the most appealing figure of New England manhood. His biographer Carlos Baker described Henry's nose that "resembled the beak of a predatory bird," and his arms that were "thickly matted with fur, like the pelt of an animal." At first blush, Thoreau conveys the impression of asexuality. In the "Higher Laws" segment of *Walden*, he begins to inveigh against sensuality, saying "we are conscious of an animal in us, which awakens in proportion as our higher nature slumbers. It is reptile and sensual, and perhaps cannot be wholly expelled." Several lines later he proclaims with orphic certainty that "chastity is the flowering of man" and a page or so later that "nature is hard to overcome, but she must be overcome." Like his friend Emerson, Henry was liable to say one thing but do quite another. Walter Harding claims that Henry's "one romance" began in 1839 with the appearance of Ellen Sewall, with whom both Henry and his brother John "fell in love." When John proposed, she (tentatively) accepted. Apparently unaware of that turn of events, Henry also tendered a proposal; her father, a Unitarian minister in Scituate, Massachusetts, disunified the plan by directing her to write a letter of refusal, about which she later wrote, "I never felt so badly at sending a letter in my life." Literary historian Henry Seidel Canby passed the incident off as Henry's "experiment in the philosophy of love." A second such experiment nearly scared poor Henry to an early grave. It involved "a dark skinned, pudgy-featured woman," as some children entrusted to her care recalled, named Sophia Ford (occasionally spelled *Foord*) who developed a fixation for Henry that sent him into a panic, in view of how, in Canby's words, he was "a major writer whose relationship with women has always been a problem." On November 14, 1847 Henry composed a letter to Waldo saying, in part, "I have a tragic correspondence, for the most part all on one side, with Miss — — . She did really wish to — I hesitate to write — marry me — that is the way they spell it. Of course I did not write a deliberate answer — how could I deliberate upon it? I sent back a distinct No, as I have learned to pronounce after considerable practice, and I trust that this No has succeeded," conclud-ing that "I really had anticipated no such foe as this in my career." In more re-cent times, Thoreau idolaters have inconclusively speculated variously that he had a deficient sexual drive, that he was a "reluctant heterosexual," and that he was indeed homoerotic. Henry obliquely addressed that speculation when in his journal he recorded, "I love man with the same distinction that I love woman — as if my friend were of some strange third sex — some other or some stranger and still my friend."

There is neither any ambiguity about Walt Whitman's sexuality nor is there any question of his ranking in the upper ten percent of America's liber-ated public personalities. If Sophia Ford threatened Thoreau with matrimo-ny, thereby taking him emotionally captive and threatening his prized inde-pendence, a woman named Anne Burrows Gilchrist (1828–1855) attempted the same thing with, of all unlikely people, Walt Whitman, with somewhat the same results. She became a widow after the death of Alexander Gilchrist, who succumbed to scarlet fever in 1861, leaving his biography of William Blake unfinished. Anne finished the book with assistance from Dante Gabriel Rossetti, who lent her a copy of *Leaves of Grass*. She not only read the book but, through some romantic leap of faith, fell in love with its author. Gilchrist wrote "A Woman's Estimate of Walt Whitman," that she later retitled as "An English Woman's Estimate of Walt Whitman." Walt wrote her an ap-preciative letter, to which she replied a year later with a declaration of love and a plan to sail to America to be near him, like it or not. Walt replied with a certain deference, and the correspondence continued for six more years during which she grew ever more ardent, and he uncharacteristically polite and reserved. In 1876 he attempted to cancel her travel plans, but she came to Philadelphia regardless with three of her four children and a goodly part of her household effects. She initially suggested marriage, and then more or less demanded it. Ironically, Walt took an immediate liking to Gilchrist and her children, although it was immediately clear that he was about to have no romantic interest in her. In fairness, it must be said that Mrs. Gilchrist was well connected literarily on both side of the Atlantic, being as she was a friend of Carlyle, Rossetti, Tennyson and their circle. Having moved to Bos-ton, she and her entourage made their emotional departure from America in 1879. There she wrote a life of Mary Lamb, daughter of Charles Lamb, the British essayist. In 1890, incidentally, Whitman, free spirit that he assuredly was, claimed to have fathered six illegitimate children.

Herman Melville had four children, one of whom (Malcolm) committed suicide at the age of 18 a day after they had quarreled. Melville's independent ways were not always conducive to family life. He married Elizabeth Knapp Shaw (Melville called her "Lizzie," "Riana," and sometimes "Winnie"), daughter of Judge Lemuel Shaw, who was the Massachusetts Chief Justice, in 1847 (sometimes reported as 1848) and wrote some 2,200 legal opinions later published in 20 volumes. He was at that time, and by all odds, infinitely better known than Melville who at the time of his marriage was 28, three years older than his bride. The union was not a satisfactory one. He found her rather dull, unimaginative, commonplace. She hoped in vain that the day might come when "he may be in better mental health," and complained that he could not manage even to keep the family finances in order. There is no question that Melville was at times given to psychic confusion, and so it was in this marriage. Lemuel Shaw, who became a distinguished jurist, also became so much of a Melville family friend that, as James E. Miller, Jr. has suggested, Herman had come to regard him as his father instead of his father-in-law, meaning among other things that he had, by some warp of the imagination, married his sister. Melville obliquely alluded to that marriage in *Bartleby*, portraying himself as a mere scrivener and his boss as a Wall Street lawyer. Shaw, in fact, had worked on Wall Street early in his legal career, so records indicate, but had dealt in chancery (a record office containing public archives) and had never made a court appearance. By 1867 Elizabeth had consulted her minister about marital problems and been advised to leave her husband, but instead remained married and outlived Melville. In recent years, it has come to light that he had, like Thoreau, an unestablished sexual orientation. D. H. Lawrence commented upon this in his *Studies in Classic American Literature* (1923), saying that Melville had "from the 'perfect woman lover' passed on to the 'perfect friend'" and had then "looked and looked for the perfect man friend."[1] His biographer Newton Arvin suggested in 1950 that Elizabeth's inclination to marry Herman (they were childhood acquaintances) "may well have been deepened by his need of Judge Shaw's paternal presence," and that "the masculine and the feminine elements in Melville's own nature were far too precariously balanced, far too unreconciled with one another, for the marriage to be anything but excruciatingly problematic both for him and for his wife." Others have enlarged on this subject, including Rictor Norton who in 2000 cited an abundance of evidence from Melville's published work. In the meantime, at least two gay bars called "Moby Dick" have inevitably surfaced, one in San Francisco, the other in Sydney, Australia.

---

1 D. H. Lawrence, *Studies in Classic American Literature*, (New York: Viking Press, 1923) 142.

John Updike referred to Hawthorne as "the young hermit of Salem," and in a *New Yorker* article entitled "The Other Sister: Was Nathaniel Hawthorne a Cad?" (March 21, 2005) Megan Marshall notes that by November of 1837, "painfully shy, he had spent the previous ten years in almost complete seclusion, composing short stories at a desk in a bedroom in hope of establishing himself as a professional writer." She provides an account of Hawthorne's having had his head turned by the first (Elizabeth) and third (Sophia) of the Peabody sisters of Salem. It was Elizabeth, as Van Wyck Brooks aptly put it, who "disinterred Hawthorne from his living grave," but despite some emotional tugs of war it was Sophia who captured his heart. The wonder is that such a withdrawn literary figure took up with women (or anyone else) at all, but it was Elizabeth, whose bookshop became a *pied-à-terre* for cockeyed transcendentalists, who has been accorded credit for more or less having invented kindergartens and who was in a position to help Hawthorne launch a career in letters. Elizabeth, whose middle sister Mary became the wife of Horace Mann, did not for a moment wonder whether Hawthorne could attach himself to women, asserting that he had "tenderness enough to make a hundred husbands." From his despised Brook Farm living experiment, Hawthorne sent letters to his Sophia, addressing her with such saccharinity as "ownest love," "dearest unutterably," and "very dearest," signing off as "thy lovingest husband." On August 22, 1841 he proclaimed, "Belovedest, my bosom yearns for thee. Methinks it is an age since thou has been in my arms. When am I to see thee again?" It was good marriage, to be sure, but it did not preclude his taking other women as they came. In an off-quoted 1855 letter that he dispatched to his friend and publisher William D. Ticknor, he ranted in a quite different voice, "America is now wholly given over to a d — d mob of scribbling women, and I should have no chance of success while the public taste is occupied with their trash — and should be ashamed of myself if I did succeed." Hermit he was, hardly one to travel in a pack.

Neither, to be sure, was Charles Baudelaire, with whom Poe is often compared, and who not only translated Poe into French, but (by his own admission) plagiarized him, regarded Poe as a pariah. By any measure, Poe was a strange case: constitutionally hermitic, inner-directed, and yet (like Hawthorne) desperately in need of a mother's nurturing. He didn't receive it from biological mother who died before he was out of his second year, nor did he receive it from his adoptive Fanny Allen who died in 1829. After that there was Jane Stith Craig Stannard, mother of a schoolmate, who was allegedly the inspiration for his lyric "To Helen," and who died in 1824 after having allegedly gone mad. Poe memorialized her as the one who "brought me home/

To the glory that was Greece,/ And the grandeur that was Rome." There was also the sort of old fashioned love affair he had with Sarah Elmira Roister (and later) Shelton whom he had intended to marry. However, while he was at the University of Virginia for ten months, Sarah traveled to Europe and married an older, more secure man named Alexander Barrett Shelton. Poe was for a time fixated upon Maria Clemm whom he called "Ma" and "Muddy" who was his chief protector beginning with the death of Fanny Allen. There was a woman suspiciously named Mary Defraud, with whom he struck up some sort of amorous arrangement (and later stalked after she had married) in New York in 1832, but which came undone because of his use of opium and his penchant for alcohol. Then there was his cousin, the harpist Virginia Clemm, a never fully developed woman with a waxen and chalky complexion and large eyes who was the prototype of some of Poe's literary heroines. After his death he took up with Francis Osgood and Helen Whitman (whose family, and Poe's drinking, got in the way) both poets. There was also Marie Louise Shaw (later Houghton) who ended their friendship in 1848 mostly by reason of his having become too eccentric. Then was Nancy Locke "Annie" Heywood (later Richmond) whom Poe favored with his poem entitled "For Annie" that ends with the lines, "but my heart it is brighter/ Than all of the many/ Stars of the sky,/ For it sparkles with Annie — / It glows with the light/ Of the love of my Annie — / With the thought of the light/ Of the eyes of my Annie"; and Elmira Royster Shelton (now a widow), both of whom were engaged to Poe — at the same time. "I was never really insane except upon occasions when my heart was touched," Poe explained in the year of his death.

The classic critical debate over Mark Twain began with a volley launched by Van Wyck Brooks in *The Ordeal of Mark Twain* (1920), when he asserted that Twain's talent was "hidden," and "that bitterness of his was the effect of a certain miscarriage in his creative life, a balked personality, and arrested development of which he was himself almost wholly unaware, but which for him destroyed the meaning of life." Brooks called Twain's American frontier "a desert of human sand! — the barrenest spot in all Christendom, surely for the seed of genius to fall in."[1] Toward the conclusion of his book, he referred to Twain as "the starved artist who for forty years has had to pretend that he was a businessman who has always wanted to be 'original' in his dress and has had to submit to a feverish censorship even over his neckties." The point-for-point rebuttal to Brooks and other like-minded pundits arrived

---

1 Van Wyck Brooks, *The Ordeal of Mark Twain* (New York: E. P. Dutton & Co. Inc., 1970) 46-47.

in Bernard DeVoto's *Mark Twain's America* (1932). The debate essentially addressed the question of whether Twain's artistic gifts prevailed over his environment. A related and often discussed question is whether Twain's talent prevailed over the allegedly domineering women in his life. Allowing for the distinct possibility of his use of pernicious irony, it may be best to allow Twain to speak for himself. "The quality of independence," he recorded in his notebook, "was almost wholly left out of the human race." In a letter to Will Bowen in 1866, he claimed that "all men — kings & serfs alike — are slave to other men & to circumstance — save alone, the pilot — who comes at no man's back [sic] and call, obeys no man's orders & scorns all men's suggestions." As to the question of controlling women, he wrote in a fugitive piece called "Experience of the McWilliamses with Membranous Croup" (1875) that "women cannot receive even the most palpably judicious suggestion without arguing it; that is, married women."

Chapter 2. Going My Way

"Comrades! We must abolish the cult of the individual decisively, once and for all."
—Nikita Khrushchev

Notwithstanding Comrade Khrushchev's diatribe, delivered in the form of an oration to a secret session of the 20th Congress of the Communist Party in 1955, individuality is still in the minds of creative and productive people everywhere a damned fine idea. The implacable Greeks of antiquity, historian Philip Lee Ralph said, "did regard their own personalities with respect and believed that they were capable of almost unlimited development. To enable the individual to realize his true potential and to live as richly and fully as possible became a prime objective as their societies progressed."[1] No less than Carl Gustav Jung, the Swiss psychiatrist and founder of analytical psychology, remarked grandiloquently that personality development "is the supreme realization of the innate individuality of a particular human being," and that "personality is an act of the greatest courage in the face of life, the absolute affirmation of all that constitutes the individual, and the most successful adaptation to the universal conditions of existence coupled with the greatest possible freedom of personal decision." Lesser-known transcendentalist Sampson Reed (1800–1880), one of Emerson's Harvard classmates, wrote in 1821 that "there is something in the inmost principles of an individual, when he begins to exist, which urges him onward." In America, at least,

---

1 Phillip Lee Ralph, *The Story of Our Civilization: 10,000 Years of Western Man* (New York: E.P. Dutton & Co, Inc., 1954) 50.

individuality shaped and guided an entire culture. Commenting on World War I, Herbert Hoover told a New York audience in 1932 that when that monstrous conflict ended "we were challenged with a peace-time choice between the American system of rugged individualism and a European philosophy of diametrically opposed doctrines — doctrines of paternalism and state socialism." Remarking on the development of the American South, historian W. J. Cash observed, "The simple man in general invariably tends to become an individualist. Everywhere and invariably his fundamental attitude is purely personal — and purely self-asserting."[1] As we have seen, the primary shapers of American letters have been individualists with assertive social opinions. As Robert Woodward and James J. Clark jointly pointed out, "the theme of social rebellion is a fundamental one — perhaps the fundamental one — in American literature."[2]

It is in American literature that one so frequently, and tellingly, encounters the loner, about whom the *OED* has a great many pejorative things to say about that and related words. A loner, it reads, is fundamentally "a person who avoids company and prefers to be alone" but it cites other usages for the term, such as "a man of few words who finds it impossible to chat and joke with the crowds," or one who might be described as "a bit of a maverick," or one "who won't be tied by party trappings." Elsewhere, it associates the term "lone" with "having no fellows or companions," one "without company," or one "with not one friend his sorrows to divide" (citing 18th-century English novelist and poet Tobias Smollett), or perhaps "to play a lone hand" (as in Quadrille and Euchre), meaning "to take on all other players." Coleridge's "The Rime of the Ancient Mariner" directs our attention to "one, that on that lonesome road/ Doth walk in fear and dread." *Lone* may also be associated with one who is unmarried, single, or widowed, or possibly "one who stands apart from others of his kind." The *OED* further defines "loneliness" simply as "the want of society or company." *Genesis* 2:18 counsels sternly that "it is not good that man should be alone," (for fear, possibly, that he will acquire some habits) and John Milton's *Tetrarch* informs us that loneliness "is the first thing which God's eye nam'd not good." Of course being alone and being lonely are two different things. *Lonely* in this context we assumed to mean "having no companionship, or society. Unaccompanied, solitary, alone." The suspicious term "lone wolf" is more or less a synonym for "loner," taken to

---

1 W.J. Cash, *The Mind of the South: Its Origin and Development in the Old South* (New York: Vintage Books, 1941) 32.

2 Robert H. Woodward and James J. Clark (Eds.), *The Social Rebel in American Literature* (New York: The Odyssey Press, 1968) vii.

mean "one who mixes little with others," and "one who keeps to himself." As someone warned someone else, "you are in very serious damage if you try to lone wolf it," a message carried in another, similar caveat: "an individualist is to be watched unless he should develop in too much of a lone wolf." Some yet unidentified person averred, "Lone Wolves are folks who don't hold group process in high esteem. They don't think others are particularly capable. They frequently think that that their ideas are the best, and find it hard to trust others to deliver 'goods' that meet their standards." In scientific parlance, the expression "lone pair" refers, so we are told, to "a pair of electrons in the outer shell of an atom which are not involved in bonding." Enlarging on that observation, an article called "Galactic Loners Produce More Stars" that appeared in NewScientist.com in June of 2005, reminds us that "an overwhelming 95% of galaxies live in communities, which teem with thousands of members." Astronomer Fiona Hoyle at Widener University explains that "galaxies in clusters interact often and during these interactions the galaxies are stripped of their gas," meaning that they "probably haven't undergone significant interaction." Michael Vogeley, another astronomer, likens this isolation to "a few rugged individuals who, without the competition of others, can live surprisingly well from the meager offerings of the land in most rural areas." Scientists, be they loners or not, have in the popular mind experienced the marginalizing that loners are made to experience. In a review of Christopher Frayling's book entitled *Mad, Bad and Dangerous?* (2005), carried in physics.web, we learn that scientists, as they are erroneously depicted in American film, "are aloof, socially inept, amoral creatures driven by pathological obsessions with the secrets of the universe and [with] the power that understanding these secrets might empower."

Such definitions and illustrations carry an obviously pejorative sense of disapproval, implying that to be alone, to be a loner, or possibly a lone wolf and all such related life options, including solitude, independence, self reliance — are inadvisable, indefensible, psychologically and socially damaging, and therefore to be discouraged. That, of course, is egregious stupidity. Montaigne said it best: "the greatest thing in the world is to know how to be self-sufficient." Indeed, self-sufficient people have the innate agility to move quickly, deftly, and decisively without any real or imagined obligation to clear their intentions with a baying chorus of dolts and dunces. That is why traveling alone is preferable, and why high aspiration all but demands working alone. As Katherine Hepburn cryptically said, "People who want to be famous are really loners — or they should be." One might interpret this to mean that folks who long to be famous are likely to be loners, or possibly to be famous is to be a loner. Whichever way this is to be understood, it also is one more reason to opt for the lone life that is advantageous, too, in the making of books. British essayist and reviewer Cyril Connolly cleverly commented, "It is better to write for yourself and have no public, than to write for the public and have no self." A woman named Anneli Rufus has assembled a sprightly and amusing book entitled *Party of One: The Loners' Manifesto* (2003) that is at once witty and on the mark. "Mainstream culture," Ms. Rufus writes, "loves nonloners. Joiners, schmoozers, teamworkers, congregants and all those who play well with others [and] scoop up the rewards." In the meantime, she says, "loners get dissed. All the time. At school, at work, at church or temple, in movies, loners are misunderstood, misjudged, loathed, pitied, and feared. Reporters and profilers calmly and constantly call us perverts, losers, stalkers and serial killers."

Not only that, but it has recently come to pass that health "professionals" are alleging that to be a loner is to put one's health at risk. A publication called *Indobase* has even suggested that "going out for a run on your own could be bad for your health," whereas going out for the same run with "a group or with a friend could be beneficial." *Indobase* uncovered this surprising disclosure by observing rodents, some of which exercised independently, while others exercised with other rodents. After 12 days of this, researchers estimated that the more socially-oriented rodents developed more than twice the brain cells. The point of all this, said one researcher, has to do with "neurogenesis," the generation of new brain cells. To run in "social" isolation, they surmised, "these positive effects are suppressed." They also concluded that rodents of a more antisocial disposition handled pressure less well than social rats.

According to a 1997 article entitled "Social Ties and the Common Cold" in the *Journal of the American Medical Association*, it has come to light that 276 ostensibly healthy volunteers were quarantined and introduced to "rhinoviruses" that resulted in sniffles. The experiment led to social conclusions, namely that loners were four times more likely than the more social types to contract a head cold. The article directs us to a turgid theory, to wit: "The hypothesis that multiple ties to friends, family, work and community are beneficial *in terms of* physical health has gained substantial support over the last decade." Notice the *de rigueur* use of "in terms of," dear to the hearts of those who do not mind their words, preferring instead to speak as others speak, which is to say *badly*. Be that as it may, the paragraph continues by noting that "particularly provocative is epidemiologic evidence that those who participate in more diversified social networks — for example are married, interact with family members, friends, neighbors, and fellow workers, and belong to social and religious groups — live longer than their counterparts with fewer types of social relationships." The paragraph ends with the surprising disclosure that "the relative risk for mortality among those with less diverse networks is comparable in magnitude to the relation between smoking and mortality from all causes." This suggests, as writer Steven J. Milloy has inferred, that loners and smokers have a comparable probability of dying from any cause one cares to nominate. To be a loner and a smoker, one might also infer, could cause death at any moment. In 2001, Yale University ran an article in its *Science Blog* entitled "'Brainy' students Least Likely to Engage in Risky Behaviors While 'Burnout' and 'Non-Conformists' Are at Highest Risk," averring, as the lengthy title suggests, that "burnouts and non-conformists had the highest levels of health risk behaviors across the areas assessed."

Citing two recent studies, an article by Shaoni Bhattacharya that appeared in the May 2, 2005, issue of *New Scientist*, carries a similar threatening message, namely that "low levels of social connectedness can adversely influence the body-lowering immune response and affecting cardiac health." Freshman college students, it goes on to say, are those who feel the loneliest, and as an apparent consequence had a 16 percent worse reaction to one influenza strain contained in a certain flu vaccine. Another study, this one based upon tracking some 3,000 men and presented at an American Heart Association convention "showed that those who had the lowest levels of social involvement — being unmarried or having few people to confide in, for example — had the highest levels of an inflammatory marker called Interleukin-6." Loners, so one hears, are even more likely to fall victim to accidents. An essay titled "Middle-Aged Loners at Greatest Risk From Fires," that appeared in *The Scotsman*, revealed that a "nationwide blight" in Scotland had developed around "men over 50" who had returned from a convivial night at the pubs and managed somehow to set themselves on fire. What to do? In one region, the article explains, "Firefighters are running a pilot scheme to check electric blankets." In another initiative, fire fighters "will now canvass pubs at night, warning drinkers of what could happen if they do not exercise care at home." Possibly, these pub-crawlers should consider getting married, but when? Sir Francis Bacon advised men not even to consider matrimony. Not everyone feels quite that strongly about it. As the twice-married 19th-century poet William Cosmo Monkhouse put it,

"There was an old party of Lyme,
Who married three wives at one time.
When asked, 'Why the third?'
He replied, 'One's absurd,
And bigamy, sir, is a crime!'

As nearly everyone knows, statisticians have for some time presented evidence that for men, at least, matrimony promotes longevity, if for no other reason than, as sociologists seem to believe, social isolation equates with higher suicide rates. A journal called *PubMed* that is a service of the National Library of Medicine and the National Institutes of Health printed a March 15, 2006 article entitled "Marital History at Midlife as a Predictor of Longevity," advancing the notion "that consistently married people live longer than whose who have experienced marital breakup," but allows for the proviso "that this is not necessarily due to the protective effects of marriage itself." It does point out, however, that "individuals who were currently married, but had previously experienced a divorce, were at significantly higher mortality risk compared with consistently married individuals." Moreover, it surmised, "individuals who had not married by midlife were not a higher mortality risk compared with consistently married individuals." That same publication carried an article in 1984, observing that men who are married to younger women live longer than men married to older women, one explanation being the no-brainer that "psychological, physiological, or social factors associated with longevity may be enhanced by marriage to a younger woman." Noreen Goldman, in an article called "Marriage Selection and Mortality Matters: Inferences and Fallacies" appearing in *Demography* in May of 1993, notes that although "hundreds of studies in a large number of industrialized countries have demonstrated that married men and woman have greater longevity and experience better health than do single, divorced and widowed persons," she questions whether "married people fare better than their unmarried counterparts because mentally and physically healthier people are more likely to marry in the first place (this is what some sociologists call 'marriage selection'), or because of the presumed social, psychological, economic and environmental benefits associated with having a spouse (sometimes called 'marriage protection')?" And what is "marriage protection"? An economist identified only as "Rahman," cited in the *Journal of Health Economics*, explains that marriage may be protective in the sense that "it may reduce stress and stress-related illness (perhaps as a result of greater social integration)." If not that, Rahman continues, "Marriage may encourage healthy types of behavior, and discourage risky or unhealthy ones (drinking, substance abuse, etc.)," commenting also "a spouse also makes it more likely that the individual receives adequate care *in terms of* illness."

If mothers don't let their kids grow up to be cowboys, so too mothers should not encourage their kids to be loners — or so the received opinion goes. A source calling itself "You Can Handle Them All," purporting to show schoolteachers how to manage different sorts of children, lists five danger signals that a loner emits, those being 1) that he "seems to shy away from everything and everyone," adding that "even a classroom visitor can pick out the loner during the first observation"; 2) that he "walks alone in the halls"; 3) that he is always extremely quiet; 4) that he "shuns participation of any kind with others"; and 5) that he "may be a good or poor student." The caveat ends by warning that such a child may "pass from year to year unnoticed." The *South African Star* warned its readers that child loners "tend to become politicians" or, saints preserve us, "join church groups," suggesting that, to the contrary, they've ceased being loners. More specifically, it cited evidence gathered at Essex University's Institute for Social and Economic Research that "10-year-olds unable to make friends, as adults sought out formal structures like political parties or the church" since "children's self-image could suffer as a result of early loneliness and they could seek status through these organizations." Moreover, the research indicated that "children who were isolated at 10 years of age were likely to be depressed adults, unlikely to have found partners and unlikely to have gained a university degree."

Does television play a role in the spawning of loners? Some people think so. David Everett, writing for *Media Life Magazine* in April of 2001 noted that there are nearly three television sets per American family, and that a great deal of programming designed to be viewed by families is instead viewed by individuals. "That's not what families are doing," he commented. What's worse, reported *South London* magazine in October of 2004, "the rise of the lonesome child is being linked to increased numbers of TV channels and multi-television household, with over a quarter (26 percent) of youngsters spending the majority of their free time in front of the box. Britain's children are becoming a nation of square-eyed loners," it warns, adding with alarm that "more than two-thirds (68 percent) of children spend more time playing alone than with friends." The noble cause of self-reliance and self-sufficiency has always been put to the supreme test during instances of playground bullying. The result, says Lawrence J. Cohen ("A Loner or Alone?" Parenthood. com, March 27, 2006) in his remarks on "how parents can help children with friendship issues," is that they encounter distressing problems (or "issues," as certain people like to describe them) such as "depression, loneliness, anxiety, even suicide or homicide," the reason being that a child "might be miserable because he's not a part of the 'in-crowd.'" One person (who shall go unidentified) suggested in 2005 one constructive method of encouraging children to refrain from becoming loners. It consists of "adding playdough to the learning areas" where there are children "that like to be alone." The theory is that "when children play with playdough, they improve on their social skills," to which we add by way of encouragement "a point well taken."

But playdough doesn't always work. Even loners have problems, or are perceived by others to have problems. An unidentified party in British Columbia recalled a marketing class where students were working up a case study of a "funeral home," whereupon the instructor asked toward whom the funeral ads were targeted. The answer was, "people who have no family or friends." The unidentified witness was aghast. "Just imagine that," he/she wrote. "An adult with no one in their [*sic*] life." And later, "What must it be like to pick up a flyer advertising cremation service, and then realize this is something you have to plan yourself?" Why not? One third of headstones are purchased by individuals over whom the stone will be placed. The observation ends with speculation that "there might be a lot of 'loners' out there.... I think it's pretty unfortunate." It might be unfortunate, yes, but only if one prefers to view it that way. Timothy Pippert, whose *Road Dogs and Loners: An Ethnographic Examination of Biological, Created, and Fictive Families of the Homeless*, presented as a doctoral dissertation at the University of Nebraska in 1999, interviewed some 45 homeless men, concluding, among other things, "that they seriously lacked strong ties with relatives and friends but [that, fortunately] they were not totally isolated," noting that "this was especially true of loners." Lone wolves must therefore be the object of deepest concern in Japan where that nation has allegedly experienced a spike in what our Japanese friends call "hikikomori," meaning "to be confined," but which has come to mean, as a chap named Son Jung-a explains, "people who are confined in their homes for a long period of time, usually over six months." In Korea there is similar distress over people who are known in that country as "reclusive loners," meaning those who "don't have friends and don't talk with family" and who "eat alone," but unaccountably "don't cook their own food." Moreover, such social ravages "sleep during the day and watch TV or surf the internet at night." But it doesn't end there. Because great numbers of reclusive loners live in rooming houses, "electronic companies are producing a greater number of small refrigerators, televisions and rice kettles." Worse still, "some rooming houses even have a rule that people living there pretend not to notice each other."

In the meantime, the Australian Bureau of Statistics reported in 2001 that whereas there were 1.8 million people (one in 11 Australians) living alone, that number is projected to reach between 2.8 and 3.7 (between one in 7 and one in 9) million by 2026. This is not always by choice. Between one quarter and one third of these people are probably over 75, and three quarters of them women. Single person households tend to delay marriage and eventually drift into separation and divorce. Moreover, by 2010 or 2011 couple families without children are predicted to exceed couple marriages with children, the main reasons being an aging population, as well as aging baby boomers' becoming "empty nesters," not to mention their declining fertility and delayed family formation. Average household size is anticipated to fall from 2.6 persons per household to between 2.2 and 2.3 by 2026. *The Los Angeles Times* reported that, according to the 2000 census, U.S. single adult households had exceeded the number of couples-with-children households. A spokesperson for the National Association of Homebuilders noticed that unmarried people are evidently planning to continue being unmarried, and are therefore purchasing homes with less privacy, fewer rooms and less square footage. There is a large part of the American population that cannot imagine living any other way. Wrote one gentleman to a website called AVEN (meaning "Asexual Visibility and Education Network"), "I've been a loner all my life. I just never understood friendship rituals. You see these groups of friends going to dinner and shopping all the time together? How does that happen?"

Good question. Whereas isolation may be atavistic, it should be pointed out that some of our animal friends are exceedingly solitary, as for example leafcutter bees that have an unnerving tendency to wander off by themselves. It did not go unnoticed during the 2008 political campaign that John McCain ominously turned up alone in an airport. Furthermore, there's not a bloody thing that can be done about it. A closer examination of tortoises in the Mohave Desert, however, has led members of the U.S. Geological Survey to conclude that, in the words of biologist Kristin Berry, "they are individuals interacting in complex communities." Berry even discovered an independently inclined tortoise so old that he was, in the words of Louis Sahagun of *The Los Angeles Times*, "probably hatched from an egg when Calvin Coolidge was president." Grizzly bears, writes Nutan Shukla from India, "tend to be solitary in habit and highly jealous of their territory and guard it regularly against intrusion by an individual of their kind."

This brings us to lone wolves of the four-legged sort, defined, according to bearcountryusa.com as "usually young males that have left the pack in search of their own territories." We are also assured that "they avoid other wolves, unless they are potential mates. When a lone wolf finds unoccupied territory, it will claim it by marking it with its scent." A new pack will form, we are told, when "other lone wolves enter the territory." As recently as 2006, the *Milwaukee Journal Sentinel* observed that in Wisconsin wolf sightings are dramatically on the rise. "Population is booming," writer Lee Bergquist reported. "Lone wolves have turned up in every corner of the state," he warned, noting "there has been no wolf incursion like this since the 19th century." Unlike two-legged wolves, the four-legged sort are benevolently protected by law, at least in liberal Wisconsin where there happens to be an abundance of deer and a population (excepting, perhaps, livestock producers) that rather likes the idea of wolves in its midst, provided that they are not actually confronted (or "challenged," as people say) by such threatening beasts. One Wisconsin woman reported locking eyes with a wolf at a distance of 20 feet in the summer of 2003. The same woman also reported having been stalked by a pair of wolves of the four-legged variety who were joined affiliatively by a third during the subsequent Christmas season. She clapped her hands and screamed at them, but to no avail. On yet another occasion her spaniel hugged her legs while two more salivating wolves cunningly observed from about 20 yards distance. One other Wisconsin observer commented that he regarded the wolf as "a beautiful animal," but regretted that the state had not successfully controlled their numbers. Back in 1865, there was a $5.00 bounty on the beasts, but after the 1975 Endangered Species Act it became illegal to kill them. Mr. Bergquist mentions also that (as is often true of the two-legged wolf variety) the four-legged wolf population was depleted by "mange, vehicle accidents and, inevitably, gunshots." A Wisconsin county supervisor, Mr. Bergquist also reported, weighed in on the wolf question, saying that "either rightly or wrongly [they] are not showing a fear of humans," citing as evidence that when a law enforcement officer sounded his siren, it elicited little to no wolfian reaction. Elsewhere in Wisconsin wolves made a stealthy foray into a town, whereupon there was a groundswell of support for moving them elsewhere. Said one mayor, "They've been seen on the street and there is a ton of little kids. People walk their dogs and they exercise; all it takes is for one person to get hurt, or one pet to be killed. I think it's a concern about safety."

We would have to agree. All the same, the Alaska Fish and Game Department disclosed that whereas there have been wolf bites reported now and then, not one person in America had been killed by such an animal. Out in Minnesota (where, as some wise guy said, if wolves and people could not co-exist, there would be a substantially fewer Minnesotans by now), there has been a humane movement to outfit wolves with radios in somewhat the way two-legged wolves are ordinarily equipped with ubiquitous cell phones. While it is still contrary to law for folks to kill wolves, 70 Wisconsin "problem wolves" were not exactly "killed" but were "euthanized" between 2003 and 2005. These and other political events have divided the population of Wisconsin between pro-wolfers and anti-wolfers. Pro-wolfers are in favor of putting guard dogs on the case, but others argue that this accomplishes nothing. Similarly, a 2002 lone wolf bulletin from Sweden brings news that it is currently illegal to hunt wolves there, "except in cases where individuals have repeatedly attacked livestock." It concludes by cautioning that "as the wolf population grows, so does the tension between the farmers and conservationists." As to lone wolves, a source calling itself wolfcountry.net reminds us that whereas "wolves belong to family groups called packs [that] usually consist of eight to 15 members," the lone wolf is "most likely to be the lowest member of the pack (the omega) that was driven out of the pack." On the slim chance that "it is lucky, the 'lone wolf' may find a mate and start a new pack," albeit the omega is one of those individuals who "absorb the greatest amount of aggression from the rest of the pack, and consequently enjoy comparatively few individual privileges." Are four-footed wolves monogamous? More or less. "There are exceptions," according to wolfcountry.net, when "an alpha animal may preferentially mate with a lower-ranking animal, especially if the other alpha is closely related (a brother or sister, for example)." Elsewhere we are informed that "rank order is established and maintained through a series of ritualized fights and posturing best described as *ritual bluffing*," a commonplace activity in singles bars. The ritual finds its conclusion, we are informed, when "a playful lupine holds its tail high and wags it."

Animal behavior does not necessarily end with the lower animals, however. There is a growing perception (some justified, some not) that there is a decided relationship between hermits, anchorites, loners (by whatever name they go) — and criminal activity. To the contrary, in a 2004 article entitled "Understanding the Delinquency and Social Relationships of Loners" published in *Youth & Society* by Stephen Demuth at Ohio's Bowling Green State University, Professor Demuth draws numerous conclusions, chief among them "that loners are less delinquent than nonloners are," allowing, however, that "there are nevertheless negative circumstances associated with being a loner," a capsule definition of which he calls a person "with no close friends." A similar study carried in *PubMed* in 1990 contends, "The lack of peer influence on the loners seems to contribute to less delinquency and drug use and more conventional lifestyle than is found among socials." Certain of Demuth's remarks, however, deserve a hearing and amplification. "Popular stereotypes of loners," he writes, having been "reinforced by recent highly publicized episodes of extreme violence, provide unsettling images of loners as psychologically and emotionally unstable and capable of serious forms of delinquency possibly as a consequence of their socially isolated status." Having pointed out that in the teenage years, young people devote less time to their parents and more time to their peers, he uses the term "social isolates" to mean "individuals with limited acceptance who suffer neglect, rejection of degradation at the hands of their schoolmates" and who "spend much of their time alone yet may drift in and out of unstable, short-lived relationships." Demuth also demonstrates that a lack of peer acceptance leads down the dark road toward "dropping out of school, juvenile and adult crime, and adult psychopathology." His observations are largely borne out by some published observations by Berent Associates in socialanxiety.com, namely that acts of violence in school are committed by the "socially handicapped," meaning that "their self-esteem is dysfunctional, they have few quality peer relationship and are low in the social 'pecking order.'" Among the "warning signs" of such behavior are "an absence of a peer group, social skills challenges, social anxiety, a sense of secrecy, irritability, communications problems, overdependence on the internet at the expense of healthy socialization, and a breakdown in parenting."

One might wonder if an overdependence upon peers and other groups does not foster a herd dependency, while tending to diminish such valuable traits as self-reliance and independence of mind and spirit. Speaking to that point was a letter with the heading, "Let's Hear It for Loners" in the British-based thisislancashire.co.uk on April 16, 1996, by a lady's objecting to having someone abusively referred to as a "loner and an odd-ball." Said the lady, "This terminology has amazed me for years! I realize that the person 'that is different' who can walk alone, entertain oneself, enjoy their [sic] company, make decisions for themselves [sic] and appreciate the material sequences of life, without having to consult another human being, is a rarity!" Having objected to a certain criminal's being labeled "a loner," the British lady rightly declared, "I was taught, along with my six brothers, to stand firm to our own points of view and not to always require confirmation or be persuaded by any other human being! This was also encouraged at school." Concluding, she asked, "Is not the person who can travel through life, making their [sic] own decisions and able to enjoy one's own company, far richer than the person who lacks assertiveness through the need for constant human contact?

Where are the characters of today? I have thoroughly enjoyed the personalities of yesteryear who have passed my way, but alas would be given the title – 'he was a loner.' How unfair!"

Unfair is right. It is not unusual to pin some hideous crime on the perpetrator's allegedly being a loner. Examples abound: *Cincinnati Enquirer*, July 5, 1998 headline: "'Loner' Charged in Killing," with reference to the murder of a six-year-old girl by a man whose occupation was a "tire mechanic," and whom (of course) "neighbors described...as a loner," despite the fact that the murderer "gave children stuffed animals and candy," appeared to assist in the search for the (then) missing child, "was a dedicated employee," told people about his recent Oregon fishing trip and "always sat and talked with the kids." On April 21, 1999, a Denver *Rocky Mountain News* headline read, "Quiet Loners Worried Other Students" with reference to the Columbine High School shootings. The perpetrators appeared to run in packs that consisted of "normal kids who did normal stuff," except that they "shot dozens of people, and then shot themselves," and spoke German to each other. They also "listened to German techno music [,] were fans of Adolph Hitler," were "10 kids in a clique" but still and all "came from families neighbors described as very fine people." As to their wearing identical trench coats, one of them admitted, "We all just started wearing them to keep warm. We all pretty much got them." Some loners these were. The *British Guardian* did one better on May 3, 1999, with a headline that read "Loner Against Society?" with a subtitle "Childhood Psychology Can Light the Fuse for Atrocities." It had to do with a fellow named David Copeland whom police had charged "with being behind the three London nail bomb attacks [and who] said he was 'working alone' for his own motives." The charges, it noted, "raise the possibility that he may be one of those rare but alarming examples of a loner capable of committing atrocities apparently in complete isolation." The article cites a psychology professor at the University of Manchester who speculated that "the spark for anyone carrying out acts of terror alone comes from childhood," suggesting that such a person would likely be frustrated over "not having any success or not having any friends." The article then brings to mind the so-called "Mardi Gras bomber" who received a 21-year sentence "for carrying out a four-year blackmail, extortion and bombing campaign against Sainsbury's and Barclays Bank," and who "in fact" had "acted alone." Acting alone, regardless of the purpose, is not a generally endorsed activity at a time when all the important activity in the world, one would be led to believe, is accomplished by committees and meetings. On November 10, 2001, a *San Francisco Chronicle* item entitled "Profile of Anthrax Mailer Portrays

Loner, Opportunist," explained that "the FBI is hoping its portrait of the perpetrator — as an anti-social 'loner' with some peculiar mannerisms in his handwriting and speech — will lead them to whoever mailed at least three anthrax-laden letters and killed [five] people." Accordingly, the *St. Petersburg Times* on that same day reported that "FBI officials said...that they believe the person who mailed several anthrax-filled letters is probably a U.S.–based male loner with a scientific bent, possibly like Unibomber Ted Kaczynski, whose letter bombs mystified law enforcement for nearly two decades." FBI profilers also surmised that 'he prefers being by himself more often than not. If employed, [he] is likely to be in a position requiring little contact with the public or other employees. He may work in a laboratory." Dealing, as he does, with anthrax, "he may have started taking antibiotics unexpectedly." Excellent point. As Sir John Pentland Mahaffy correctly observed, in Ireland (at least) "the inevitable never happens and the unexpected constantly occurs." The *Christian Science Monitor's* "Domestic Loners Top Suspect List in Anthrax Attacks," (December 19, 2001) ventured to say, "The rise of these lone attackers can be linked to a right-wing terrorist philosophy that sprang up in the early 1990s, known as 'leaderless resistance'" that was "advocated in a tract by former Ku Klux Klan leader Louis Beam, it calls for 'phantom cells' rather than taking orders from an organization." It subsequently mentions "a domestic-terrorism expert at Simmons College in Boston" who in turn holds that "these small cells or individuals operate independently from each other, and basically just take their marching orders from what they read in the newspaper." Hence, running such a character down is no simple task, partly "because there's no one to talk, other than that lone individual."

From the Republic of Finland came an October 14, 2002 piece entitled "Shopping Mall Bomber Described as a Loner," reporting on a shopping mall explosion slightly north of Helsinki that killed seven people (including the bomber) and injured 70 others. Police believed that the perpetrator was a 19-year-old chemistry student [not the best of signals] whose friends described him "as a quiet and withdrawn young man who would sit at the rear of the classroom and who rarely took part in student events." On May 27, 2003, *The Christian Science Monitor* included a piece called "'Lone Wolves' Pose Explosive Terror Threat" that had to do with Sayed Abdul Malike who in New York, according to report, "tried to buy enough explosives to blow up a mountain." *The Monitor* characterized Malike as a "lone-wolf terrorist sympathizer," meaning "people who are not part of organized groups like Al Qaeda, but who are inclined to act in sympathy with their aims." It notes "experts" who "say the major terrorist attacks in the United States have been perpetrated by deranged individuals who were sympathetic to a larger cause — from Oklahoma bomber Timothy McVeigh to the Washington area sniper John Allen Muhammad." It went on to note, "Malike's case is illustrative of the challenges posed by lone wolves — and their vulnerabilities." Since Malike had to ask advice on how to build a bomb, federal agents surmised, "He could very likely be a lone wolf." It ends with the familiar caveat that, "since lone wolves can be hard to detect, law enforcement is dependent on public vigilance." On February 1, 2005, CNN.com published an article titled simply "Lone Wolves" written by Henry Schuster, a senior producer at CNN's Investigative Unit, specializing in "the people and organizations driving international and domestic terrorism." Wrote Mr. Schuster, "Lone Wolves are typically Americans with an extremist agenda [we are particularly impressed when anyone says *agenda*], usually anti-government. They are certainly not the only domestic terrorists, but they are scary nonetheless." He concludes by citing the case of Tim McVeigh as an example of "how dangerous a lone wolf could be," warning that, "in the world of terrorism, lone wolves are harder to hunt." A Chinese English language paper called *The Standard* published an article written by Mike German, a former FBI agent assigned to domestic terrorism, on McVeigh after his execution for his Oklahoma City bombing that took 168 lives, calling him "the prototypical lone wolf terrorist," and commenting at the end of his piece that "lone extremists pose a challenge for law enforcement because they are difficult to predict. It's like searching every haystack for a needle." At a site called news24.com on March 22, 2005 there appeared an anonymously submitted article called "Teen Gunman Was a Loner," about a 15-year-old Minnesota youth who shot his grandfather, a woman, and seven others at his high school, then turned the gun on himself. The account described him as "a quiet, much-teased loner, who had professed an admiration for Adolph Hitler." On August 11, 2005 Associated Press published an item titled "Potential 'Lone Wolf' Attackers Concern Police," about a 23-year-old Pakistani believed to have intended to blow up a New York subway station, citing police as exclaiming that "they are concerned about angry, isolated men...as much as terrorist networks like al-Qaeda, adding that one of the "ongoing concerns is the emergence of 'lone wolves.'" It ends by saying that, aside from al-Qaeda operatives, "the lone wolf, when influenced by day-to-day events, is harder to stop, harder to know about, much more difficult to defend against."

Whereas there may well be loners, lone wolves, solitary chaps who go through life without deliberately harming anyone, chances are that one will never hear about them. On October 22, 2005, CNN reported on the 16-year-old kid who murdered a 52-year-old woman in or near Martinez, California, by bludgeoning her over the head with a piece of crown molding as part of a botched scheme to secure stolen credit card numbers to finance (or "fund," as some prefer) his marijuana-growing enterprise. Police assumed that he acted alone. The assassin was, CNN reported, "described by classmates as a goth loner who followed the occult and dressed in black from the polish on his fingernails to his trench coat." Reported another classmate, "When he walked by, everybody talked about him — like, he definitely didn't blend in." Small wonder. Reporters who visited the suspect's home "saw goats and chickens [wandering] around the property, a potbelly stove, a bathtub and dozens of baseballs littered the yard," so the Associated Press said. The *New York Daily News* printed a gruesome account of a 41-year-old ex-con who raped, tortured and murdered a woman in Queens. The headline carried the all too familiar message. "Queens Nabe [neighborhood] in Shock Over Lurking 'Loner.'" Said one nabe, "He just kept to himself. He dressed in military stuff. He's just a quiet, strange guy." Apparently so. By "military stuff" he meant that the accused "was a self-styled police buff, dressing in fatigues or black SWAT team-type uniforms, tucking his trousers neatly into black combat boots, sometimes wearing paraphernalia that identified him as a federal agent or U.S. marshal." He was also observed visiting a local store, with a mind to purchasing some dog biscuits. "He would buy dog food, newspapers, lottery tickets and turkey sandwiches," said its owner, with an air of suspicion. Marshall N. Heyman, Ph.D., Director of the Behavioral Assessment Systems Center in Falls Church, Virginia, found in his February, 2006 study of presidential assassins that such offenders were likely to suffer from a sense of "inadequacy in dealing with social...challenges." Then on March 31, 2006, the Anti-Defamation League published a story subtitled "'Lone Wolf' of Hate Prowls the Internet," referring to "one of the most radical and influential voices on the racist right" who hoped "that a violent revolution [would] topple the United States government, which he "[considered] a Jewish-occupied government." The accused, the piece went on to say, "sees himself as a propagandist sowing the seeds of a racist revolution, and [who] predicts that 'lone wolves" will reap the harvest." The *London Times* published a 2006 item called "Deadly Rampage of Loner 'Who Dreamt of Being a Serial Killer," about "a loner who stabbed four strangers to death and left two others gravely wounded." The accused, after one of his intended victims wrestled a steak knife from him, replied pensively, "Sorry. I am a schizophrenic. I can't help it." According to reports, he "had no friends but enjoyed playing computer games [but] could not cope with growing up to become a man." Reuters reported after the 2007 Virginia Tech University shootings that took the lives of 33 people including the student gunman himself, that "experts in such crimes" testified that "people who commit mass murders...are frustrated loners bent on revenge who blame others for their failures." Police, meanwhile, said, "He was a loner, and we're having difficulty finding information about him."

This is not to suggest that we defend criminal behavior, but that we take umbrage at calling every criminal a loner. There is no question that, in the public mind, individuality is subversive enough to carry with it identification with criminality, on the assumption that anyone who stays to himself must necessarily be up to some pernicious activity. Adrian Savage, in his February 3, 2006 article in a site called *The Coyote Within* entitled "Being Yourself Matters," celebrates and encourages individuality, non-conformity, and the eccentricity that often accompanies them. "Maybe it's because I'm English," he says, "that I feel at home with all types of eccentrics and non-conformists. To me, they're like spice in food: essential to add zest and interest to what otherwise be too bland. They're also responsible for most of the truly good ideas we take for granted." On that point, Jan Harold Brunvand in the *Study of American Folklore* (1978) lends credence to the theory that widely accepted ideas spring from individual minds. "The theory of individual origins and communal re-creation," he writes, "holds that an item of folklore has a single inventor at any level of society, but that it is repeatedly made over as it is transmitted by word of mouth."[1] Whereas business and corporate life, about which we will have a good deal to say in the next chapter, leans heavily toward conformity and team playing, some in the world of commerce would argue otherwise. Eric K. Winslow and George T. Solomon have authored a rather maverick treatise entitled "Entrepreneurs Are More Than Non-Conformists [;] They are Mildly Sociopathic" (*Journal of Creative Behavior*, Vol. 21, pp. 202–23) positing that entrepreneurs share such traits as risk-taking and non-conformity, and are, as the title announces, inclined to be at least somewhat sociopathic. That may come as no surprise. Erudite folks may happen to recall that Reed Sampson went farther than that when he recorded in his essay "On Genius" (1821), that "there prevails an idea in the world that its great men are more like God than others." In 1859, John Stuart Mill's *On Liberty* referred to individuality "as one of the elements of well-being." Mill declared in his third chapter (devoted to individuality) that "I insist thus emphatically on the importance of genius, and the necessity of allowing it to unfold itself freely both in thought and practice," suggesting elsewhere that

---

1 Jan Harold Brunvand, *The Study of American Folklore* (New York: W.W. Norton Company, Inc., 1978) 28.

"the worth of the State in the long run is the worth of the individuals compos-ing it."[1] Oh, surely not. The worth of the state, as is commonly believed, rests in the corrupt hands of politicians and useless bureaucrats.

Resistance to such rubbish will most logically originate from indepen-dently minded individuals (although, as we shall see, there is some dis-agreement with that assumption) who challenge the status quo, earning for themselves various printable names as dissenters, contrarians, and (more generically) non-conformists. We know Emerson's famous quip (cited ear-lier) that "whoso would be a man, must be a nonconformist." Our biblical parents Adam and Eve, as independently minded as anyone since their time, may have been the first dissenters of record, having disobeyed God's com-mand that originates with His earnest caveat to Adam when (in the *New English Bible* rendering) he "took the man and put him in the garden of Eden to till it and care for it. He told the man, 'you may eat from every tree in the garden, but not from the tree of the knowledge of good and evil; for on the day that you eat from it, you will certainly die.'" We all know what followed that most famously flagrant act of *dissent*. The *OED* defines dissent variously as "to withhold assent or consent from a proposal, etc.; not to assent; to dis-agree with or object to an action" as well as "to think differently, disagree, differ from (an opinion or) with (a person)" or maybe "to differ in religious opinion; to differ from the doctrine or worship of a particular church, esp. from that of the established, national or orthodox church," or quite possibly "to be at dissention or variance; to quarrel," or maybe even "to differ as to, or from," or in some instances "to differ in sense, meaning or purport." Sowing dissent in the ranks, one need hardly say, is a perilous activity that can evoke reactions that range from benignant annoyance to murder.

The Reverend Archie Rowe of Coleford, England, reminds us "in our own land, Dissenters or Nonconformists have included such influential groups as the Quakers, the Anabaptists (who were the forerunners of the Baptists) Presbyterians, Unitarians and Congregationalists and, a little later, the Methodists." Mr. Rowe continues, "the Quakers were particularly known for their opposition to social injustice," and that the Quaker Elizabeth Fry "did so much to bring about prison reform," that William Wilberforce "fought for the abolition of slavery," that "others introduced the Building Society sys-tem and the Trade Unions," charitably concluding that "dissenters have been responsible for some of our best schools, hospitals and children's homes." Nonconformists, if such we call people and the people for whom they speak, do not necessarily earn enthusiastic societal approbation. Whereas Martin

---

1 John Stuart Mill, *On Liberty* (New York: W.W. Norton & Company, 1975) 106.

Luther King publicly proclaimed "the hope of a secure and livable world lies with disciplined nonconformists who are dedicated to justice, peace and brotherhood," Eric Hoffer, that independently-inclined longshoreman-turned-armchair-philosopher, observed that "nonconformists travel as a rule in bunches. You rarely find a nonconformist who does it alone. And woe to him inside a nonconformist clique who does not conform with nonconformity." Said curmudgeon Bill Vaughn, "If there is anything the nonconformist hates worse than a conformist, it's another nonconformist who does not conform to the prevailing standard of nonconformity." It was literary comedian James Thurber who raised the ultimate question: "Why do you have to be a nonconformist like everybody else?"

Dissent is part of the loner's stock in trade, not because he deems it his calling in life to assume a contrarian view of anything that comes to mind, but because he at least thinks for himself, and does not allow outside pressures to interfere. Unlettered John Bunyan (1628–1688) composed his *Grace Abounding* (1666) while incarcerated at the Bedford jail as punishment for his nonconformity to the Church of England. One of the classics of dissent in English literature is Daniel Defoe's "The Shortest Way with the Dissenters; Or, Proposal for the Establishment of the Church" (1702). It should be pointed out that in his day, Defoe was, by people who purported to know him, treated as a pariah and a traitor in the political sense of the word, and that he lived for better or worse in the seamy literary underworld. His novels, such as *Moll Flanders* (1722) and *Roxana* (otherwise known as *The Fortunate Mistress*) in 1724, are depictions of the wretched life about which he knew a thing or two. Adopting the pose of a Tory, he argued in "The Shortest Way with the Dissenters" that the only way to deal with them was to eradicate them. It was quite as simple as that. It's ironic last words crescendo into a mighty italic outburst, concluding with *"And may God Almighty put it into the hearts of all the friends of Truth, to lift up a Standard against Pride and ANTICHRIST! That the Posterity of the Sons of Error may be rooted out from the face of this land, for ever!"* Bunyan sounded as if he were the Almighty Himself holding forth through some cosmic megaphone.

A commentator with the unlikely name of Eddie Hogg gently reminds us that "every American should know what a Nonconformist is[;] this nation was built by such sturdy people. The Pilgrim Fathers were early nonconformists. A nonconformist in the narrow sense of that term was a person who could not give [vent] to the doctrine and practice of Anglicanism." He concludes by observing, "The nonconformists were Puritans, called so because they distrusted the reformation of the English Church from what they called the 'dregs of popery.' These dregs would be the whole structure of medieval worship; the wearing of vestments; the use of the alter, kneeling before the elements of the Lords [*sic*] Supper; the use of the apocrypha in worship, and many other usages that did not have the warrant of scripture." Indeed the shortest way of handling American dissenters, be they religious or political, has been widely discussed in classrooms and courts. We remember William O. Douglas (1898–1980), an associate justice of the U.S. Supreme Court, partly because of his advocacy of civil rights and free speech. In the "Court Years 1939–1975" segment of his *Autobiography* (1980), Justice Douglas commented that "The radical has never fared well in American life, whether he was dubbed anarchist, socialist, Bolshevik or Communist. Public passions have always run against him; and that feeling has radiated from judges as well as from newspapers and the people on Main Street." This, he argues, is partly accountable to the "America [that] has long been and remains a very conservative nation." There came a time, he recalls," when "the states, like the federal government, made lists of 'subversive' organizations; and some, like New York, disqualified members of such organizations from public employment — for example, from working as a teacher. A teacher held ineligible was entitled to a hearing; but he or she could not challenge the finding that the organization he or she was accused of joining was 'subversive.'"

It is oftimes difficult to say who is subversive and who is not. A site called ourladyswarrior.org, purporting to represent the Catholic Church, recently published a black list of "organizations and persons who purport to hold the Catholic Faith but actually dissent from the Truth and instead embrace error, all the while proclaiming themselves as Catholic." Among its offenders is one allegedly "promoting ordination of women among a plethora of other *social justice* issues"; another that condemns "opinions which dissent from Church teachings"; another that explains "how to spot dissident beliefs hidden within spoken or written material"; another that provides "our recommendations of books and publications which expose the truth about the dissenters"; another that exposes a "New Age theology called 'Jesus Consciousness'"; another that provides "official Vatican condemnation of Fr. Nugent's and Sr. Gramick's teaching regarding homosexuality"; another that provides an "Official Vatican condemnation of Liberation Theology, a belief which incorporates principles of Marxist atheistic Communism; another that provides an "official Vatican warning regarding the writings of Fr. Teilhard de Chardin"; another "denying that Catholics for a Free Choice merit[s] any recognition or support as a Catholic organization"; another that contains an "Official Vatican warning regarding the writings of Fr. Jacques

Dupuis['s] book on religious pluralism"; another that provides an "Official Vatican warning regarding the so-called ordination of seven women." There was yet another expressing "disappointment that the new edition of Father McBrien's book on Catholicism did not sufficiently correct several *deficiencies* that the committee had identified in its examination of the first two editions of the book undertaken in the early '80s." The document continues by providing an "in-depth analysis" of liberalism, heresy, apostasy, schism, modernism and anathema — as they relate to dissent. It then lists "types of spirituality [that are] defined and presented so that one may see their influence on dissenter spirituality," warning that "you will be shocked at the large degree of paganist concepts incorporated by the radical dissenters. There are common threads of sacred nature (eco- or bio- spirituality) since nature is a god or god-like and that we are 'one with creation'." It eventually asks, "While none of this paganism is remotely Catholic, haven't many seen classes advertised in the parish bulletin for the Enneagram, Tai-Chi, or yoga?" It proceeds to counsel against such things as paganism, Hinduism, pantheism, Buddhism, Brahmanism, Taoism, gnosticism, theosophy, wicca (that it calls "witchcraft by a new name"), Satanism, occult meditation, eco-spirituality, witchcraft and church feminists, psychics and witchcraft, Sophia wisdom, Sophia Christ, Gaia, mother earth, sacred creation, eco-feminists, pagan politics, eco-spirituality, green spirituality freemasonry, superstition, charkas, healing touch, reiki and tantric magic, maze craze, enneagram, freemasonry and something called Toronto blessing. What is an *enneagram*? Bruce Sabalaskey defines it as "a new age pagan tool with occult roots which purportedly categorizes your personality to tell you how to obtain heath ('integration') and avoid neurosis ('disintegration')," warning that "usually pagan influenced spirituality centers will sponsor all Enneagrams, Centering Prayer, and Labyrinths." One might, by way of contrast, compare such tactics intended to quell, nay eradicate, dissention by reconsidering Mahatma (meaning "great souled") Gandhi (1869–1948) the former attorney who, distressed by the religion that gave rise to Pakistan, argued the unity of all men under God. A religious lunatic who found fault with his sublime forbearance ultimately assassinated him.

Guardian Newspapers reported in "China Tightens Net Around Online Dissenters" (February 6, 2004) that in an all-out assault upon independent thought and its expression, the Beijing regime turned an estimated 30,000 thought police loose, with instructions to round up online dissidents, and corralled 54 persons for disseminating opinion not endorsed by authorities. Citing an Amnesty report, the article claimed that detainees were charged with such alleged crimes as "organizing online political petitions, proselytizing for the outlawed Falun Gong movement, and spreading 'rumors' about Aids and SARS." They faced sentences, so the piece continued, "of between two and 12 years in prison," adding that four have died in detention and that there are reports of torture. A 23-year-old female student named Liu Di, also known as the *Stainless Steel Mouse*, who found fault with the government for suppressing governmental control of the Internet, received a warning from university sources saying, "People in high places have told us that you hold radical views. Stop what you are doing." Shortly after, she was arrested and convicted without trial and detained in prison for a year before a worldwide outcry prompted her release. Regardless, "authorities" ordered an internet café to maintain a log of all computer users and their identification numbers as well as a report on every site they visited in the last 60 days. Those same authorities arrested a young man named Du Daobin, whom they took into custody after his initiating a petition calling for the release of Liu Di. "He left for work, but never came back," his wife reported. "Two days later the police searched our house and took our computer."

What with misleading and stereotypical portraiture, loners have had anything but an easy time of it. Furthermore being loners is (to be quite honest about it) somewhat precarious. If they're driving down a highway, and develop an overwhelming urge to cut a u-turn, they do it, and they do it without explaining themselves to anyone or securing the permission of their betters. With or without consent from some higher source, and for the benefit of Alcoholics Anonymous members, a group called "Loners-Internationalists Correspondence Service" has benevolently come to the rescue of AA-loners, especially *sea-going* AA-loners, provided they are willing to 1) read and write English, 2) provide a permanent mailing address, and 3) be willing to share experience, strength and hope via correspondence" — something that, being loners, would not be in their short range plans. On the subject of travel, a correspondent at gapyear.com recounts a travel adventure with an unlikely collection of people who regard themselves as loners. It necessarily, therefore, failed and fell apart quite soon. "I've always been a loner when it comes to traveling," he recalled. "I tried traveling with a group once, but after just six hours in a bus across Sinai, never agreeing on an itinerary, we'd decided to head our separate ways in Cairo. It's just so much easier doing it alone: you can go when you want and leave when you want, and if you don't have a plan there's nobody to bug you about your lack of organization."

Out of the February 26, 2006 *Philadelphia Inquirer* came an article by Art Carey titled, "This Way Up: Only the Lonely Know," wherein he raises the subject of Loner Liberation, with its amusing battle cry, "Loners of the world, separate!" Carey cites some memorable exchanges with his woman friend "Julian," age 52, "a recovering lawyer and aspiring novelist" who is alleged to have said, "there are those who need to surround themselves with chatter and commotion to validate their existence. I feel most fully alive when I'm by myself, alone able to hear myself think." Continuing, "I like my own company; I'm pleased with my own conversation. Like Cicero, I am never less alone than when alone. Like Thoreau, I have never found a companion more companionable than solitude." Added Julian, "I never fit in. I didn't want to play Barbie with the girls and I didn't want to roughhouse with the boys. I just wanted to sit on the sideline and read." Said Carey, "Send Julian an invitation and you'll plunge her into a funk. Like me, she dreads parties, receptions and large social gatherings." How bad is that? An anonymous blogger said recently, "Being a loner means you are always free. Free to be yourself, without having to keep up appearances or act the part that is expected of you. Being a loner means that you are accountable only to yourself and to those you choose to respect....If you think being alone is lonely, try being in a bad relationship. I've been there...and I would much rather be alone."

Precisely. A software engineer named Bryant Choung, reported Joanna Glasner in *Wired News* on April 5, 2006, bravely set out to "satirize social discovery by launching *Snubster*, an oxymoronic anti-social networking site that encourages independently-minded folks to 'create public lists of people and things that rankle them.'" The site even has a provision for "sending an e-mail to someone newly added to the list to tell them [*sic*] why they're being snubbed." *Snubster*, Ms. Glassner reports, "is among the latest in a series of cyber places created to poke fun at social networking." She adds, "*Isolatr*, [is] a spoof site that claims to be 'helping you to find where other people are not.'" Another such possibility, she reports, "is *Introverster*, which represents itself as 'an online community that prevents stupid people and friends from harassing you online.'"

Rather than uniting (an improbability) with other lone wolves, it might be a better idea to seek an environment temperamentally prepared to accommodate independently minded anti social types. Instead of enrolling in some brick and mortar university, one can study (as it were) online. Jennifer Mulrean reported for encarta.msn.com with a column called, "Is Online Learning for Loners?" The answer is yes, albeit it's no place to hide from customary classroom give-and-take, either, since one is expected to participate actively in online exchanges of opinion is a way of letting everyone know that he's still out there and still grappling with the course at hand. "Self-motivation,"

Ms. Mulrean warns, "doesn't have to mean isolation. You might be surprised to learn that some online programs are set up so that you actually have more interaction with the teacher and other students than you would by sitting in a lecture hall. But if you study at home, you may as well work at home." Similarly, a news source called projectmanagertraining.com explores what it calls *peek-a-boo management*, wherein managers "must use project management techniques specifically adapted to at-home work" to verify that the lone wolf completes his/her chores within an estimated time. Indeed, one must constantly monitor loners for fear that they run off by themselves and perpetrate some antisocial act such as peeing on a hydrant. Even the U.S. Army understands this potential problem and is on 24-hour alert before accepting loners into the military. It was not without serious misgivings, in fact, that such outsiders were invited to defend our nation. On Valentine's Day, 2001, there came a statement purporting to originate from Washington, warily acknowledging, "The Army's new 'Army of One' campaign is attracting millions of troubled loners," recruitment officials said Monday, adding that "Historically, Army enlistees are creepy, antisocial drifters,' [allegedly] said Sgt. Glenn Decinces of the Army's Recruitment Office. 'After years of trying to attract stable, achievement-oriented patriots with the slogan 'Be All You Can Be,' we finally gave up and decided to consciously go after the freakos we've always drawn." If loners cannot find a home in the military, then where are they to go in quest of peace, security, and universal acceptance?

Home. That's where. "Home is the place where," (Robert Frost declared in "The Death of the Hired Man") "when you have to go there, / They have to take you in." London may be such a place, according to LondonNet, which on October 27, 2005, declared, "London Likes Loners." The article explained that, yes, "Londoners have always been independent types." This is quite probably so. Consider, for example Oscar Wilde, Neville Chamberlain, T. E Lawrence (aka "Lawrence of Arabia"), Jack the Ripper, Sherlock Holmes and Professor Moriarty. Without their solitude, they would be nowhere. Citing the 2005 Unilever Family Report, "nearly half the population of Chelsea [and] Kensington" does indeed live alone. This information has been received and regarded as altogether good news by social planners, since it is "meant to outline lifestyles, health and social networks of people who live alone, as well as ask who lives alone and why." The report also revealed, quite surprisingly, that roughly "94% of Londoners prefer to live alone before cohabiting and starting families, and that more women are comfortable being alone than men." Still more surprising is its estimate that, "within the next fifteen years, the most common type of household, at 35%, will be made up of people living by themselves."

Living alone tends to reinforce and protect oneself against virulent invitations to occasions that one would just as soon avoid, nay, *desperately* avoid. Garbo, incidentally, reportedly said, "I vant to be alone"; she actually said, "I vant to be *let* alone." This was merely a throwaway line in a film called *Grand Hotel* (1932) and Miss Garbo may have meant neither one. She also said, "Give me a viskey," but she may not have meant that, either. Whether Miss Garbo was a loner, we may never know; at least she portrayed one in the movies. But when true lone wolves say they want to be alone, by George, they mean it. Consequently, they evade such trying occasions as dinner parties, weddings and funerals. Dinner parties are particularly difficult, because they place more pressure upon one's sociability and time. Dinner parties demand about six labor-intensive hours, roughly distributed among the pre-prandial, prandial, and post-prandial. It can be, and usually is, an enervating six hours. One is pressed into the company of people who do not interest him on any of multiple levels. Lone wolves understand that it is far better to beg off or even ignore the invitation, rather than to be the first guest to vanish at a provenient moment. If one decides to leave the occasion when everyone else does, he is in danger of sentencing himself to more dinner parties. Another tactic, and a last ditch one at that, is not to live up to one's advance billing as a dinner guest. That is a regrettable way to have one's name deleted from guest lists, but it is at least effective. Not to do so is to allow socially ambitious women (mostly) to preempt one's weekends indefinitely.

Social gadfly James Boswell's *Life of Johnson* (1791) attributes the remark that "a dinner lubricates business" to William Scott (aka Baron Stowell). However, if one has neither business nor anything else to lubricate, there is no object in subjecting himself to a six-hour dinner death march. One strategy for a guest is publicly to espouse some unpopular opinion in such a way that it will muddy the waters of sociability and permit the guest gradually to ease with nearly imperceptible grace toward an exit. The question is how best to slip out the door, preferably at a moment when other guests are lost in the rhetorically orgiastic throes of dialectical passion. Dinner parties are hotbeds of opinion and postulation that afford many such golden moments that aid the prisoner surreptitiously to recover his social freedom. Margaret Halsey said "it is *comme il faut* to establish the supremacy of an idea by smashing it in the faces of those who try to contradict it. The English never smash in a face. They merely refrain from asking it to dinner." One of the rewards of ostracism is to devote what would have been dinner party time to some far higher purpose, such as contemplating a ceiling. It is difficult to explain why, through what subliminal motive, one would presume to demand the presence of someone who might well wish to be somewhere else, doing something else. Some people view an RSVP not as a courtesy but as an *order*, such as an invitation to a colostomy.

One resourceful dinner party hostess, so reports Microsoft's *Home Magazine*, occasionally invites of a group of six to eight persons, then proceeds to divide them into teams who are assigned cheerfully to prepare dishes in a small kitchen. Margaret Montet has excitedly reported, "The best party I've ever thrown was a murder mystery dinner party. I invited friends and colleagues from various parts of my world, and they mixed! They mingled! Even I had fun. We talked about it for months afterwards." She continued, "The hard part was getting the right number of people to RSVP and commit to the party." One can just imagine. As to the murder aspect, "all the guests were mingling and discussing things [such] as their actual selves as well as their characters. Some wore costumes, some brought props, and some used accents to give their characters color. One of the participants remarked, "Those of us who had accents, or chose to use them, had a blast trying to stay in character. The game definitely kept us guessing." Other dinner ideas: command guests to sing, respond to trivia questions and tell a joke. Ms. Montet's next party? "I selected a mystery that takes place in an office setting," she says, "so that the only costume needed will be business attire (with some possibly wacky touches).... The biggest problem is deciding whom to invite!"

Granted, that's a tough one. A worse problem still is to receive an invitation, because it's one more unnecessary and cloying inconvenience with which one is left to deal, but deal one probably ought. This can be done in any of several ways. One can accept a dinner invitation and then suffer through all six programmed hours of it; one can accept the invitation and leave undetected after ten minutes; one can simply ignore the invitation; one can invent some excuse for not accepting it; one can explain to the hostess that he has, alas, no social life (something that Max Beerbohm in *Zuleika Dobson* [1911] called "that admirable fidelity to social engagements which is one of the virtues implanted in the members of our aristocracy") and has furthermore not contemplated any immediate plans to create one. Should worse come to worst, one must remember never to wear a coat or other outer garment to a dinner party, for fear that it will be carried for safe keeping to a room and will later be awkward to find in order to effect a hasty but surgically precise exit. Hosts have been known to raise a sort of good-natured fuss for an early departer who tries to find his coat in a room littered with other coats. One slightly amusing activity for a reluctant guest is to vanish in such a way that the other guests are unaware of his departure for minutes, hours, or possibly ever. In the meantime, the departed one is quite far down the road, so to speak. Such a deceptive prank is a clever achievement similar to breaking out of a high security incarceration unit. Whatever one does, invitations are a general annoyance, not to say *threat*, to lone wolfery, thanks to those women who thrive on social inanity. One solution to the dinner party dilemma might be to invite only women. In the meantime, whether one accepts or evades acceptance, he loses. Not to become socially involved is to invite hostility that, as we have seen, is all too often aimed at independent, self-reliant people who by their nature are neither adequate nor acceptable as guests. They are simply not guest material, and from that useless point of view, they are useless. This is not because they are necessarily self-absorbed, but because they don't fancy having their time wasted and don't rely upon other people for support and approval. Beerbohm wrote somewhat simplistically that "mankind is divisible into two great classes: hosts and guests," whereas there is nothing especially noteworthy about either one, inasmuch as the former attempts to control people for relatively short time periods, and the latter submits to it. What one often finds are reluctant hosts and reluctant guests who more resemble *submissive sheep*. Some people, let us be clear, aren't interested in forming new friendships because they are in no sense necessary. Nor is playing on a football team. Nor joining a country club. Nor enlisting in an army. One should never intrude upon someone else's private time. Leave that someone alone. A similar but ever worse problem for a lone wolf is to be the unlucky recipient of a wedding invitation; one of those notifications is still more difficult to pass off, since a wedding is supposedly the paramount day in a woman's petty life. It's worse than a letter from the IRS questioning the accuracy of one's income tax report. The 16th-century English poet John Heywood composed an epigram entitled "Wedding and Hanging," where, given a choice, a husband opts for the latter. Probably the best way to respond is by dispatching a wedding gift and then forgetting about the wedding itself. Weddings are a dilemma for the lone wolf, because he can find no cause to celebrate what appears to him as a perfectly dismal idea. He cannot bear to witness them. Indeed, one ought more sensibly celebrate at funerals and mourn at weddings. Funerals ought rightly to be a celebration of the deceased's soul sent gloriously to an indescribably better existence. The transmigration of a soul is not something that occasions mourning. Weddings, on the considerable other hand, are ill advised for a whole range of reasons. Unless the groom is someone the wolf intensely dislikes, it is with extreme regret that he stands by helplessly while the groom ceremoniously, even voluntarily, places his head in a marital noose. This is a painful thing to witness. Eventually, he will be looking for a way out. In the opening chapter of Thomas Hardy's *The Mayor of Casterbridge* (1886) we discover a man putting his wife up for auction. In the meantime, make no mistake, weddings are strictly and exclusively women's affairs. They are occasions to which women are summoned off the streets as if by some powerfully invisible magnetic current, and to which they crave some sort of ritualistic role to play. They enjoy, for example "helping" the bride in and out of her fairy gown. Weddings are something about which, heaven knows why, even little girls seem to daydream endlessly and act out, as if, even in childhood, they will not have certified themselves as women until they put this dreadful ritual behind them with a mind to being proclaimed *Queen for a Day*, and gloriously whisked away to some obscure and dismal destiny. Such rituals require a certain amount of concertedly metaphysical contemplation, as if nuptial planning is the first time the prospective bride ever planned anything whatsoever.

Let's see: in no order of significance, there are a number of greater or lesser considerations which wedding contemplators must thrash out among themselves, such as the selection of invitations, the wedding date, the location, the various celebratory dinners, the thresholds, the champagne, the butterflies, the lugubrious public addresses, the newspaper coverage, the limousines, the receiving lines, the dowries, the reservations, the bubbling fountains, the skirt-lifting gynecologists, the rice, the flowers, the lawn-mowings, the toasts, the flower girls, the bride's maids, the tents, the registries, the rehearsals, the keepsakes, the showers, the caterers, the tears, the maid of honor, the person who administers oaths, the maids of dishonor, the gowns (to be worn only once), the waiters, the lavish gifts, the sobbing witnesses, the inebriates, the cakes (was it not Margot Asquith who revealed that a certain Lady Desbrough had spread "enough white lies to ice a wedding cake"?), the bar keepers, the clichés, the fireworks, the peripatetic photographers, the living doves, the string quartets, the hairdressers, the psychiatrists, the security men, the dirty dishes, the pre-nuptial agreements and the divorce papers. Anything else?

Oh, yes. The groom: by any measurement the least significant person at this insidiously feminine carnival, and the one whose influence is least in authority. If a bride is Queen for a Day, he is Chump for a Day, the fall guy for as long as the marriage survives, which may not be long. Someone (and we don't know who) said, "It's not true that married men live longer than single men. It only seems longer." There is a women's cable television channel appropriately called *We* that in July of 2006 carried the frantic wedding of a frantic woman and a decidedly bewildered groom who, at that golden moment when some senile clergyman sonorously proclaimed them husband and wife, looked for all the world as though he had received a death sentence sent down by some court of final assize. No wonder. An altar is no place for a lone wolf, nor is it a place for what would appear to be a great proportion of otherwise ostensibly eligible bachelors. It may be of some encouragement to note that over many years fewer Americans have seen fit to marry, possibly in view of marriage's dismal odds that, according to government figures, show marriages explode or implode at approximately the rate of 50 percent and perpetuate infinite damage upon innocent children who did not ask to be born. For the loner, however, marriage is quite out of the question and for a number of sufficiently good reasons. After those 50 percent of marriages come undone, one wonders about the condition of other half. If the first half of marriages is decidedly dead, the second half is at death's door. Matrimony is a fearfully confining but (in a sense) addictively stable existence that married people find difficult, maybe impossible, to relinquish. Yes, it is unsatisfactory, but it's something to grin and bear. Yes, it is monotonous, but to some it is preferable than courageously striking out on a new life. Yes, it is liable to involve some sort of abuse to body, soul, and spirit, but that is to be expected. Marriages are unsatisfactory for a number of other reasons, one of which is that men are by nature polygamous, although a few can be domesticated through fear, intimidation, hectoring and so forth. The wonder is that, following divorce, men are more likely to remarry than are women. It has in recent years come to pass that when the parties are not married, any free range sexual activity with other partners has been interpreted by received public opinion as "cheating," when it is in no sense the breaking of any sacred covenant. To desist is merely cheating oneself. Certain men may remain monogamous, but they are uncomfortable and profoundly discontent, to say the least, in doing so. Equally disadvantageous, whereas marriage is occasionally depicted as a partnership, it is more likely to develop into a monstrous liability when, for example, a spouse becomes mere dead weight, an anchor that exacts its considerable price in disillusionment, discouragement, demoralization. When should a man marry? Sir Francis Bacon, possibly citing the philosopher Thales (who apparently left no written words of his own), expressed it perfectly: *A young man not yet; an elder man not at all.*

There are other things for the lone wolf to whisk into his bin of ash and other detritus. This involves undoing certain aspects of one's personal history. Religion, as a practical, possible, even mystical guide to behavior, is more a hindrance than a help. "Things have come to a pretty pass," William Lamb is alleged to have said, "when religion is allowed to invade the sphere of private life." Liken it to liberating musty attics laden with outworn accoutrements from times long past when one knew no better than to retain them. Houses of worship, although they may offer mystic comfort and solace to some of their stalwart communicants who are prepared to receive it, are hardly more than veiled businesses and breakfast clubs that may serve as forums to sell refrigerators, disseminate utter nonsense, spread gossip and seduce women. This is not entirely an undesirable thing, since it is unusual that one might accomplish all four without leaving a room. Holy places are not ideal platforms for wolfian solitude and divine self-expression, not to say direct-line hypostatic union with a divine creator, however. They do impose a sense of structure for those whose lives seem to require it. One can, for example hang one's hat (as it were) upon the Christian mysteries and assemble every seven days or so with his fellow suppliants to place his tenuous hold on stability at least temporarily upon automatic pilot. This presumes that it is both necessary and desirable to embrace generally held religious positions. "There's no reason to bring religion into it," Sean O'Casey wrote in the first act of *The Plough and the Stars* (1926). "I think we ought to have as great a regard for religion as we can, so as to keep it out of as many things as possible." Encountering the same people and hearing the same message recited by the same robed sage, an eternal gray eminence standing in the same place and wearing the same expression, affords the comforting delusion that the world is theologically motionless. There comes a moment, however, when the independent thinker has had enough of other people's views. People commonly refer to "my pastor" (or whatever name they deem appropriate) in the same sense that they refer to "my plumber," "my accountant," "my endodontist," "my drycleaner" and so forth, as if to suggest that they are all more of less equally indispensable persons on whom they can rely. The theologically-inclined among us may just as well read and reflect upon moral and religious documents, unassisted — then form their own conclusions. Dr. Samuel Johnson (Boswell's Johnson), in his *Lives of the English Poets*, recounts a hilarious incident involving Dean Swift and one Lady Berkeley in the midst of one of her "private devotions," having recently perused the Hon. Robert Boyle's *Occasional Reflections Upon Several Subjects* (1665). "Swift," Johnson wrote, "had by no means the same relish for that kind of writing," and in retaliation inserted his own "Meditation on a Broomstick," then closed the volume, "after which he took care to have the book restored to its proper place."

On the next occasion with Lady Berkeley he commenced to read his composition "with great composure of countenance," whereupon she stopped him and pensively repeated the words *Meditation on a Broomstick*, remarking "bless me, what a strange subject," after which Johnson observes that "there is no knowing what useful lessons of instruction this wonderful man may draw from things apparently the most trivial."[1] Likewise, American maverick Benjamin Franklin, one might recall, prudently devoted Sunday to study, meaning, we take it, that he was striking out for new spiritual continents where he might temporarily drop anchor. Having for example assiduously read the religious skeptic Anthony Ashley Cooper, third Earl of Shaftsbury, as well as the deistical Anthony Collins, he proclaimed that he had "become a real Doubter in many Points of our Religious Doctrine." The indomitable Franklin, a philosophic sojourner who traveled metaphysically alone, remained unafraid to pick the universe's most securely padlocked uncertainties for his private amusement and edification.

It is more arduous than ever for lone wolves to thread their stealthy ways through old university corridors since the insidious erosion of free expression made itself felt. It has destroyed the aspirations of more than one student. Whereas in the past one of the purported glories of university life had been the free exchange of opinion (regardless of how inane that opinion may have been) among ladies and gentlemen, our campuses are now infested with Orwellian *thought police* who tolerate only officially-sanctioned views (regardless of how preposterous these views are) that trace their seamy origins to tinhorn politicians (another redundancy) who write those views into law, with a mind to evading anyone's ire, so to be reelected and allowed to remain gorging, like the hogs they assuredly are, at the public trough. Oddly enough, there are countries where any crackpot who denies that the Holocaust is a fact of history, will be remanded to prison for a term sufficiently long to revise his opinion. Whereas there is nothing remotely comic about the Holocaust, there is something amusing about one who denies it, and even more comic, any government that incarcerates its citizens for espousing outrageous convictions. One wonders where that practice will end. One public university freshman student reported privately that during an "orientation" (read *indoctrination*) she and her classmates-to-be were served notice that, unless they subscribed with the straightest of faces to certain politically correct views, they would be better served to study (or whatever students do) elsewhere.

---

1 Sutherland, James (Ed.), *The Oxford Book of Literary Anecdotes* (New York: Pocket Books, 1975) 65-67.

This unfortunate situation is, of course, particularly alarming and offensive to anyone who is of independent intellect and who wishes to acquire a richly abundant comprehensive education and be left to sort out his own convictions. Worse still, the muddleheaded bureaucrats who mismanage our overpriced universities tacitly endorse thought control. The essential motive is to keep from stepping on anybody's feet, something that is impossible to guarantee on a university campus where the population comes in all colors and persuasions in addition to (one might say) *all genders*. Another intent is to oblige large numbers of students to support (or claim to support) any silly notions that politically (in)correct faculties are proffering at the time from their public lecterns. Academic freedom's primary purpose has been to allow all points of view to have an airing without summoning the academic Keystone Kops. Universities are, after all, a forum for generally younger people to test their ideas and eventually develop their own value systems. Dorothy Rabinowitz of *The Wall Street Journal* contributed an article on July 7, 2008, entitled "American Politics Aren't Post-Racial" involving Purdue's University's failed attempt to bring action against a student *for reading a book* borrowed from that university's library. The student, who was then working his way through school as a janitor, had the gall to open the pages of a volume entitled *Notre Dame vs the Klan: How the Fighting Irish Defeated the Ku Klux Klan*. He unwittingly found himself charged by campus thought police with "openly *reading the book* related [to an] historically and racially abhorrent subject," and doggedly "continued[,] despite complaints[,] *to read a book*" that he moreover kept on reading. The student then properly notified the American Civil Liberties Union, which contacted university attorneys and settled the matter.

The New York Times noted that in June of 2007 a documentary film entitled "Indoctrinate U" was out there in circulation, arguing "with vivid examples, that the nation's colleges are squelching freedom of expression and are no longer free marketplaces of ideas." The suppression of free dialog and the offensive movement toward obedient collective behavior were on the move well before that. Thomas Hine, in his book entitled *The Rise & Fall of the American Teenager* (1999) notes that an imbecilic Newark, New Jersey, school superintendent in 1913 decreed that the purpose of public education was to produce team players, and that it is "not individuality, but social unity" to be stressed, since unity "results in efficiency and is rarely, if ever, obtained except by thorough uniformity of some kind," adding that "children must be taught to live and work together cooperatively; to submit their individual wills to the will of the majority; and to conform to social requirements whether they approve of them or not."

Ergo, Greek letter "societies" (as we shall see in subsequent chapters) have done every bit they can to control their constituencies even to the extent of directing them in virtually every aspect of their young and therefore impressionable lives. For a university to suppress open discourse is unthinkable. As William Fankboner has written, "censorship is eliminating all intellectual and artistic vitality with a vengeance [while inhibiting] the easy give-and-take of human discourse." Philip Atkinson has traced the origins of political correctness to the 1880s, although it obviously finds its origins in the long history of American anti-intellectualism. It is, he reminds us, "a spontaneous declaration that particular ideas, expressions and behavior, which were they legal, should be forbidden by law, and people who transgressed should be punished." He believes what everyone knows, that the purpose of this tyranny was "to prevent [people from] being *offended*; to compel everyone to avoid using words or behavior that may upset homosexuals, women, non-whites, the crippled, the mentally impaired, the fat or the ugly." Political correctness, he says later, "is merely the resentment of spoilt children directed against their parent's values." Professor Herbert Shapiro of the University of Cincinnati has argued that "those insistent on economic and political orthodoxy have repeatedly sought to eliminate dissent from the discourse taking place within the university." He continued, "academic freedom has often had an imperiled existence as professors and students have only with difficulty been able to seriously question the arrangements of the status quo." In the meantime, without a free and unfettered exchange of ideas, universities may just as well shutter their doors.

Learning, as any lone wolf will be delighted to hear reiterated, is a solitary experience and better achieved alone than in the company of classmates, even classmates who, for a change, have been accorded a freedom of speech, which may be one of the few things that Al Gore did not invent. Even some *dummkopf* who has wasted his mind in some intellectually impoverished college of "education" might happen to know that everyone learns in his own way and in his own time. Einstein flunked college physics, and was neither the first nor the last to do so. Intellectual achievement cannot successfully be made to fit a given time allotment because the desire for an education of any sort originates from within and develops at its own pace and intensity. It is never successfully imposed from without. Consequently, everyone must decide for himself precisely what, if anything, he wants to know, and then set about knowing it. Every autumn, millions of new "students" arrive on American campuses, evidently because someone has told them to go there and possibly has even agreed to pay all the costs pursuant thereto. These same neophytes are the ones who, within a year or so, have variously flunked out, drunked out, drugged out, wandered off or otherwise disappeared without a forwarding address. The farther one has passed beyond the age of 22 without a bachelor's degree in hand, the more difficult it will be to get one and the more doubtful it will be. Education may in a sense be wasted upon the young, but at the same time one would not wish to be treated to education's privileges only after, say, the age of 50, when its manifold benefits would have been largely passed. A substantial, liberal university education may possibly hasten the maturation of college students who are nothing if not late adolescents, many of whom are not fully in control of their minds, bodies and glorious destinies. Loners, if no one else, understand that half the battle is fighting off that adolescent immaturity and staying well away from fraternities and sororities that, contrary to their extravagant claims, do not work to a young person's advantage in any way whatsoever. Independents need not be reminded of that. We will have more to say about communal campus life in the following two chapters. Meanwhile, the decision about what to study, and why, is understandably perplexing to newer students. That question may be settled in at least two ways. The first is to enroll in substantial courses that address substantial fields of learning of universal concern to any educated person, such as those which offer some familiarity with mathematics, history, economics, literature, chemistry, anthropology, physics, a second language, philosophy, fine arts, music and such. Brighter students dismiss the trendy rubbish that universities hurriedly serve up to convert some current fad into a "revenue stream." Independent minds refuse instruction from any misguided faculty person whose mission is to proselytize. The second is to select a field of primary interest through a simple method, namely by determining what interests one has in combination with where one's ability lies. No one can do everything. If one's interests and abilities lead toward playing the violin, then that violin is the answer. The objective in the educational enterprise is to become a broadly educated and civilized individual, with the emphasis upon the *individual*. Fretting over one's vocation can just as well be put off. There is always the possibility of graduate education, and there is always the high probability that an individual with a sound, basic education, because of a proven ability to assimilate and master, can be put to nearly any task with extraordinary results. It may or may not come as a pleasant surprise to the loner "community" that the university of the future will come through the magic of cyberspace, although for obvious reasons that is difficult to imagine. Were it a reality, then a loner could qualify for university degrees without leaving his solitary lime tree bower. Learning is nevertheless a solitary, mental journey that one necessarily travels alone. Universities have substantial libraries, and most of what one learns in a university comes out of that library (if it permits its books to be read), rather than out of a classroom. The most one can expect from a classroom is a little coaching, if that. To get near to a library, one must go there, not through cyberspace, but through inches and miles. One also hears the dubious argument that being in a real, actual classroom allows one to give and take with other students, should there be any. Students, in reality, rarely have anything of value to say, but a great deal to ask. In the end, education provides one with the necessary skills to resolve questions without relying upon some schoolmaster. It is the residual influence of a solid education that comes eventually to one's fundamental requirements and rescue. B. F. Skinner summarized it perfectly: "Education is what survives when what has been learned has been forgotten."

Although it need not be, television broadcasting is still the wasteland that Chicago lawyer Newton Minnow, then chairman of the Federal Communications Commission, claimed it was in his embarrassingly inarticulate address before the National Association of Broadcasters on May 9, 1961. Essentially what television producers have chosen to present, he said, is "a procession of game shows, violence, audience participation-shows, formula comedies about totally unbelievable families, blood and thunder, mayhem, violence, sadism, murder, western badmen, western good men, private eyes, gangsters, more violence and cartoons." He then rightly described television advertising as "screaming, cajoling and offending." Such language provoked the perpetrators of a program called "Gilligan's Island" to christen its vessel the "S. S. Minnow." Nearly a half century later, television is perilously close to one hundred percent rubbish, totally unacceptable to any enlightened, independent thinker who long ago turned what little attention he had wasted on television, into such rewardingly diversionary things as fine music and intelligent reading, neither of which have anything to do with Newton Minnow and his mythic motorboat. That television broadcasting immediately directed itself at the lowest common denominator was hardly surprising. "Television?" said C. P. Scott, editor of the *Manchester Guardian* in 1928. "The word is half Greek and half Latin," he said dismissively. "No good will come of it." He was substantially right. In 1936, however, he reported optimistically that "Sir Thomas Beechham believes that television can do much to improve the musical taste of the nation." David Sarnoff, then president and chairman of the board at RCA, predictably shared (or said he did) the same view when he confidently predicted that "television drama of high caliber and produced by first-rate artists will raise the level of dramatic taste of the American nation." Little, if any such thing, happened; the industry spared little time or ceremony in escorting its miraculous medium straight to hell. Cambridge graduate David Frost, the video interviewer who profited smartly from television broadcasting, quipped sardonically that television "is an invention that permits you to be entertained in your living room by people you wouldn't have in your home." For devotees of fluff and blunder, one can even "study" television broadcasting in some universities, and thereby ardently evade receiving a real education. In all fairness, one should allow that television has had its purposes, such as stupefying patients trapped for hours in triple-booked medical offices. It has also labored splendidly to mutilate the English language beyond redemption, and make the world safer for Miss America contests; create ceremonies honoring those who have borne the television industry to new lows; transform courtrooms into cultural barnyards; glorify yokels who preserve the dubious reputation of stock car racing; tell the world when to laugh on cue, and when to cease laughing. Best of all, it has taught the world how to stop thinking and start gazing with slack-jawed intensity at what gibberish might then happen to foul the airwaves and sully the mind. The loner, being nothing if not a deft navigator though culture's polluted waters, can steer wide of this sewer with relatively little difficulty.

Shopping malls too might well shutter their electric doors, since they have allowed themselves to represent the contagious vulgarity of modern urban American life with its seedy commercialism and its pandering to what is essentially middle class tastes that loners, among others, are likely to find alarmingly depressing, and for more than one reason. There are mobs of eternally strolling shoppers there, for one thing, and no person of independence will want to allow himself to move in a herd through a commercial waste land. For another thing, such places are likely to broadcast revolting sounds that may appear to a target audience of people who regard shopping as a sporting activity, despite that uneasy feeling that one senses when he is about to be chiseled out of his money. Moreover, one develops a keen, if arrogant, sense of embarrassment, or what's worse, humiliation, at being seen in such a place, despite that some people consider it a form of emotional recreation rather than a deadening encounter with neon and noise. The first of all shopping malls, we are given to understand, was the Country Club Plaza that opened near Kansas City, Missouri in 1922. The first enclosed mall popped up in Edina, Minnesota in 1956. It was in the 1980s, however, that shopping malls sprang like poisonous weeds almost everywhere in America.

John Schumaker, writing for the *New Internationalist* magazine in July of 2001 saw shopping malls as insidious places where "hyper materialism also features prominently in the emerging plague of existential disorders such as chronic boredom, ennui, jadedness, purposelessness, meaninglessness and alienation." Schumaker later reported "surveys of therapists reveal that 40 per cent of Americans seeking psychotherapy today suffer from these and other complaints, often referred to as all-pervasive 'psychic deadness.' Once materialism becomes the epicenter of one's life it can be hard to feel any more alive than the lifeless objects that litter the consumer world." In a recent study of US university students, 81 per cent of them reported feeling lost in an 'existential vacuum.'" One should caution that *existential* signifies different things to different people, even to the point of meaning anything one wants it to mean. As a general consensus, however, it assumes that one is born into a world that is without transcendent meaning, and that one must impose meaning nevertheless by living his life according to some purpose that he determines.[1] One would hope that, among the range of wholesome and creative purposes, one does not condemn himself, like one of Dante's damned, to stroll eternally in a shopping mall. The loner's priority, after all, is to be alone. Shopping malls do what they can to prevent that from happening, since their objective is to capture the attention of great mobs of nomadic shoppers whose tastes they may be able to erode. At a mall, the credit card is king, and is the undoing of persons unable to control their expenditures. A mall is the antithesis of the loner's natural habitat which is likely to be a darkened, possibly unheated, space with lighting enough to consume books and other papers while contemplating fine music and advisedly shutting the rest of the world out. Emerson speaks to us again from "Self-Reliance": "It is easy in the world to live after the world's opinion; it is easy in solitude to live after our own; but the great man is he who in the midst of the crowd keeps with perfect sweetness the independence of solitude."

Funerals are trying occasions for nearly everyone, with the possible exception of ghouls and people in the burial business. For loners the disposition of the dead raises a troubling set of dilemmas, the first of which is that loners do everything possible to avoid congregating for nearly any purpose. If they approach every other situation alone, it follows that they will ap-

---

1 The *OED* calls existentialism "a doctrine that concentrates on the essence of the individual, who, being free and responsible, is held to be what he makes himself by the self-development of his essence through acts of the will." Its main philosophical exponents have been Kierkegaard, Jaspers and Sartre. The movement has its Christian applications, but it has also suggested that since there is no God, one is totally free to develop his life and identity through whatever means he has at his disposal.

proach death, including their own, in the same fashion, namely as a private, internal matter. Another reason is that they may be of the persuasion that funerals, rightly considered, should logically be sufficient reason, as we have suggested, for rejoicing and celebration now that one of the human number has transmigrated into what philosophers have nearly unanimously viewed as the gateway to an eternal life as it may variously be construed. Failing of that, the deceased himself may be of the opinion that he's had a quite good life and that he's had quite enough of it. Attendees at his funeral rites might just as well tip a bottle of the best and send him packing, as it were. Richard Hough's 1980 biography of Lord Louis Mountbatten, aka Viscount Mount-batten of Burma, finds his lordship proclaiming, "I can't think of a more won-derful thanksgiving for the life I've had than that everyone should be jolly at my funeral." Be that as it may, if there is mourning, the mourning is likely to be directed to the mourners themselves, not at the deceased who is well beyond needing it. Another difficulty is that families of the deceased often insist that their guests be made to admire a corpse. For some people who do not necessarily react to corpses the way other people do, this may pose an upsetting problem, or "issue" as some people like to say. Dead bodies (and quite a few living ones) are grotesque and disgusting, and are best disposed of discretely and rapidly, preferably through cremation. Besides that, funer-als are hideous. Mencken tells us, *in passim*, that the word mortician "was suggested by a physician, for undertakers naturally admire and like to pal with resurrection men [grave robbers who supplied cadavers to physicians and medical students]. From the earliest days they have sought to bedizen their hocus-pocus with mellifluous euphemisms." There was a somewhat amusing circumstance on the Pacific Coast years ago when, acting upon a decedent's instructions, the independently-minded pilot of a small aircraft took charge of the decedent's ashes and took wing over the Pacific, so to distribute those ashes fenestrally from the aircraft, as per the decedent's wishes. When the pilot lowered his window, alas, ashes flew everywhere except out of the cabin. Disgruntled, he returned to land, whisked the ashes into a container and dumped them into a rubbish bin. Better that than to view a corpse. It is an abomination (many times worse than a dinner party or a wedding) visited upon innocent people. The reasonable thing to have done is allow funereal decisions to rest, *antea*, with the deceased. The loner, meanwhile, may ease the day for himself and those around him if he simply meets the funeral party at a cemetery and engages them in sanctimonious chatter. After a few appropriate words, both the corpse and the loner vanish into the underground.

Chapter 3. What Price Affiliation?

> "Committee — a group of men who individually can do nothing, but as a group decide that nothing can be done."
> — Fred Allen

Joiners are joiners on the tenuous assumption that they can function better in a mob than as individuals. If they are uncertain, unimaginative, unoriginal, unmotivated and unassertive, then they have ostensibly made the correct procedural choice. They can always be under the thumb of someone who is certain, imaginative, original, motivated and assertive. Most joiners travel in packs and are remarkably other-directed. Without human support from all sides, they are lost. There is nothing wrong with this, providing that consent to living their lives as followers. They exact satisfaction in the knowledge that they're a small (if all but useless) part of a big, not especially dynamic, faceless team mismanaged by moronic bureaucrats whose objective is to control whomever and whatever is controllable. To the bureaucratic mentality, such words as "different," "creative," "alone," and so forth, are faintly if not intensely pejorative and may herald the coming of some threatening person who does not derive profound satisfaction from having ingratiated himself with crowds and groups. Nor is there anything inherently wrong-headed with joining a baseball team or an army since these outfits cannot exist without willing participants; nor, of course, would there be teams and armies without volunteers to take orders from, and function as, a team. Without teams, some would not have the consummate joy of witnessing football games and other carnages. But stay. The Orpheus Chamber

Orchestra and sometimes the Prague Chamber Orchestra perform magnifi-cently — without a conductor. Elsewhere, however, many people will be more than pleased to have played a spear-carrying role, regardless of how insignificant. Not everyone, after all, can carry the flag and lead the charge. We have all been heartened, nay *inspired*, by heroic hometown life histories that run thusly: "Ed Walnut has retired from National Lunchbucket where he drove the same forklift for 68 years." He has, so to speak, taken the check-ered flag in more ways than one; but by George, he was a company man to the day that management showed him the door.

In the dismal world of corporate life, some think first of William H. Whyte Jr.'s landmark book entitled *The Organization Man* (1956) that raised a few brows at its initial appearance,[1] albeit Whyte advanced some observa-tions that today one would merely *assume*. He mentions, for example, that "the organization man" is he "who most urgently wants to belong," and he who keenly feels a "growing preoccupation with group work." Team life (marriage is an example) is part of a dubious strategy aimed at transporting oneself seamlessly and safely as possible into a benevolent team structure from cradle to grave. The motive is to blend in, join in, and pitch in. Whyte himself said that, as organization men view it, "through an extension of the group spirit, through educating [*sic*] people to sublimate their egos, orga-nizations can rid themselves of tyrants and create atmospheres in which the group will bring out the best in everyone." On the surface of it, it may seem attractive at least to people who happen to have, we regret to say, pro-nouncedly *affiliative* tendencies. They well understand that you gather five, ten, twenty people together and concentrate, let us say, on some common problem, then out if this sustained session of Group Think there will emerge, as if by black magic, abundant evidence of mass intelligence that an associate of ours calls "pooled ignorance." Researcher Geert Hofstede[2] refers to Group Think as "a state where people think so alike that they do not challenge or-ganizational thinking, and [that] there is a reduced capacity for innovative thought." He adds that "this could occur, for example, where there is heavy reliance on a central charismatic figure in the organization, or where there

---

1 A Marine Corps veteran, William Holly Whyte (1917–1999), joined *Fortune* magazine in 1946 and eventually became an editor there. *The Organization Man*, that was rendered in several languages in addition to English, is reputed to have sold over two million copies. Whyte considered himself an "urbanologist," more or less reaching the conclusion that "what peo-ple want is other people," and determining that whenever there are seven people per foot of walkway within one minute" it creates "a nice bustle."

2 Hofstede developed a hypothesis for differentiating one culture from another, using as criteria "power distance," "individualism," "masculinity," "uncertainty avoidance," and "long term orientation."

is an evangelical belief in the organization's values." The many, after all, are always superior to the few. We all accept that. That is why we rely upon plebiscites to resolve stubbornly metaphysical questions.

There is more than safety in numbers; there is also community, commitment, compensation, camaraderie and (worst of all) conformity. But there may also be concern (and even worse) consternation over surrendering to group will. Alfred North Whitehead (1861–1947) who taught mathematics at the University of London and philosophy at Harvard, asked by whose authority did moral standards arise in any place at any time, conclude that "it is what the majority then and there happened to like." Majorities, sad to say, have often, especially by intellectually independent thinkers, been held up to scorn and ridicule, albeit it is difficult to exceed the detestation of the majority that the distinguished Norwegian playwright Henrik Ibsen (1828–1906) gave emphasis in Act 4 of *En Folkefiende* (*An Enemy of the People*) through the disarmingly subversive voice of his Dr. Stockmann: "The majority *never* has right on its side...never, I tell you!" says Stockmann. "That's one of the social lies that an intelligent, independent man has to fight against. Who makes up the majority of the population in a country — the wise men or the fools? I think you will agree with me that, all the wide world over, nowadays the fools are in a quite terrifyingly overwhelming majority. And how the devil can it be right for the fools to rule over the wise men?" He continues, "The majority is strong — unfortunately — but *right* it certainly is not! I'm right — I and a few others — the minority is always right!" The good doctor later asserts that "all these majority-truths are like last year's salt pork — moldy, rancid, half-cured ham!" and still later that "the doctrine that the common herd — the masses — the mob — are the backbone of the People — that they *are* the People. That the common man, this ignorant and uneducated part of society, has the same right to sanction and condemn, to govern and advise, as the intellectually superior few." Just at the end of the play, we find Stockman summarizing his case, saying, "The strongest man in the world is the man who stands most alone."

Ibsen, of course, was not alone. On September 11, 1918 Eugene Victor Debs (1855–1926), the Terre Haute Indiana socialist, union organizer and pacifist of whom Ibsen's Stockmann would likely have disapproved, nevertheless articulated nearly the same opinion in an address he delivered at the Federal Court in Cleveland Ohio. "When great changes occur in history," Debs propounded, "when great principles are involved, as a rule the majority are wrong. The minority are right." Oh, surely not! The anathema to creative, individual problem solving on the part of loners and social separatists is the menace of bureaucracies, those people who manage to botch anything they can find to botch, and insist upon layers of meetings during which critical questions never surface, and problems always go unaddressed. As Ronald Reagan memorably remarked, "every once in a while somebody has to get the bureaucracy by the neck and shake it loose and say 'Stop doing what you're doing.'" The bureaucrat is not doing anything; that's the point. "The perfect bureaucrat everywhere," wrote author, critic and editor Brooks Atkinson, "is the man who manages to make no decision and escape all responsibility." Jim Robertson, who has written much about bureaucracies for a source called *Terra Libra Holdings*, has astutely commented, "Bureaucratic organizations tend to attract workers who obey orders and follow rules...as well as those with the psychological defect of needing to control others." He adds that, "bureaucracies compulsively create more rules," even though "there is little incentive to improve efficiency. They create more and more jobs for rule-creators, rule-enforcers, and rule interpreters," and moreover, "don't like freedom-oriented individuals." Elsewhere, Robertson correctly reminds us that "bureaucrats rate you successful when you surrender your individual diversity and person power to them," adding that "bureaucrats rate you as successful when they can convince you to admit to them that you [need] their help," even when you desperately don't want it.

Joiners have a tendency to regret that more of the world is not properly joined, as if being mutually dependent is a preferable way to stumble through life. In an article called "The Lonely American Just Got a Bit Lonelier," for the "Ideas and Trends" section of *The New York Times* on July 2, 2006, Henry Fountain expressed his profound regret that "for as long as humans have gathered in groups, it seems, some people have been left on the outside looking in." What a crying shame. He continues, saying that Americans are "lacking in people to tell their deepest, darkest secrets," and references a recent study conducted by sociologists at Duke and the University of Arizona, revealing that most adults have only two people with whom they believe they can communicate, and that approximately one quarter have no one at all. Fountain notes the rise of the great American internet as a cause for celebration, since it brings scattered family members into a single Old McDonald electronic barnyard. He also cites a correlation between how many friends one has and how long one may reasonably expect to live.

On a larger scale, Jason Kaufman's "Rise and Fall of a Nation of Joiners: The Knights of Labor Revisited" (*Journal of Interdisciplinary History*, Spring 2001) argues, to make a protracted story brief, that the decline and fall of the KOL was in part accountable to its not having fallen within the charmed "golden age of fraternity" inasmuch as "the birth of the fraternal movement preceded the Knights' by at least a decade," albeit "the Knights' founders were active participants in other fraternal orders," something that he apparently interprets as a positive sign. The Knights of Labor, for those who may have forgotten some sides of American history, began assembling workers in 1869 and became a national organization nine years later. The KOL attempted to bring women, minorities, and (strangely enough) employers together in an effort to foster the eight-hour day, abolish child and convict labor. It allegedly represented over 700,000 workers at its peak in 1886, but thanks to a litany of managerial blunders, ceased to exist by 1900. Kaufman notes that "one of the most divisive issues within the Knights' short history concerned the fraternal oath of secrecy required of all members," adding that "fraternal orders customarily possessed coteries of handshakes, rituals, and signs for members only." The KOL was sufficiently threatening to provoke the Catholic Church, Kaufman reminds us, to become "suspicious of organizations that required members who swear allegiance to any power other than to God and the Church." In other words, all such enthusiastic purveyors of brotherhood, allegiance, and unanimity had begun to bicker over whose brotherhood, allegiance and unanimity was (so to speak) *on the table.*

Writing for *The Philanthropy Roundtable* in 1999, Everett Carll Ladd, until recently the double lettered director of the Roper Center for Public Opinion Research, authored what he called "A Nation of Joiners," i.e. that "peculiarly American form of behavior." Ladd's opinions call to mind the Viennese economist, management consultant, and author Peter Drucker's prolix belief that "nothing sets this country as much apart from the rest of the Western World its almost instinctive reliance upon voluntary and often spontaneous group action for the most important social purposes." Ladd documents the prevalent decline of civic minded Americans, observing that a mere 18 percent belong to any voluntary group, whereas Americans supposedly lead other more or less civilized nations in the percentage of its citizens who belong to religious organizations. "America continues to stand out as a nation of joiners." That said, Ladd concludes with satisfaction, noting also "the latest global data point to a widespread expansion of associational engagement." In other words, the more joiners, the better it is for us all. In a minor note, "PubMed," the online voice of the National Library of Medicine and the National Institute of Health, in 1984 reported on the treatment success of joiners and non-joiners in an effort to curb cigarette smoking. The idea was to stop smoking and start joining. "Non-joiners," it held, "were found to be more anxious, less educated and [and lacking in] self-efficacy expectation than treatment joiners." The message: surrender your joint, and join. This is anything but an unpopular view. "Social involvement is good for your mental and physical health," Mary Ellen Strote of *Look Smart Mom* reports, "and it doesn't matter whether you get involved in a church group, civic association, hiking or sports team. Establishing friendly ties lowers stress, increases immunity and boosts the amount of support you receive." We could hardly agree more. "Social 'networks' also can help you with practical challenges like finding a job, helping your community function better or learning a sport." Ms. Strote directs our attention to one Tom Stander, identified with the Saguaro Seminar[1] at Harvard, who tells us earnestly, "civic engagement is the health club of the new millennium. If civic engagement is not your idea of existential fulfillment, try joining a book club, a kennel society or your own private mafia."

Precisely, then, what characteristics do such joiners share, except that in general they join anything that permits joining? William E. Geist of *The New York Times* assembled a particularly arresting article called "For the Groupers, Sands of Summer Beckons in Spring" on the desperate effort that groupers waged to rent summer space on Fire Island or the Hamptons in the spring of 1981. Why the desperation? Because everyone else was doing it. That's why. The all-out stampede to rent summer space, he reported, had "already reached its peak as weekend hoards descend on those areas by car, train, bus and ferry" so not to be excluded from doing what, at least at that time, everybody else had in mind. Failing of that, others may have invited the owner of a summer place to come into the city for dinner, or perhaps to present himself at what were known as "grouper parties" organized, as Geist expressed it, "for the purpose of finding a group of young or 'semi-young' singles to share the rent on a summer place." For these socially conscious young New Yorkers, it was the place to be, ergo they must be there at nearly any cost. It was, said one attendee, "like a sorority rush," as frantically interested parties arrived for amounted to a cut session organized by a group that had by that time rented one property or another and were looking for the right sort of person to shoulder the cost burden of what they called "shares and half shares." One such person placed a classified in the *Village Voice*, soliciting "friendly, attractive, intelligent, professional people. Men 28–40, women 26–35." Elsewhere, the call went out for "West Side people," "intelligent achievers," "recently di-

---

1 The Saguaro Seminar on "Civic Engagement in America" concentrated upon "expanding what we know about our levels of trust and community engagement" and on "developing strategies and efforts to increase this engagement." Its "BetterTogether" report concentrates upon how to "re-engage America civically."

vorced," "winter skiers," "non-smokers in 30's," "natural fooders," "gourmets," and "chamber music players." The idea, obviously, was that in a place like New York with its compulsive, overarching need to conform (has there ever been a Republican sighting?), a large sectors of its population were to consider precisely what everyone else was doing, then do it more expensively, so to make a louder statement than anyone else. It is entirely possible that such a movement could begin like spontaneous combustion and with scant warning reverse itself, and direct that everyone, *post haste* and on cue, depart Fire Island and the Hamptons so to return to the city. Part of the intention is to conform without having it appear that one is conforming. This can be done if someone takes credit for starting a mass movement that has people leaping from hotel windows simply because everyone else is doing it. It can also be accomplished if one cultivates the technique of waiting until a public parade has begun to form, then jump to the front of it like some baton-twirling drum major on the Fourth of July. Loners and other independently motivated people by whatever names they go, quite obviously, have no truck with such desipience.

A group calling itself ChangingMinds.org has a few thoughts on conformity, which it defines as "the desire to go along with the norms of a group of people, so that you will be accepted as an in-group person" rather than be "rejected as an out-group person." It argues that since we are at heart tribal animals, we "have a deep need to belong to a group of some sort," so to send the message that "I am like you. I am following the rules. I am not a threat." Importantly, as we shall observe in the pages to follow, ChangingMinds advises that "the degree to which other people conform to the rules[,] indicates their desire to be a group member," reminding us of "pop fans who dress like their idols." It continues by saying that there are people who attempt to blend with whatever group they happen to find themselves on a given occasion. To wax more theoretical about it, a paper entitled "Custom Versus Fashion: Path-Dependence and Limit Cycles in a Random Matching-Game" authored by Kimono Matsuyama in May of 1993 holds that whereas both conformists and nonconformists can exhibit a number of different patterns of behavior, it remains true that "conformists set the social custom and Nonconformists revolt against it," as for example when nonconformists become what Matsuyama calls "fashion leaders" who never-the-less "switch their actions periodically," while, as one might expect, "conformists follow with delay." Obviously, conformists fall predictably into line, but they delay long enough to be assured that others are falling into the same line so that they won't make a tactical mistake and jump into line only to discover that it's the wrong line. The worst thing a conformist wants to do is misconform, thereby sending a signal that he has an independent streak concealed somewhere within.

Glen M. Parker's *Team Players and Teamwork* (1996) examines what aspects converge to form the best (or shall we say worst?) team participants. The book includes a discussion of 1) four kinds of teamers, 2) the right balance of styles for optimum productivity, 3) instruction on how to cause team players "to support, challenge, and inspire one another to achieve stellar results," and 4) "a useful framework for identifying team roles," as suggested by "more than fifty team-obsessed organizations, among them Xerox [whose shares are worth about one fifth of their 1999 price], Honeywell [whose common stock sells for about half what it did in 1999], 3M [whose common has tumbled in that same period from about $32 to $2] and General Motors," whose common share price has plunged from about $90 to about $5), and has teamed itself nearly out of existence. According to the KUKA Robot Group, DaimlerChrysler did the next better thing when it dumped its team players and got into real robots. Remember that Erich Fromm, in *The Sane Society* (1955)[1] said, "The danger of the future is that men become robots." A brilliant idea it was, albeit, assembly line workers had been morphing themselves into robots for quite some time — until robots themselves took over. DaimlerChrysler, by this time had all but served team players their walking papers. One may recall that Isaac Asimov developed his three fundamental "rules of Robotics" in his *I, Robot* (1950)[2], to wit: One, a robot may not injure a human being, or, through inaction, allow a human being to come to harm. Two, a robot must obey the orders given it by human beings except where such orders would conflict with the First Law...Three, a robot must protect its own existence as long as such protection does not conflict with the First or Second Laws." KUKA could scarcely contain its joy when it proclaimed that DaimlerChrysler had welcomed robots into its Mercedes plants, wherein the KUKA Rooter had managed to bring with it a seamlessly "coordinated teamwork between robots," permitting them "to work faster, and with greater precision and versatility," even to the point where KUKA's monsters could seize an automobile body and present it like a leg of lamb in any position for ease of access by humans (what few remain) and by what KUKA calls "machine team members," meaning automatons who require no

---

1 Born in Frankfort, Fromm received a Ph.D. from Heidelberg in 1922 and launched a career in psychotherapy, viewing freedom as the primary characteristic of the human condition.

2 Asimov's *I, Robot* is a short story collection, the title of which originated with his publisher. He wrote nearly 500 books, and has been credited with having elevated the reputation of science fiction. Azimov earned a Ph.D. in chemistry at Columbia in 1948.

pay, no medical benefits, no grievances, no labor contracts, no overtime, no strikes, no retirement packages, no latrines, no bloody nothing.

Be all that as it may, the pressure is still on to join and be joined in all of one's thoughts and activities. A handful of individuals calling itself defensetech.org published a 2005 article called "Bureaucrats 1, Guerilla Geeks 0," about a tesseration of techies who descended upon Houston, FCC license in hand, with the intention of establishing a low-power radio station called Austin Airways for the benevolent purpose of keeping local hurricane Katrina evacuees inside the Astrodome apprised of relief efforts on their behalf. When local bureaucrats got wind of this nefarious plan, they first demanded that the techies come forward with 10,000 portable radios before commencing their broadcasts. The tech people found a way to comply with this absurd request, when another bureaucrat denied them the use of the Astrodome from which to broadcast their emergency low power FM station, explaining that the Astrodome would not provide them with electricity. When Austin Airways offered to provide its own battery power, the bureaucrats turned them down again. Meanwhile, some of the evacuees were reportedly overjoyed that they might receive emergency information relating to such things as employment, food, housing, lost children, clothing and so forth. It didn't happen.

At about the same time the *Washington Post* set out to learn by what politically correct name bureaucrats were calling their Christmas trees. It became a bureaucratic *cause célèbre* and moronic comedy of errors. "The calendar the federal government gave us said 'Christmas holiday,'" reported Staff Sergeant Lorenzo Parnell of the D.C. National Guard, "so we're saying it's a Christmas tree." Good thinking — until certain Christians voiced "concerns" (i.e., complaints) about rendering Christmas as a secular holiday, which it had been for quite some time. Then the *Washington Times* revealed that His Grace, the House Speaker J. Dennis Hastert had accordingly directed bureaucrats on the Capitol's West Lawn to unveil to their contentious arbor as the "Capitol Christmas Tree," in a letter to Alan M. Hantman who happens to be the "Architect of the Capitol" that was built in 1792, and needed no more architects. Hastert, visionary statesman that he was, wrote, "I strongly urge that we return to this tradition and join the White House, countless public institutions and millions of American families in celebrating the season with a Christmas tree." Excellent thought, excellently expressed. The *Post* article explains that the first such tree in 1964 was indeed called a "Christmas tree," albeit "was named a *holiday tree* in the mid–1990s to acknowledge other cultural traditions, sources said. Nobody knows who ordered the change or when it occurred."

Nor, of course, is the mystic, nay heavenly, cloud of theology exempt from the menace of bureaucracy. Indeed, religions are themselves bureaucracies — some of the worst. In 2007, The *Anglican Journal* published an article by Leanne Larmondin titled, "Bureaucrats Query 'Licentious' Service," having to do with a proposed joint religious service shared by conceivably antagonistic Lutherans and Anglicans in Waterloo, Ontario in 2007. As Ms. Larmondin explains, the religious event "began a long journey through a bureaucratic maze of one local liquor control board, two provincial ministries and a provincial ombudsman's office before acquiring permission to hold a worship service, complete with sacramental wine, in the arena." Since the service involved roughly 4,000 persons, and since obviously no local church was large enough, the only place for the happening was the Waterloo Recreation Centre. The unenviable task of planning was largely in the hands of a woman named Eileen Scully, who went head to head with at least ten bureaucrats with a mind to making it legal through various bureaucratic balderdash to consume wine in the Centre. Meanwhile, the Lutherans refused to serve oxymoronic "non-alcoholic wine," on the premise that to do so collided with their "theology," if such exists. Then the matter fell into the hands of a provincial ombudsman, and from there to the provincial alcohol and gaming commission's bureaucrats who invented a number of idiotic bureaucratic questions such as the size of the arena; the number of exits therein; the matter of whether people would be seated, roaming around or possibly climbing stairs while partaking of Christ's body and blood; and whether there would be children present. Finally, some "ministry" (whatever that may signify) turned the matter over to its attorneys who discovered the province's Religious Tolerance Act, a document that resulted in a permission from some bureaucrat to carry on with the church service on the proviso that the consumption of alcohol did not cause these Anglicans and Lutherans to engage in what it called "acts of licentiousness," that by this time might have been a real possibility. If it did indeed set off a wave of moral abandon, the incident seems to have gone unrecorded, which is probably just as well.

Divorced-Dad-Daily.com on April 7, 2006 published an article it called "Some Bureaucrats Want to Expand Discriminatory Thinking. Are You Surprised?" It has mostly to do with federal bureaucrats skewing demographic numbers (as they are quite capable of doing) allegedly to placate feminist groups — not the kind of people one wants to rankle. It cites 2001 statistics confirming that men earn roughly 80 percent of engineering degrees and 75 percent of computer science degrees, with the result that "universities, non-profits and the government pour money into programs" with the intention of remedying what bureaucratic jackasses view as regrettable gender discrepancies that cry out for bureaucratic intervention. It goes on to say that when Harvard president Larry Summers speculated (in public) that innate gender differences might play a role in the formation of these numbers, his musings (along with some other vendettas) cost him his job, academic freedom be hanged. The nerve! Shortly after that, *The Wall Street Journal* noted, the University of California at Davis disinvited Summers as a speaker after "more than 150 faculty members protested his appearance, saying Mr. Summers 'has come to symbolize gender and racial prejudice in academia.'" What he should have said, with tubs of rhetorical bubbles and political correctness, was that the lopsided numbers were the direct result of discrimination against women by the infidels who comprise the Engineering faculty. Elsewhere, the article cites supposed evidence of women's being treated "differently" at some universities that, thank heaven, go identified. To the contrary, the article notes, women earn about eight of ten degrees in "education" (albeit these degrees are not worth the paper upon which they are written); they also take eight in ten psychology degrees, six in ten degrees in accounting and biology. If what is good for the goose (as we all uphold) is good for the gander, then bureaucrats might piss away some of their bottomless piles of public money toward herding men into these sometimes dubious fields of supposedly academic inquiry. Furthermore, it notes that women earn something like 58 percent of bachelor's degrees (with black American women it is closer to two-thirds), that might infer that women enrollees be reined in while men be encouraged by any of several delicious rewards, among them flattery, freebies, and flagellation. The article does allow that "the increasingly poor performance of young men is the most significant, troubling trend in American education," and that if one were to imagine that the trend were reversed, such that "men's academic achievement were soaring relative to women's," then women's groups would howl their outrage. The article posits that, for some time, the only way to avoid having bureaucrats bring litigations against universities was to allow athletic precipitation to be an index to enrollment; for example, if 58 percent of students were women, then 58 percent of student athletes must also be women. It makes perfect sense, as Voltaire might have said while chortling up his sleeve. Since (we might speculate) fewer women might have an inclination toward athletics, the only thing to do is lower the number of young men in athletics as well. The piece directs our attention, pursuant to precisely this end, to evidence that "more than 90 universities cut men's track and field, and more than 20 cancelled wrestling." Were this choplogic carried into academic matters, bureaucrats would, as the article suggests, eject women from certain courses so that the ratios complied with bureaucratic miscalculations. Furthermore, bureaucrats would have recruiters pursing male applicants and discouraging women. It makes corking good bureaucratic nonsense. Another strategy, and a damned fine one, will be to advise one million women undergraduates to terminate their studies, with a mind to bringing these imaginary numbers into imaginary balance. Once again, we have before us the inglorious result of turning real or imagined problems over to a committee of joiners, all of whom are stumbling over one another in frenzied passion to comply so that their pooled ignorance misshapes public policy. All herds and no hermits, they are; the result is laughable, except that it's not, even by bureaucratic non-standards, very amusing.

In another education-related matter, a letter posted by Chuck Muth purportedly representing a group called "Citizen Outreach" on March 29, 2006, rises to the defense of a Nevada charter school known as *Halima Academy* against bureaucrats operating under the supposed aegis of the Nevada Department of Education which sought to bring the school down, citing alleged failures to provide bureaucratic paperwork. The allegations were thick as goat fleas, namely 1) that there were two teachers (actually three) on the governing board, whereas there should be three; 2) that the school failed to submit a resume (actually it had) for one of those three teachers, 3) that the school failed (it had not) to schedule enough meetings; 4) that those meetings were assembled without a quorum, 5) that no members of the governing board attended a "technical assistance workshop"; 6) that no member of the governing board ever attended the meetings of another school's governing board; 7) that the governing board did not obtain a "criminal history report " meaning that the director and two other employees were supposedly not in compliance with all 14,000 words of the Nevada Revised Statute providing that certain employees must "submit to the governing body of the charter school a complete set of his fingerprints and written permission authorizing the governing body to forward the fingerprints to the Central Repository for Nevada Records of Criminal history for its report on the criminal history of the applicant"; 8) that the school had not (it had) submitted an audit; 9) that one child had been, on testimony of that child's parents, admitted to the ninth grade before having competed the eighth; 10) that the school had failed to submit an "At Risk Report"; 11) that the school had (it had not) failed to renew an "Errors and Omissions" rider on its insurance coverage and, for good measure; 12) that the school did not assign someone to attend a bureaucratic "in service" program on how to comply with still more bureaucratic horse apples. The school responded that it was in only its second year of operation and whereas it understood that it must supposedly comply with prevailing laws, "most of the issues presented here are simple mistakes or communications errors." Halima Academy was organized as a last gasp effort to save 100 or so high-risk kids, not a few of whom had truancy records and others who had so-called "learning disabilities." Most of the learning disabilities, obviously, belonged to the dimwitted committee types who precipitated and then aggravated problems that only deterred the Halima Academy from going about the business of assisting troubled children.

John Stuart Mill's *On Liberty* refers to such bureaucratic bullying as a "tyranny of the majority" aimed at suppressing the creativity and innovation of independent citizen. To submit, said the old fellow, is to confirm "the servility of mankind towards the supposed preferences or aversion of their temporal masters." On April 12, 2006, *Whistleblower Magazine* published an unsigned article on a journalistic inquiry by Joseph Farah, Sarah Foster, Dana Perliner, Steven Greenhut, Walter Williams, Charlotte Allen, David Kupelian and others in an investigation called "The End of Private Property: How bureaucrats steal homes, trample the Constitution and destroy lives" pertaining to the so-called "Kelo" Supreme Court decision that allows wholesale political seizures of private homes, businesses and even houses of worship, for the purpose of building such bureaucratically favored projects as privately financed office buildings, condominiums, gambling casinos, restaurants and boutiques. The article claims that over 10,000 such properties have been condemned or have been threatened with condemnation for the purpose of enhancing private enterprise. Besides the city of New London, Connecticut, the examples cited were Oakland, California, that implemented its eminent domain by seizing a 57-year-old private business to pave the way for a housing development; Boynton Beach, Florida, that destroyed a 50-year-old business to make way for other business enterprises; Richmond Heights, Missouri, where bureaucrats are grabbing 200 homes to be razed in favor of newer housing; Spring Valley, New York, that shortly after the *Kelo* decision petitioned the Supreme Court of that state to authorize destruction of 15 midtown properties so that a private "developer" might construct residential and business properties; Ventor City, New Jersey, where the mayor proposes the demolition of 126 buildings, some supposedly $200,000-homes and a few apartments, the better to replace them with luxury condos, parking garages and stores; East Baltimore, where bureaucrats are helping themselves to some 2,000 properties, for the high purpose of creating something called a "biotech park"; and Boston, where, two days following Kelo the move was on to grab waterfront property from owners. Dr. Walter E. Williams, the curmudgeonly but always informative John M. Olin Distinguished Professor of Economics at George Mason University in Fairfax, Virginia, has pointedly referred to the *Kelo* decision as the U.S. Supreme Court's having accorded local governments the authority to "take a private person's house and turn it over to another private person."

On a global level, Mary M. Shirley's *Bureaucrats in Business* (1995) addresses the matter of government bureaucrats who seize entrepreneurial opportunities in what are sometimes poorer countries at the expense of private entrepreneurs. As Ms. Shirley writes, bureaucrats "operate a casino in Ghana, bake cookies in Egypt, assemble watches in India, mine salt in Mexico, make matches in Mali...bottle water in Senegal," and, one might add, sell liquor in Ohio and other less than progressive states. She refers to such monopolies as SOEs — state owned enterprises. She also notes that in Tanzania, for example, "central government subsidies to SOEs equal 72% of central government spending on education, and 150% of central government spending on health." To the contrary, she notes with approbation that countries such as Chile, South Korea Mexico have divested SOEs aggressively, giving rise to more free enterprise competition. Bureaucrats are one thing; private managers quite another. Accordingly, Ms. Shirley concludes, "inefficient state enterprises are costing developing economies dearly, especially the poorest among them," adding that private enterprise "offers potentially large benefits, including more goods and services of better quality at lower prices, increased availability of resources for health, education and other social spending; and improved fiscal stability — all of which contribute to more rapid economic growth."

In the meantime, Adam Thierer (senior fellow at the Progress and Freedom Foundation) and Wayne Crews (vice president at the Competitive Enterprise Institute) composed a piece called "The World Wide Web (of Bureaucrats?)" for the October 9, 2005 *Wall Street Journal* on the foiled United Nations attempt to seize control of the internet, beginning with the alarmist message that *Kofi Annan* [is] *Coming to a Computer Near You!* The article takes proper umbrage that the internet that has "long run as a global cyberzone of freedom — where governments take a 'hands off' approach — is in jeopardy." Under such international control, suppression of "free speech and expression" (as the article calls it) would be the first order of business. Moreover, various regulatory bodies the world over have attempted to suppress materials that would otherwise attract no subversive attention, such as the Australian court that, as Theirer and Crews point out, "has ruled that the online edition of *Barron's*...could be subjected to Aussie libel laws." At the time of this article, the U.N. was contemplating the second phase of what it called a "World Summit on the Information Society (WSIS) that began in 2003 in Switzerland and then lumbered like a sick cow into a "second phase" two years later in Tunisia with a mind to bringing the internet to bay, subjecting it to some 190 legal codes the world over. The report that WSIS issued to the world was, needless to say, a masterpiece of bureaucratic blubber, brilliantly illustrated by the following effusive declaration that seemed to jump up its own bung: "We reaffirm the principles enunciated in the Geneva phase of WSIS, in December 2003," it says, "that the Internet has evolved into a global facility available to the public and its governance should constitute a core issue of the Information Society agenda. [Who, we ask, does not love an agenda?] The international management of the Internet should be multilateral, transparent and democratic, with the full involvement of governments, the private sector, civil society and international organizations. It should be an equitable distribution of resources, facilitate access for all and ensure a stable and secure functioning on the Internet, taking into account multilingualism." To compose such an abomination was a triumph of bureaucratic rhetorical obfuscation. Thierer and Crews cite a reaction to the WSIS by the U.S. State Department's David Gross who, surprisingly for a bureaucrat, responded cogently and literately, without even one "issue," "window of opportunity," "cautious optimism" or "in terms of," saying quite directly that, "we will not agree to the U.N. taking over management of the Internet," because "the Internet was developed in the U.S. [by Al Gore, by any chance?] and is not a collective 'global resource.' It is an evolving technology, largely privately owned and operated, and should stay that way."

Needless to say, U.S. governmental agencies are just as much given to bureaucratic balderdash as the UN essentially is. Donna Howell of *Investor's Business Daily* wrote a piece entitled "Lawmakers Give Bureaucrats Low Mark" on March 16, 2006, saying, "Five agencies got an A+. Eight flunked. The government gave itself a D+ overall for computer security in 2005." Ms. Howell reported that the United States Agency for International Development (USAID), oddly enough, registered 100 percent, along with A+ performances by the Environmental Protection Agency, the Labor Department, the Office of Personnel Management and the Social Security Administration. Homeland Security and the Defense Department flunked, as did Agriculture, Energy, Health and Human Services, Interior, State and Veterans Affairs. The wonder is that any agency in the federal and state behemoth can possibly defend itself on any grounds. One would like to have confidence in government's ability to evaluate its own performances, but such efforts may inexorably lead in the direction of still more bureaucratic doubletalk and paper shuffling.

The *Macmillan English Dictionary* tells us that the plural noun neologism *sheeple* appeared first in *The Wall Street Journal* in 1984, and may be defined in the simplest way as "people who are easily persuaded and tend to follow what other people do," or more pointedly, "people who act in direct reaction to saturation advertising, going out and buying 'must have' fashions and fads of the moment," or more directly still as, "people who don't tend to think for themselves but basically follow the crowd or believe what the media tells them." Barbara Anderson was the *WSJ* writer who coined the term, however, apparently as a deplorable right wing expression used to belittle gullible people who have a naïve confidence in the government's supposed authority to commit any sort of perverse outrage that it wants. Likewise, an August 4, 2005 editorial in the Pittsburgh *Tribune Review* found fault with the onslaught of the Republican Party's annual summer meeting, supposedly organized around the slogan, "Give us a chance, we'll give you a choice: Strengthening Lincoln's Legacy." The editorial entitled "The GOP Gathers: A Herd of Sheeple," questioned what "chance," what "choice" and what "Lincoln legacy" was out there, in view of how "the just-passed highways bill is an embarrassment"; how "the energy bill isn't any better. (to wit, support for ethanol — which requires more energy to make than it produces — is idiocy incarnate)"; how "the Medicare prescription drug plan is a 10-pound sledgehammer driving a finishing nail"; how Social Security reform has been "diluted and largely shelved"; and how the immigration policy is "confused, misguided and [threatening] to national security." The editorial concludes by saying that the Republican Party, having forgotten the meaning of conservatism, needs to return to its being "a party of principle," but that this will never occur, inasmuch as "sheeple, not prone to independence, run with the herd." On October 19, 2005 Walter Williams developed a rather provocative essay in the same vein called "A Nation of Sheeple" in townhall.com where he argues that American people have gradually been "softening up" to certain governmental edicts, for example President Bush's willingness to engage the military to assist with the Hurricane Katrina catastrophe and with quarantining parts of the nation in the event of an avian flu outbreak. Another was the anti-smoking movement that began on sections of commercial aircraft, then spread like measles to the entire aircraft, front to aft. Then there was the aforementioned Kelo decision where "politicians have learned

[from] and become comfortable with the fact that today's Americans will docilely accept just about any legalized restraint on their behavior." Another was what Williams calls "federal intrusion in our financial privacy through the Bank Security Act," namely, that bureaucrats are nosing through everyone's bank statements. An anonymous contributor to the threadwatch.org website, could scarcely have agreed more, citing an instance of sheeple in action, using the example of a woman who presented herself at her bank where she had allegedly been a customer for some 70 years, and had allegedly done business there at least once a week, confronted a teller who had worked at the bank for 20 years, attempted to withdraw $1,000, only to have the teller insist upon matching the signature on the customer's withdrawal slip against the signature on file. The sum and substance of these anecdotes is the outrageous Americans have become a nation of herds willing (especially) incrementally, to tolerate any nefarious (if it be that) encroachment upon what might be called their *best interests*, rather than some bureaucrat's blundering notion of social engineering.

Bureaucrats have long criticized independents in their midst, largely because independence is the virtue they most want to obliterate since it interferes with their passion for controlling everything and everyone. Even in the not so wonderful, out-of-control lower middle class world of NASCAR there are those who take pleasure in an individual contestant's having been driven (if one will pardon the pun) out of competition by some of the larger racing "teams" that control most of the racing and its high end prize money. A *Sporting News* article called "Victory Loves Company; Loners are History" authored by Lee Spencer (October 15, 2002), makes exactly that observation, holding that no singleton, however Herculean, will ever again prevail in NASCAR's Byzantine season point system because "no privateer will win the title again [since] Winston Cup [as it was then known] racing has become a collection of big-money, multi-car operations that rule the sport," adding later that "the multicar 'haves' are making this and subsequent chases a battle of armies rather than drivers." Ms. Spencer calls to mind the late NASCAR lone ranger Alan Kulwicki the University of Wisconsin engineer who, with three others, died at age 38 in an airplane crash on April Fool's day in 1993 while en route from a public relations junket in Knoxville to Bristol, Tennessee where he had intended to compete in a stock car race. As a loner, Kulwicki won 24 pole starting positions and five races with what was comparatively a shoestring operation, and scarfed up the NASCAR Winston Cup title in 1992 over Bill Elliott, Davey Allison and Harry Gant. Those halcyon days, the pundits claim, have come and gone. Spencer quotes Paul Andrews who was

Kulwicki's crew chief in 1992, "you couldn't be a winner week in and week out," he replied. "The multi-car teams have lots of resources, like wind tunnel time and engineering staffs." The message is ubiquitous: join forces, or else. That includes everything from the bizarre world of NASCAR to the metaphysical morass of today's theology. In a Lenten missive Sister Mary McGlone, a member of the General Leadership Team of the Sisters of St. Joseph of Carondelet, writing metaphorically on the subject of "Salt and Light vs. Losers and Loners," for *The Catholic Key* (February 7, 1999) advising us to "coerce, manipulate, compete, nurture, unify" in that order. Sr. Mary refers to "salt," she explains, because Jesus himself supposedly referred to his followers by that name. She concludes by asserting somewhat fuzzily "we need to nurture the just and charitable relationships which make us a people of the light, and preserve enough salty presence to light the fires," because that is "the commitment needed to transform a world of losers and loners into a real community." Her remark puts us in mind of Henry Adams' memorable observation that "one friend in a lifetime is much; two are many; three are hardly possible. Friendship needs a certain parallelism of life, a community of thought, a rivalry of aim."

Team players, of course, do not see life and work in quite that way. Of particular interest is John C. Maxwell's authoritatively titled *The 17 Indisputable Laws of Teamwork* (2001) that contains a great many messages of special interest to loners and other independent spirits. It argues, of course, that the best approach to accomplishment is to assemble a team and place a challenge before it. "One is too small a number to achieve success," Mr. Maxwell[1] declares, and then moves on to other unequivocal principles, among them that "everyone knows that teamwork is a good thing; in fact, it's essential." None of those three declarations are beyond dispute, nor is his assertion that "no lone individual has done anything of value," a declaration that is manifestly absurd. How many bureaucrats and their drones did it require to compose the *Commedia*? How many to paint the *Mona Lisa*? Elsewhere he advises, "some people aren't outgoing and simply don't think in terms of [beware of bureaucrats who toss an "in terms of" your way] team building and team participation." Whether one is "outgoing" has nothing to do with foisting creative work on a committee that, given enough time, will screw it up. Later he poses a more than provocative query: "Why take the journey alone when you can invite others along with you?" Answer: You're bored with their company

---

1 Maxwell also authored *21 Irrefutable Laws of Leadership* and the *Winning With People Workbook*, having been influenced by Dale Carnegie's *How to Win Friends and Influence People*. He studied at Ohio Christian University, Azuza Pacific University and the Fuller Theological Seminary.

and have absolutely zero confidence in their ability to do anything except sit around a table taking notes and nodding approval when anybody says anything, regardless of how preposterous. Says Mr. Maxwell, "nobody can do it alone." Is that why women visit bathrooms in pairs? "It's all about the team," he also posits, to which we ask, *what* is all about the team? Utter the pejorative word *team*, and what comes to mind? A room full of lumbering lard-asses who will require 24 to 36 hours to destroy an excellent idea, far better left in the hand one individual.

Maxwell can find plenty of company out there, as for example in a quite outrageous essay team written by Karen G. Evans and Gary L. Wamsley titled "Where's the Institution" that one can find between the covers of George Frederickson and Joycelyn M. Johnson's team-edited *Public Management Reform and Innovation: Research, Theory an Application* (1999). Evans and Wamsley brazenly assert that we "generally must accept that the individual in both the modern and post modern world cannot survive alone," since "like the Tin Woodsman, the individual rusts into immobility in isolation." They elsewhere venture that "since the closing of the frontier at the end of the last century, the opportunity to live the largely mythological American life of splendidly isolated individualism began to disappear." We earnestly trust that is not so, and lack any evidence to the contrary. All of those ardently cooperative teams laboring like squirrels in the back committee rooms at Enron, General Motors and the Ford Motor Company were unable to team-think themselves out of massive self-destruction, while the fuzznut bureaucrats at FEMA and their committees fiddled while New Orleans all but floated out to sea. New York bureaucrats and their committees for five years have been scratching their heads and asses over the question how next to allocate what had been the World Trade Center site. Evans and Walmsley, meanwhile, continue to claim with obvious pride, "Our [your?] life has become corporate life [we don't question that for a moment], and this corporate life works in ways that deny our full intellectual and creative capacity." If your corporate life denies your full intellectual and creative capacity, we earnestly suggest you try something else, like building a cabin in the woods and sustaining life with the nuts and berries that fall gratuitously from the abundant environment into which you have placed yourselves.

Glenn Parker's *Team Players and Teamwork: The New Competitive Business Strategy* (1990) tells us that a collaborator "is a goal-directed member [of what?] who sees the vision, mission or goal of the team as paramount but is flexible and open to new ideas, is willing to pitch in and work outside his defined role, and is able to share the limelight with other team members." In other words, he's a team guy from his toenails up, the sort of person who enjoys bouncing ideas off the mindless dunderheads who pack his committee. Imagine 50 Joe Bidens in the same room. But such layered ignorance has its regrettable limitations, such as the person trapped on a committee that offers nothing but a proliferation of platitudes. He desperately wishes he were somewhere else, preferably alone. In the eyes of Mr. Parker, he is best described as an "ineffective team player," an obviously ambiguous expression, meaning that he's a player on an ineffective team, or possibly that he's an ineffective player on a team, in which case he's not a player at all. How to handle such a lone wolf of this ignominious sort? Parker suggests asking him, (as tactfully as conceivable), "Why are you on this team?" to which he may respond that he obviously *isn't*. If circumstances reach this regrettable point, Parker suggests that the time has come "to confront the person," with a mind to asking him how, in the name of inefficiency, he would not be thrilled to be a part of any team that would agree to tolerate him in its midst. This candid conversation, Parker tactfully advises, "is best done privately." We're just now beginning to understand the gravity of this problem. Chances are the renegade never pledged a college fraternity and therefore missed an opportunity to be shoved into humiliatingly communal situations wherein he was ordered to perform certain indignities against his better judgment, and perform them cheerfully. But suppose that this crackpot neither gets along nor goes along? What then? Parker again comes to the rescue. His response? "Zap the person." What? *Zap the person!* Whereas he would have been a disgrace to his fraternity, is now a disgrace to his corporation. "Some people must go," Parker says with an obviously heavy heart. "Some people just cannot be rehabilitated." We confessed to having been in denial, but we are at last manfully prepared to come clean, to affirm Parker's stern dictum. Tell us, Parker! "They must be transferred [but where, oh leader?], reassigned [to the loading dock, perhaps?], or simply fired." That's more like it. Terminate the chap. Send him packing. Our poor loner, to borrow words of Shakespeare's Bolingbroke, has been sentenced to "Eating the bitter bread of banishment."

At least his company might have packed him off to some penal colony where his solitary habits might have been altered to the point that he had completely renounced and abandoned his here-to-fore erroneous sense of self-reliance, then learned how, and without malice, to become a complete company man, subservient to a troupe of arrogant, know-nothing blockheads who like to detain people in rooms for long periods, and adjust their thinking to coincide with the group in whose hostile midst they uncomfortably find themselves. It doesn't end there. If corporate control artists haven't peeked through everyone's bedroom windows by this time, they are well on their way to commandeering their employees private time by requiring them to appear at team-building fun places. Such a one, located in an undisclosed location, is NASCAR driver Ward Burton's wildlife retreat where aberrant sectors of modern society can learn to open fire on clay birds, learn to love nature — and begin feeling better about corporate life. It is a lesson in how to stop worrying and (as people used to say) learn to love the bomb. Joyce Gannon of the Pittsburgh *Post Gazette* covered some of this regimented stupidity in a July 10, 2005, business news item called "Off-Site Excursions to Build Productivity Take Workers to Unique Venues," wherein she mentions the enforced gathering of some 150 hospital emergency room workers summoned together with ambulance squad members to have a little fun in the woods where, after rolls and coffee, they might team up and (of course) split into groups (what else?) of four, then file out smartly to certain locations from which they take arms at clay birds. The whole idea, said a hospital spokesman was to allow ambulance drivers to play Daniel Boone beside an emergency room doc. Call it a *bonding experience*, without which group efforts forfeit their togetherness. Ms. Gannon notes that "organizations are spending huge sums to send employees off-site for sports, games and activates designed to help them forge bonds that will ultimately improve teamwork and productivity back in the office," inasmuch as the aforementioned activities are prescribed with a mind to discovering parallels between fun and work. "It's about bringing a team together and encouraging and helping each other," says a gentleman from a Las Vegas outfit called "Thrillseekers Unlimited" that arranges such outings as these as well as "extreme" vacations that include such attractions as bungee-jumping and fast rides in NASCAR hardtops. She also mentions a San Francisco firm called "The Go Game" that devises "web-based problem-solving activities for teams of co-workers to play out of the office at venues as diverse as beaches and malls, using cell phones to obtain instructions," since groups are not encouraged to formulate their own direction. Says Mrs. Gannon, "teams are assigned such tasks as producing a 20-second video advising new employees on how to get a raise, in which one member plays the boss, one works the camera and the others play the roles of employees." The charade ends, she adds, when "the whole company views all the videos and votes for the best." Ms. Gannon was told that "even inexperienced shooters like employee team outings, 'because you get to make noise and break targets' after which, "someone else cleans up your mess." Another observer noted with sly bureaucratic approval that in a shooting competition, "if we have an accounting department versus an

IT [whatever that may be] department, the computer people always analyze the distance before they shoot," noting that engineers do that, as well. The accountants, being accountants, "just stand and stare." It is entirely possible, some anonymous yoyo points out, that having fired guns all day next to some nameless dork, one might well conclude, "Hey. This is more than a one-dimensional accounting person." Indeed so. It may be a one-dimensional accounting person firing a gun at a clay pigeon because, like a conscripted soldier, he's been more or less commanded to do so on pain of losing his livelihood on grounds that he simply wasn't *fitting in* sufficiently well.

But even that problem has it remedies. James Woudhuysen, we are told, is Professor of Forecasting and Innovation (What won't they think of next?) at a place called De Montfort University in Leicester, and has worked up an essay entitled "Team Players: The popularity of workplace teams indicates how work is elided with play," that presumes to draw even a pathetic bloke into workplace teams through the application of what Woudhuysen calls "ecstatic transcendence" in the miraculous world of interactive workplace drones. If over their howls of protest loners be inexorably driven into workgroups, this one may be the least offensive, although online managers have a tendency, even a policy, to exploit the personal lives of its contributors, something that may not rest well with lone wolves who are loath to tell anyone a bloody thing about their private lives. Nevertheless, as the good professor reminds us, this sort of cyber work is "a mutually therapeutic and supportive activity" that, if delivered properly "could bring about the laid-back, leisurely, genuinely economy to which we all aspire." How does this come about? By a whole new way of looking at committees and their miserable participants, wherein "contributions are defined more by content than by cosmetics [we like the sound of that] when the team works electronically." When that happens, *bingo*: "Like a football team [we like the simile] one at work recognizes individual talent, but subordinates it [we hear you] to the discipline of the whole." Which is of course the basic idea: working in a team. Holding hands. Blowing each other's noses. Laughing and sobbing uncontrollably together, even though we're half a world apart. " A work team," the professor continues, "demands humility of the participating Self [we understand that] in the service of 'scoring' and so winning the affections of the surrounding work audience. And a really professional work team, nowadays, is guided by a manager who is a coach." Football. Coach. We're beginning to see the light, albeit dimly. But does any work get done? Isn't there a profit to be made, without which there would be no interactive television? "For the past two centuries," the professor explains, "workers broadly sublimated the Self to the objectives and deadlines surrounding profitability; but there was a strict divorce between the worlds of work and play." We regret to hear this. "Play," the professor continues, "was something to be done after hours." But today? "Society has moved on. "It elides work and play." It's about time, if you want our opinion. Teams, the professor feels, are like a sandbox "for a small group of friends." Citing the Boston Consulting Group, he explains that work teams are "about affection, affiliation, acknowledgement, recognition and self-worth." Indeed, the BGG believes that a team is 'a circle of need, desire, and ultimately of love.'" So do we. *How might we join?* "Join as many teams as you can," the professor responds, "in a therapeutic hunt for what New Labor ministers call self-esteem." By George, that sounds like a capitol idea. Finding love, and getting paid for it. "Serving" (as enlightened people say) on a committee without having to look at, or listen to, all of their babbling and the same time not managing to say anything, is a bloody fine idea.

Not everyone approaches group activity in quite the manner that Professor Woudhuysen does. The British government, as one might presume, is a little more spartanly businesslike about the whole matter. In its directive titled simply "Working Groups," it says with admirable and unexpectedly unbureaucratic unimaginative directness that they are "small, task-focused groups of Alliance [whatever that may be] members responsible for turning the priorities, set by the Planning Group, into action." If that is not sufficiently mind-deadening, it continues by earnestly recommending that "for each priority set by the Planning Group, a working group is established. The Planning Group invites Alliance members with the appropriate experience, resources and influence to join working groups which will then be responsible for delivering on the priorities." It concludes on a relatively liberal note, allowing that "the working groups operate in whatever way is most effective." Does that mean that they're quite a liberty to retire to a forest and ambush clay pigeons? If not, fear not; there is a one-size-fits-all software out there that will successfully wrap its fangs around any loner, nay, any *nation* of loners. The BBC reported on February 7, 2006 that "employers want good team workers who can communicate properly and have cultural awareness," reiterating later that "employers are likely to be looking to graduates who can demonstrate softer skill such as team working, cultural awareness [again], leadership and communication skills, as well as academic achievement."

David Essex's "Team Players: The Lowdown on Collaboration Software Tools," in the August 9, 2004, *GCN Home* explains that "collaboration software tools are applications that enable real-time communications and document sharing among workgroups or larger user organizations." It sounds like a whole lot of fun. The operative words here are "collaboration," "communications," "workgroups," and "organizations," which, of course, are "issues" that Essex addresses. True, but they are aimed also at collaboratively-minded herd animals more than eager to team-up either in person or out there in the cyber world. He provides a brief history of cyber collaboration, noting that many of the "applications" of yesteryear "were tolled together and accesses by employees and customers through centralized portals" that he describes as "the Web toy that everyone wanted but didn't know how to use." Impediments to mass collaboration, we surmise, must have been exceedingly frustrating to those *who so longed for it.* To the rescue, he says, came "web-based software with less lofty yet more practical ambitions" of which "governments are beginning to take advantage." All we can say is: *at last.* "Rather than trying to smother everyone in a sort of electronic group hug [we like that: *group hug*], what's now called *collaboration software* facilitates the short-term communication needs of project items." We understand. We begin with short-term; before we know it, we're into long-term. Mr. Essex continues, "People's first instinct is to start group discussions in e-mail." We can well understand that, having begun many a contagious conversation that raged out of control and soon accommodated tens, then hundreds of voices, all chattering at the same time. "When the volume becomes unmanageable, and documents are passed around," Essex continues," "they hanker for more elegant tools designed for the unique demands of effective, electronically mediated teamwork." Precisely. Not merely teamwork, but something far better than teamwork; *electronically mediated* teamwork. Call it, if you will (business school graduates say "if you will" three or four times a minute) *twenty-first century electronically mediated cyber communication.* Be that as it may, several talkative team workers have taken to purchasing software that addresses their passion for talking with each other. "The local Rotary Club," we are reliably informed, was "the first on board with [one such] service, dubbed the Community Connector."

If that doesn't work, there's always WhirlyBall that, according to Shelley K. Wong of Associated Press, consists of "two teams of five players, who pass [a] ball with handheld plastic scoops and score points by tossing it at a target on an elevated backboard — all the while driving an electric vehicle steered with a lever." All this plays out on a 4,000 square foot rink equipped with an electric floor. WhirlyBall, according to Ms. Wong "combines jai alai, basketball, hockey and electric powered bumper cars" and has its sinister purposes, however, as for example the Seattle accounting firm that incorporates it in its job interview rituals that Ms. Wong calls "a surprise test of how prospective employees cooperate." She also notes that the credit department managers at Zebra Technologies in Vernon Hills, Illinois use bumper cars as a cunning tool to encourage "office camaraderie." One can just imagine. Of course, there are personality types that can be herded virtually anywhere to participate in anything, regardless of how mindless it may be. Ask Paul Donato, a financial analyst at Cigna the health insurer: "We're sitting in our cubes trying to do work, working on computers, pumping our proposals," he told Wong, "and now we're sitting in a bumper car approaching our co-workers at 12 miles an hour[,] ramming them and hoping the ball falls out of their little stick. It's totally different[,] but it's a really good time," especially it you are half stir-crazy from being cooped up inside a corporate cubicle for years on end. Leaping out of an office window might offer some relief from that ignominious fate. "It's really become a rage with corporations," said Kim Mangum who manufactures everything one needs to go Balling. Wong reports that it has taken hold at corporations like The Hartford Financial Services Group, United HealthCare and Aetna. One manager testified that "WhirlyBall is the talk of the water cooler for weeks." But wherever you go, there's always a wet blanket. Wong notes that Lynda McDermott, president of New York's EquiPro International, had the gall to say that she hasn't heard of the sport and doesn't see how it applies to the workplace." EquiPro, in the meantime, "advises team-building programs for clients including Pfizer Inc, Procter & Gamble Co. and Time Warner" each of them presumably filled with employees eager to have someone's badgering them, with or without their having been softened up with a bracing interlude of WhirlyBalling. Better to seek refuge in a cubical than to confront that. As some aphoristic dodo once philosophized, "There's No 'I' in Team," a damned fine message, concisely expressed. Bravo. There are those so committed to team trivia that they aspire to drive individuality out of the committee room, which is the last place any individual wants to be.

There was a guardedly interesting recent "roundtable" (lone wolves stay as far from roundtables as possible) on the subject of "Producing Team Players" at the Seattle Central Community College, during which one of the "educators" (we're leery of people who call themselves *educators*) and employers averred that industry needs (we have heard this before) employees with "experience working in teams," nonetheless "strong commitment to individual performance is all too often a correlate of high achievement." That may be, but let's overlook it. The study of mathematics, the educator went on to say, "highlights individual effort over teamwork," albeit "parts of school mathematics (routine problems) do not require or benefit much from group work."

Unfortunately too, "college admission is based on individual effort, including SAT scores, course grades, and writing samples. Parents want high schools to focus on preparation for college, and are thus very nervous about high-lighting teamwork as a priority." Moreover, "assessing an applicant's poten-tial as a team member is often not a priority in business hiring practices," and to worsen matters, "people who may do a good job as part of a team my have difficulty getting in the front door." The anonymous person's testimony ends, alas, with the Parthian message that "the era of the lone gunman is over."

That happens to be the opinion of Jeffrey Glaze, editor of AtlantaEvent. com who in an undated article called "Community Vs. The Loner," argues in Darwinian terms that lone guns are in peril of being subsumed by "predators that travel in packs," as are the predators themselves — unless they travel in bunches. In the world of business, he says, it's safety in numbers that takes the form of business-to-business networking. The Jersey City asset manage-ment firm of Abner, Herman & Brock, writer Sandy Serva of *Buyside* noted in March of 2003, reported that in the world of asset management there is indeed "safety in numbers." Accordingly, the company gathers up its senior managers "several times a week" to make asset decision for its customers who include "high net worth" folks (minimum $250,000). At AH&B, the team system, oddly enough, appears to be effective, if that is not too much to be believed. As Ms. Serva says, "While it seems that such discussions might invariably lead to some table-pounding, the group terms these disagreements as 'constructive debating.'" Fortunately too, "all this talking doesn't leave the group mired in deadlock," partly because in instances of disagreement, "we will challenge each other in a respectful manner."

The same is emphatically not so within the bureaucratic paradise that misshapes our eternally blundering federal government. On the financial page of the May 10, 2004 *New Yorker*, James Surowiecki makes a number of observations ironic in a publication that seems to feel that it is more impor-tant to elect impossibly naive Democratic candidates to look after matters of national security, at a time when "the American intelligence community is a mess." Community it is not. That it may be a mess is no surprise, since anything governments touch turns to a mess, if it isn't a mess to begin with. The problem, Mr. Surowiecki correctly says, is that "we have fifteen agencies responsible for gathering and analyzing intelligence" and who "on a good day...duplicate each other's efforts," whereas "on a bad day, they hoard in-formation and undermine their cohorts, seeming at times more preoccupied with reputations, budgets, and internal power struggles than with the na-tion's security." This non-community, he goes on to say, "has "a history of bureaucratic turf wars, occupational secrecy, and sibling rivalry — a kind of dysfunction that seems typical of the public sector." You bet it does. "Independence encourages responsibility," Surowiecki also correctly says, "but there are some things that people can do better together than they can apart." Let's see. Sex, perhaps? "Excessive internal competition," on the other hand, "eliminates these advantages. It encourages people to hoard information, betray their colleagues, and pursue their own ends." That, let it be understood, is what individuals are wont to do. It is one reason why they do not hide in packs and committees. Surowiecki cites a curious anecdote from the world of advanced cogitation in Motown's upper rooms. "A former chairman of General Motors," he recalls, "once described the process of building a new car there as a series of spiteful exchanges between the engineers and the assemblers: "O.K., you build it if you can, you S.O.B," some maverick shouted in a committee meeting when group-think faltered as a *modus operandi*. Mr. Surowiecki, of course, acknowledges this, concluding that "it is senseless, after all, to hire hundreds of thousands of people to find stuff out and then urge them to keep what they know to themselves."

Bureaucracies, recall, beget more bureaucracies, the purpose being to create meetings for the sake of creating more meetings. Anyone who has worked for a corporation, including a university, well knows that if there is a problem to be addressed, no one will have the nerve (in public) to explain the problem, why it is a problem and what the hell to do about it. Instead, the strategy is to talk around the problem and propagate more meetings, with more wasted time, paper, energy and words. Example: Why are "students" flunking out of community colleges in alarming numbers? Because they are 1) stupid, and 2) unmotivated. You won't hear anyone say that, because it will respond to the problem and the reasons behind the problem, something we don't want to do. What we *will* do is organize a subcommittee to look into the problem, return in 30 days, and respond with doubletalk and vague proposals that will be 100 percent inappropriate and ineffective. Better still, we can always apply for a federal grant that will piss away more taxpayers' money and accomplish exactly nothing. Another bureaucratic activity: finding something that functions perfectly well and then "improving" it, which is to say, screwing it up. This activity then sets the bureaucratic stage for determining why that thing is screwed up. On it goes. Every new computer's "operating system" merely complicates its operation. New television receivers are so technically advanced that (without first consulting the fine print of an operating manual) they permit themselves neither to be turned on nor (what is more significant) to be turned off.

The touchy-feely "Center for Service and Leadership" at George Mason University has formulated some down-home strategies to make the bureaucratic mentality friendly to the insecure souls who might like to join in, but who are just too darned timid. It's a herd-minded person's nirvana and a lone wolf's despair. One begins by fostering a certain "desire for acceptance" by letting the suppliant know that "the group is safe." So far, so good. One then sets about gathering information that will reveal the 'similarities [good] and differences [bad] among them, while keeping the atmosphere both simple and non-controversial. We're behind that, all the way. " Serious topics and feelings are avoided," we are warned. After this, the motive is to orient people to each other and to the pointless "tasks" to which they will be assigned. Then it's time to see to it that "each member must relinquish the comfort of non-threatening topics and risk the possibility of conflict." Over time, alas, "conflict inevitably results in their personal relations." We feared that, but somehow saw it coming. What's worse, "there may be wide swings in members' behavior based on emerging issues [our favorite word] of competition and hostilities," wherein "some members may remain completely silent while others attempt to dominate." What remains is for these apprenticing bureaucrats to "move from a 'testing and proving' mentality to a problem-solving mentality." It's about time. What's supposed to happen next is what the Center for Leadership and Service calls "norming," meaning that everyone must hug everyone else on the committee in the knowledge that, since they're all herd-people, they may just as well cultivate "a sense of group belonging and a feeling of relief." We're feeling immeasurably better, thank you. Now that we've been *normed*, let's get on with it. Now that we're "on the same page," as they say, we feel a sense of relief, having begun "to experience the sense of group belonging and a feeling of relief as a result of resolving interpersonal conflicts."

"The election is over.
The ballots are cast.
I'll hug your elephant.
You'll kiss my — ."

The next thing we do is ignite the "data flow between group members" the better to "share feeling and ideas, solicit and give feedback to one another." Excellent. This is how life should be lived: lots of feedback. Touchy stuff. *Feely.* By this time, the "members may begin to fear the inevitable future breakup of the group," and, with that inexorable sense of cosmic *dread*, begin doing funny things, like collapsing frequently or dissolving unaccountably into tears. One would hope, as the group developers suggest, that they "engendered" enough "interdependence" so that some of the better adjusted among them can work "independently." Well, not exactly. We mean "independently in subgroups." You had us worried for a moment. By this time, "group identity is complete." Hooray! The final stage is adjourning, which means "the termination of task behaviors and disengagement from relationships." We doubt whether we're prepared for this. We are warned that it can become "a minor crisis" for which, quite frankly, we are unprepared, although we have been availed to a "disengagement process" that, as may be deemed appropriate by some subcommittee, may involve an awards ceremony during which everyone bestows a gratuitous honor on someone else, as may befit the extent to which the receiver distinguished himself by his (oh yes, *her*) utter uselessness, the supreme accolade that one may receive as a bureaucrat and team player.

Let us suppose, on the other hand, that we were menaced by a *worst case scenario* (as business school grads and management types fondly call such circumstances) involving a loose consortium of lone wolves, outsiders, inner-directeds, independents, isolatos, singles, nerds, dweebs, trend-bucking buckaroos, dorks, geeks, loners and other of such inordinately antisocial riff-raff who comprise the dregs of American society. And suppose these goons declare an old-fashioned sit-down strike? This can spell trouble. *Large trouble*, for bureaucrats and other control artists throughout our great nation and its legions of herds and submissive sheep who snap to attention at the mere sound of authority faintly heard like a distant trumpet somewhere in the remote distance. Stranger things have happened. A group calling itself Accel-Team, righteously devoting itself to "advancing employee productivity" (we like the sound of that) has distributed what one might call an anonymous "white paper" (we also like the sound of that, because on the surface of it, it seems to solve with a certain academic finality, the most trivial of complaints) called "Employee Motivation, the Organizational Environment and Productivity," that might as another *reductio ad absurdum* be retitled as the "Revenge of the Oddballs." In plain English, it addresses the regrettable reality that in "every [any?] organization there are often informal group pressures that influence and regulate individual behavior." We don't like the sound of this. The paper continues by warning that "informal groups formulate an implicit code of ethics or an unspoken set of standards, establishing behavior" and furthermore are given to "subtly exercising control over its members regarding the amount of output."

Speaking of time wasting, in 1997 Harvard's Derek Bok Center for Teaching and Learning[1] began promoting the not-so-good idea that it would be wonderfully beneficial to allow students to teach themselves by (we wince to say it) forming into small groups. Attached was a caveat, not without good reason, that carefully warned "students who fear that group work is a potential [potential?] waste of valuable time may [but won't] benefit from considering the reasons [there aren't any reasons] and benefits [ditto]. The five "reasons and benefits" (such as they are) seem tailor made for incipient bureaucrats and other social planners: 1) generating a broad array of possible alternative points of view or solutions to a problem (sounds reasonable, if improbable); 2) giving students a chance to work on a project that is too large or complex for an individual (At Harvard? How could that be?) 3) allowing students with different backgrounds to bring their special knowledge (Diversity! We love it. Only recently have we noticed that folks are not necessarily out of the same mould, although sometimes we wish it were not so); 4) giving students a chance to teach each other (While the professor supposedly in charge takes a short siesta, perhaps? Splendid idea.); and 5) offering students a structured experience [what might a structured experience be?] so they can practice skills applicable to professional [To what professions might we allude?] situations. The document, as if in an afterthought, proceeds to list still more alleged benefits, among them that students who have a tough time speaking to more than five people at the same time, will now seize an opportunity to become quite loquacious in front of large captive slack-jawed audiences; that it will afford other students who for some reason who having been hanging back to join in and speak their minds; that it's an ideal occasion for all but unidentified and terminally passive nerds to escape anonymity, if only for a few minutes; that it's a great moment in world history for students to instruct each other *qui docet discut*, and at Harvard tuition prices. Sounds like a darned good deal to us. Before the session ends, they might perchance rouse the professor from his slumber and explain to His Excellency what they've learned.

> Tis the voice of the sluggard, I heard him complain:
> "You have waked me too soon, I must slumber again."
> — Isaac Watts, *The Sluggard* (c. 1715)

---

1 The Bok Center invests its trust in the notion that people work more effectively in groups, stressing the management of group processes, the encouragement of ideas, group leadership, group functioning and the problems that arise as a result.

Finally, students theoretically prepare better if they participate actively, although those idealistic assumptions are, as they say, "open to question." One of the attendant problems ("challenges," we now say) in this marvelous activity is that students (if any) will naturally team up with their friends (if any), thereby excluding the same dorks, outsiders, isolatos, creeps, lone wolves, unclubables and so forth to whom we have spitefully referred. They, of course, will be more than happy not to participate at all, having been under the sadly mistaken impression that they enrolled in a course that at the front of the room was a professor with a head on his shoulders and his mind switched on. Suppose, *worst case scenario* again, that some inner-directed person finds himself assigned to your group? What says the Derek Bok Center for Teaching and Learning about *that* thorny question? Let's consult the document under the heading, "Students That [*sic*] Don't Fit." We quote: "You might anticipate your response to the one or two exceptions of a person who really has difficulty [taking the whole enterprise seriously, maybe?] in the group. After trying various remedies [such as telling that person to blow off, perhaps?] is there [another] out — can this person join another group? [We hardly think so; he rejected the *first* one.] Work on an independent project?" Maybe so, but he enrolled for the course on the assumption that it was a series or organized and pertinent lectures on some pertinent topic delivered by a pertinent scholar. Now you're asking him to do it all himself. For this he paid high tuition? What gives?

We'll tell you what gives. It's "all about" (as the cliché artists claim) joining in, be it for better or (more likely) worse. The high-toned *Youth, Education & Technology News* carried the inevitable verdict on October 28, 2005, with a headline that proclaimed "Millennial Generation a Group of Joiners," confirming what we had long dreaded, that "high school and college students — the so-called millennial generation — are joiners, say students, teachers, and sociologists alike." Said another way, it's "United We Stand; Divided We Flop." What's potentially if not actually worse, the YE&T says that "they're starting and joining school-based clubs at a much higher rate than students before them," a sinister signal if we ever heard one, albeit "they also seem more interested than their predecessors in [and we can hardly fault this] public service and cultural and ethnic issues." There are, of course "ulterior" motives, such as currying favor with college admission types that, as we too well know, are heavily into "issues," particularly of those *issues* relate to "diversity," a term that they assume credit for having, along with its durable definition, invented. The article allows that "some call this generation the 'joiners,'" whereas "others have referred to them as the 'play-date generation.'"

Play Dates (for the uninitiated) is a book by Leslie Carroll purporting to show two and three year olds how to socialize. Said one high schooler of his Latin Club, "I just like the sense of community it brings," to which we add *consensus gentium*. Similarly, an article that appeared in the December, 2005 scottish-enterprise.com reported that kids at a Dundee school "are leading the pack [a particularly relevant word] as dynamic team players — using the test in educational software from Team Play Learning Dynamics" thanks in part to the Michelin Development Fund. It seems that "second year pupils at St. Savior's High are using game based learning software to find out about team building, communication and leadership while mastering computer skills." The project, was "inspired by the idea of using games to help people learn and communicate, the company set to work using the expertise of psychologists and games designers to add the finishing touches." The once-familiar phrase "working with" is a code expression that means yielding one's ideas to the wisdom of some blundering bureaucrat or half-cocked committee. One of the teachers at St. Savior's remarked that "the way the pupils have responded to working together in teams, using problem solving skills, and communicating with each other is fascinating." We can only imagine. A chap named Jim Piggot, the CEO of TPLD (Team Play Learning Dynamics) was beside himself. "We already know," said Mr. Piggot, "that game based learning and interactive team building encourage people to work together, while developing leadership and team building skills." Meanwhile, Simon Goring of Michelin Development Dundee remarked that the whole program "aims to encourage skills and entrepreneurship and promote the long-term future of the city." Some glorious day in the distant future, we (as through a glass darkly) envision the world as one cosmic chain gang presided over by a committee of automatons that have learned their "people skills" through their devotion to computer gaming and their complete and universal submission to groupthink as shepherded by the infallibility of artificially sweetened balderdash. There will be no space for individuals, independent thinkers, recluses and their mysteriously dark chambers with their objectionable books, monographs and their profoundly excellent music. The motive is to join all people into some grayed and blurred pseudo-consensus. Wrote George Orwell in *Nineteen Eighty-Four*, "War is Peace, Freedom is Slavery, Ignorance is Strength."[1]

---

1 This infamous Orwellian slogan may be read less as an outrageous irony, and more as a paradox, as are other expressions (as his biographer Jeffrey Meyers reminds us) as "big brother is watching you," "thought police," "doublethink," and "unperson."

To the contrary, scarcely anyone in the world of free enterprise is unfamiliar with John Frances "Jack" Welch, Jr. whose ambition was to transform General Electric, where he hired on as a Ph.D. in chemical engineering from the University of Illinois, into "the world's most competitive enterprise." He managed to pump the company's market value from an estimated $12 to 26.8 billion in 1981 to roughly $280 to 300 billion in 2001. Purportedly anti-bureaucratic, Welch instead advocated a different bureaucratic mode. Certain Welch idolaters, in the meantime, have characterized him as "the Vince Lombardi of business," drawing compensation estimated at $93.1 million in 2000. Be all that as it may, Welch or someone writing in his name, advanced a document called "25 Lessons from Jack Welch" that recommend what might be viewed as an anti-bureaucratic, bureaucratic *what's what*. Item 11, for instance, bears the heading "Get Rid of Bureaucracy" advising managers to "turn [employees] loose, and get the management layers off their backs, the bureaucratic shackles off their feet and the functional barriers out of their way." It's the kind of sentiment one likes to hear. Elsewhere he advises, managing less is managing better," and that "close supervision, control and bureaucracy kill the competitive spirit." To encourage the most out of employees, he says, "you must remove anything that gets in their way," such as a bureaucracy "that prevents the free flow of ideas, people, [and] decisions." Item 17, however, urges us to "Make Everybody a Team Player," arguing that "managers should learn to be team players," and that it may be necessary to "take steps [such as what?] against those managers who wouldn't learn to become team players." Problems associated with team playing, however are apt to persist. "I don't want any yes-men around me," Sammy Goldfish, aka Samuel Goldwyn of Metro-Goldwyn-Mayer, is alleged to have said. "I want everybody to tell me the truth even if it costs them their jobs." In the meantime, Welch opined, "small companies have huge competitive advantages" because they are "uncluttered, simple, informal," and because they thrive on passion and ridicule bureaucracy." Bob Nelson's *Rewarding Employees* newsletter reported in 1999 that at a GE plant in Puerto Rico, "cross-departmental teams are organized to discuss how suggested changes or improvements will affect each part of the operation," further noting that "hourly workers (associates) run the meetings, while managers (advisers) intervene only at the request of the team," the result allegedly being that "productivity has increased 20% since the approach began." There is no gainsaying, however, that a corporation remains a corporation, and that the inevitable interaction that goes on there still demands constant collaboration between hundreds of people who are by necessity obliged to play ball with everyone else. There remains scant room for the loner and professional oddball as corporate leader.

Ray O'Leary, a retired Marine Corps officer of our acquaintance remarks, "by the time one makes 3 or 4 star general the loners and oddballs have been weeded out by the fitness report/selection process." He continues, "There may be an occasional Brigadier General who slipped through but he will probably go no further. Eccentric, yes. Let me name a few: MacArthur, Patton, Stonewall Jackson, the Brit Field Marshall Montgomery (who was Irish by the way). The top command is always warriors. I like the remark attributed to Frederick the Great: My officers carry two of the four following qualities: Aggressive or Lazy, Intelligent or Stupid. The aggressive and stupid are dangerous. The intelligent and aggressive, while making good decisions get in the way of the people who are trying to carry them out. He said he liked the intelligent and lazy; they make good decisions, and let people carry them out without interference. Marine Corps [generals] are with rare exception warriors. I once asked an Army Reserve [colonel] retired to explain the Army's most recent motto 'An Army of One,' one of the most stupid things I have heard in my lifetime. He said I have got to realize that warriors seldom reach top Army command; one must have a corporate mentality to get to the top. This motto sounds like one produced by some flack working for a big corporation."

It probably was, but of all this great nation's great bureaucracies, the military's may well be one of the biggest, second only to our federal government, itself so hopelessly mired for so long and deeply in bureaucratic sludge that no one can seriously believe it will ever dredge itself out of the muck. Our friends at the University of Illinois have published what they call an "ACDIS Occasional Paper" dated May, 2003 that ostensibly examines "Civil-Military Relations in Pakistan," but which treats more than anything the role of military bureaucracies in relation to civil society, if such can be uncovered. What it essentially argues is that the military "is considered one of the most powerful institutions" in its "defining, formulating and executing external or security policies," and that to no one's surprise it is also "considered to be more assertive and tends to pose a certain [number] of challenges [read *threats*] to civilian authorities." The paper then turns to Samuel P. Huntington, "one of three leading theorists on civil-military relations" who tells us that "two sets of values are assumed to be characteristically military," to wit: "bellicosity and authoritarianism," and therefore it is no surprise that the average combatant has a tendency to be "opposed to democracy and to desire the organization of society on the basis of the chain of command." It may also come as no surprise Huntington notes, that the military mind as-signs a high premium on obedience, a supposed virtue about which others of more independent inclinations may harbor certain reservations. As Thomas à Kempis rightly pointed out, "It is much safer to obey rather than rule." In an even more telling remark, Huntington holds that the "military ethic is thus pessimistic, collectivist, historically inclined, power-oriented, nation-alistic, militaristic, pacifist and instrumentalist in its view of the military profession." He also argues, as do others in the field, that it is the statesman and not the warrior who theoretically possesses "superior political wisdom," and that the professional soldier's role is to obey rather and rule. His role is to "stand ready" to go where he be sent, and perform what he is instructed to perform. This function, in Huntington's view, renders the military "politi-cally sterile and neutral" in its service to the state. Considered as a bureau-cratic force in civil society, however, it should be added that the military's professional ability to plan and execute national defense strategy also pro-vided it a place in the government defense policy formulation, and that it therefore became part of the government bureaucracy. Dwight Eisenhower adroitly made the transition from soldier to statesman with what appeared to be a certain ease (which it was not), presiding over huge and therefore in-efficient bureaucracies in both roles. After West Point he became a military commander in World War II, and by 1942 became chief of army operations in Washington, then commander of European theater operations, followed by Supreme Commander of the Allied Expeditionary Force. He directed the French invasion of 1944, that earned him a promotion to five star general that in turn made him army Chief of Staff after the war, after which he became president of Columbia University,[1] then returned to military life in his role as Supreme Commander of Allied Forces in Europe, whereupon he organized NATO forces, resigned in 1952 to run for president on the Republican ticket and made good on his campaign promise to end the Korean war.

Efficient and organized by nature, Robert S. McNamara who served as Defense Secretary under the Kennedy and Johnson administrations between January 21, 1961, and February 29, 1968, often found himself up to his gills in bureaucracies, after which he left ostensibly to become president of still another bureaucracy, that being the World Bank. It was in 2006 that de-fense strategist Edward Luttwak recalled that when McNamara, who had

---

[1] This seems ironic, in retrospect, since Eisenhower seems to have entertained anti-intellectual convictions. Richard Hofstadter has noticed that *Time* magazine and other publications identified Eisenhower's presidential victory as evidence of "a widespread unhealthy gap between the American intellectuals and the people."

served only thirty days or so as president of the Ford Motor Company, came to Washington with his so-called whiz-kids in tow, it was with a mind to eliminating fat from the military juggernaut. The reaction among military bureaucrats, (in Luttwak's words) was to say, "what you call 'cost-effectiveness' and 'efficiency' is driving us toward doing things that would be great if we were in the civilian world; but we're not." Luttwak continued, "it's wrong in war, where the enemy will be able to use the weak points that any machine has, and exploit them." In other words, from the perspective of the military bureaucracy, what would pass for civilian efficiency was not "war-effective." McNamara, who entered the Army Air Force at the rank of captain in 1943 and left three years later at the rank of lieutenant colonel, had some idea how the military operated, and did indeed simplify the system, insisting upon a single defense policy instead of several, and did allegedly save some $14 billion between 1961 and 1966. McNamara was by temperament anything but a bureaucrat, however, and in his 1995 book entitled *In Retrospect*, aired his profound regret for Vietnam policies for which he was in part responsible.

Neither McNamara nor anyone else, however, would definitively get control of the military bureaucracy which received a scathing evaluation in a 1982 paper called "Organized Anarchies: Military Bureaucracy in the 1980s," jointly authored by Alan Ned Sabrosky and Karen A. McPherson of the Foreign Policy Institute, with James Clay Thompson, a political scientist at the University of North Carolina. "The military bureaucracy today," they wrote, "is a highly complex and differentiated structure whose interplay of institutional and interpersonal policies produces an 'organized anarchy.' Its anarchical character is reinforced by ambiguities in the international environment and defense policy priorities; the misdirection of problems and misuse of participants within the bureaucracy; the misleading and overloading of the system with information and demands; incompletely understood intrabureaucratic processes; and a combination of selectivity and inattention in the entire decision-making progress."

It is all unfortunately true, and being true, one does not know whether to laugh or cry. In the fall of 1986 cadets at the Air Force Academy in Colorado Springs had the extreme pleasure of celebrating the 25th anniversary of Joseph Heller's *Catch 22*,[1] and had the additional pleasure of hobnobbing with

---

1 *Catch-22* had been banned in certain parts of the country, sharing that honor with Ray Bradbury's *Fahrenheit 451*, Darwin's *On the Origin of Species*, Flaubert's *Madame Bovary*, Anne Frank's *The Diary of a Young Girl*, Fitzgerald's *The Great Gatsby*, Harper Lee's *To Kill a Mockingbird*, Orwell's *1984*, Salinger's *The Catcher in the Rye*, Shakespeare's *Romeo and Juliet*, Twain's *Huckleberry Finn*, and Wright's *Native Son*.

Mr. Heller himself. Writer Andrew Malcolm, who covered the occasion for *The New York Times*, referred to Mr. Heller's novel "that captured the insanity of war and the human condition while adding a phrase [catch 22] to the English language. There was even a birthday cake for Yossarian, the novel's puzzled protagonist. "These warriors-in-the-making applauded, cheered, mobbed and padded after" Mr. Heller, "the man who made fun of an insane military bureaucracy" as if he'd added (and maybe he did) a new dimension to the literature of war, then discussed "the evil Colonel Cathecart, who kept raising the number of bombings necessary for rotation home, Major Major, who would only see people in his office when he wasn't in, and Milo Minderbinder, the mess officer who could see profit in almost anything." In the collective wisdom of the English Department, however, *Catch-22* became what some might call a *learning tool*. Said the department chair, "we want these men and women to be a thinking part of a large military bureaucracy [if such be possible]. We don't want them to be victims of the Colonel Cathcarts of the world. To put it bluntly, you don't want dumb officers out there protecting your country." To be sure, there are more than a few out there. Mr. Heller was good enough to cite a couple. "I understand," he said, that "the Air Force Academy has a catch-22. To repair a uniform it must be freshly cleaned. But the cleaning staff has orders not to clean any uniforms needing repair." He also cited one army officer in Vietnam allegedly informing the press that, "I'm happy to announce our casualties have increased greatly and are now on a level with those of our marines."

There are, of course, bureaucratic stupidities of a financial nature, such as those identified by *Business Week* on July 31, 2006, among them that "The U.S. Military has lost billions to fraud and mismanagement by private contractors in Iraq who do everything from cooking soldiers' meals to building hospitals to providing security." The article underscores concern among taxpayers that instead of protecting the lives of our service personnel, the money was siphoned off in some major league scams. It draws upon a remark by Jeffrey H. Smith, a CIA Clinton "era" (there must be more descriptive terms for those regrettable years) general counsel, who said what one might expect to hear, that "what has happened in Iraq is just disgraceful." *BW* then notes a certain California firm that allegedly built six of a projected 150 "health centers," raking in $190 million, allegedly $30 million over budget. There is also mention of the Government Accountability [We didn't know that the government had any accountability.] Office's reporting the Defense Department salvaged "about $2 billion" over the last five years from contractors' "dishonesty or mismanagement."

In the meantime, there is dissention in the ranks over the matter of officer promotion in a bureaucracy so Byzantine, so says a publication called *News Insight* (September 7, 2006) in a piece entitled "Military, Bureaucracy Stand-Off on Promotions," that "a very broad base [of officers] makes the pyramid appear unscalable." Moreover, in true bureaucratic fashion, the three services each have their criteria and differing objectives that allow the bureaucracy to call attention to these inconsistencies to frustrate any simplified solution. The NI rhetoric is as inscrutable as the problem it purports to address. The article refers to "cadre review," *cadre* apparently meaning a nucleus of indoctrinated military insiders. Consider the following bureaucratically fuzzed-up assessment of the promotion question: "As the services view with each other," says the writer designated merely as "Our Correspondent," the "bureaucrats are busy ensuring that this [what?] in no way hurts their interests and hold over the country's defence [*sic*] forces. Unwilling to let the forces corner poses [how does one corner a pose?] with officialdom, the bureaucrats are busy pointing out inconsistencies in the proposals, not to forget [who is not to forget?] the financial riders [what financial riders?]. Whether this mess will end [the problem or its rhetoric?] and a concrete action would [will?] emerge is anybody's guess."

It's also anybody's guess what maintains public support for the bureaucratic existence and dysfunction of the National Aeronautics and Space Administration (NASA), which superseded another bloated federal flapdoodle called the National Advisory Committee on Aeronautics (NACA). NASA made as its public business the possibilities of manned space flight (although it apparently need not have been manned at all) along with interplanetary explorations into space, experiments with earth-orbital satellites, rocket ships and more or less ordinary aeronautics. What put NASA on the grotesque federal budget was alarm generated by Russia's launching of the artificial satellite *Sputnik 1* on October 4, 1957. This ignited a temporary passion for the promotion of mathematics and "science" in American public schools. Thanks to the almost total unpreparedness of American colleges of "education," as well as America's traditional anti-intellectual landscape, this never happened. Today, high schools cannot so much as graduate students who cannot read, write nor kick a field goal. Along with other bureaucracies, NASA has mastered the art of squandering public money (the thing that it does best), although NASA, to its eternal credit, did at least propel a chimpanzee into space, and bring the little chap back in one piece — something that it hasn't always been able to do with its astronauts. For its 2007 budget, for example it is requesting a mere $16.8 billion. Maggie McKee reported in the *NewScience* news service on May 4, 2006 that this modest proposal fell into the hands of another bureaucracy, this one called the "US National research Council," that in turned referred it to a bureaucratic debacle subcommittee of individuals who were standing around scratching their privates while discussing "spending priorities." But let's be fair. NASA was about to build something called the "James Webb Space Telescope" for a mere million bucks, but later decided it would cost $4.5 billion to keep it pointed skyward for about ten years. It was cheap at the price, considering that the Hubble Space Telescope (how many telescopes do we need?) has cost about $11 billion to keep it flying for the last 16 years. One NASA bureaucrat had the audacity to suggest "the impact of these cost overruns had done so much damage to upset the balance of the program." He should know. There are subcommittees that report to an advisory council that reports directly to him. The problem, we are told, that NASA can't afford enough "scientific advisors" to sift through its budgetary morass. This deplorable situation, McKee writes, was "roundly criticized by the astronomical community." Another bureaucrat wisely summarized the matter this way: "There is a kind of wise use of human resources and programs that seems to be missing in this budget." Bingo! Any follow-up remark? Yes? "They did it in a hurry," he conceded, "and without consulting the *community* in how to make the impact the least bad." Then NASA decided to do the most rational of things: it called a two -day meeting in Baltimore, mindful that two day meetings are better than one day meetings, just as two hour meetings are better than one hour meetings, and so forth. We don't have a problem with that, simply because we routinely take twice as much time to perform any task as may seem reasonable to the efficiency-minded. Furthermore, 100 people (including not a few NASA "officials") reportedly turned up to hear the committees drone on for two days. That too was a promising sign. A source identified as GCN reported on March 6, 2006 that the U. S. Inspector General happened to notice that NASA issued some 82 contracts to 29 contractors, worth a total of some $630 million. Ms. McKee's article ends on a brighter note, reassuring us that "the agency may decided to change the budget [thank heaven] based on the advisory councils recommendations," and furthermore (this is the good part) "both houses of Congress must approve the budget — a process that is expected to take several months." It probably requires several months for a blowhard bureaucrat to empty his bladder. In the meantime, NASA's famous launches have been interminably delayed for any number of damned good and sufficient reasons, to wit: someone forgot to put fuel in a rocket; someone forgot to usher the drunken (as it indeed turned out) astronauts on board; someone forgot to light the wick; someone forgot what day it was; someone forgot to point the rocket in the proper direction (i.e., up his rump); someone forgot to be anyone but a simpleminded bureaucrat and squanderer of public resources. A recent Rand Simberg essay called "The Path Not Taken," published in *The New Atlantis* ("A Journal of Technology & Society"), avers that "aside from a single American astronaut on the International Space Station, who got there because he went up in a Russian capsule, NASA's manned space program is currently on hold," and that "NASA's present space activities remain mired in thought patterns that are decades-old artifacts of the Cold War." He also calls our attention to something that we full well know, about "the billions of dollars of budget overruns," for example the shuttle that "cost several billion dollars to develop, and continues to cost billions of dollars per year to operate — even when, as now, it isn't flying at all." *The Right Stuff*, to cite the title of Tom Wolfe's glorified space age novel published during the Johnson years, refers as much as anything to the NASA's cult of personality, calculated, no doubt, to deflect criticism by depicting astronauts like the down home good American citizens and nice guys next door which some of them were. Meanwhile, regarding the discontinuance of NASA's space shuttle fleet, another bureaucrat vowed that his outfit would fix the "foam problem" and get the vehicle back in the air by "early next year." The *foam problem* has to do with insulation that had been breaking loose from booster rockets for the last 20 years — or more. Give or take a few more billions and a few dozen meetings, these diddlewits will fix their foam.

"There is no automatic program review," a NASA bureaucrat conceded, "to address what we are not doing that we should be doing." You can say that again. Another report admitted that NASA "decided not to replace a 'Criticality-1' gizmo, even though it supposedly understood that said part had "life or death implications for shuttle astronauts." By August of 2005 the bureaucracy had grounded all of its space ships "because there were five areas that didn't work right," prompting *Space News* to admit that "there are people here at very high levels that have been asking, why not just shut the darn thing down?" By March of 2006 there came a report suggesting that NASA ought to consider assuming responsibility for the boatloads of taxpayers' money it was igniting in bureaucratic bonfires. It happened that a certain "inspector general" discovered "problems with NASA's "enterprisewide" management system. Imagine. NASA then junked the name of its "Financial Management Program," and began calling it the "Integrated Enterprise Management Program," the better to deal with the Pennsylvania company that persisted in submitting "inaccurate, incomplete or unsupported invoices," albeit at least two sub-bureaucracies "had different procedures for similar work, and inconsistent contract oversight practices." In May of that year it came to light that the long-awaited James Webb Space Telescope that bureaucrats said would cost a mere one billion tax dollars, would now run in the neighborhood of 4.5 billion. It didn't matter anyway, because it was paid in public dollars. In April 2007, NASA's Mars Global Surveyor blew up because of what it called "human error," namely that a battery quit, causing a computer to shut down. Life has never been easy at NASA. One of their right stuff female astronauts was arrested for allegedly trying to kidnap another woman involved in a love triangle. If that wasn't bad enough, in July 2007, NASA revealed that its astronauts were buzzing around in space while they were crocked. Of course, the matter went to the attention of a bureaucratic panel. *The New York Times* said the panel learned to its presumed dismay "about heavy drinking by crew members just before flights," and that "alcohol is freely used in the crew quarters, where astronauts are quarantined [but not much] at the Kennedy Space Center in the three days before launch." NASA said that it was somehow not structured to deal with potted astronauts, "nor is any medical surveillance program by itself likely to detect them or change the pattern of alcohol use." On a related note, there were "concerns regarding substandard task performance." At NASA, the blunders never cease. Warren Leary of *The New York Times* reported on December 22, 2007 that NASA has postponed its joyride to Mars until 2013, citing an "undisclosed conflict of interest" (bureaucratic specifics unavailable) involving the bureaucracy's disconnect between "one proposal and the assessment group," whatever that may mean. What it means to taxpayers is a mere $40 million tacked on to NASA's (conservative, no doubt) cost estimate of $475 million.

Chapter 4. Yours Fraternally: Bringing in the Sheep

> Now, as Nature made every man with a nose and eyes of his own, she gave him a character of his own too; and yet we, O foolish race! must do our very best to ape some one or two of our neighbors, whose ideas fit us no more than their breeches!... but the silly animal is never content, is ever trying to fit itself into another shape, wants to deny its own identity, and has not the courage to utter its own thoughts. Because Lord Byron was wicked, and quarreled with the world, and found himself growing fat, and quarreled with his victuals, and thus, naturally, grew ill-humored, did not half Europe grow ill-humored too?"
> —William Makepeace Thackeray, *The Paris Sketch Book* (1840)

When in early autumn students dutifully pack off to some university or another, it is (or at the very least *was*) for any of several inestimably valuable ends, central among them to "find" themselves. By that we mean discover their identities, their peculiar strengths and liabilities, their intellectual commitments, their range of beliefs. They step awkwardly into that twilight world between youth and maturity for what may be the first time, to become self sufficiently comfortable, to encourage an open mind toward conflicting academic positions, to marshal evidence necessary to develop a program of at least tentative positions amid a bewildering range of ticklish matters such as philosophy, ethics, religion, science, morality, mortality and associated metaphysical problems. It should be a wonderfully memorable journey, afloat in sea of great expectations. It is best undertaken alone, for the independent soul has, as Virginia Woolf has written in *Mrs. Dalloway* (1925) "the privilege of loneliness; in privacy one may do as one chooses." "Higher" education is one of life's great adventures, an intellectual grand tour into regions of the mind hitherto unexplored.

What awaits them may be something quite offensively different, however. A person may choose to pass those significant four years in the supreme privacy of his own company, or may elect a more aggressively social program, meaning he may consent to being herded through those years in the manner that dogs herd sheep — only worse. To do so, obviously, places his privacy and his identity in jeopardy. One is put in mind of that tiresome evangelical hymn set to inexorably mournful measures and titled "Bringing in the Sheaves," (possibly attributed to *Psalm* 126:6 that reads "He that goeth forth and weepeth,/ bearing seed for sowing,/ shall doubtless come again with joy, bringing his sheaves with him") sometimes mistaken for "Bringing in the Cheese," "Bringing (or banging) in the Sheets," and even "Bringing in the Sheep."

> Bringing in the sheep, bringing in the sheep,
> We shall come rejoicing, bringing in the sheep.
> Bringing in the sheep, bringing in the sheep,
> We shall come rejoicing, bringing in the sheep."

Sheep, indeed. Our young seekers after truth may have unwittingly and naively stumbled not into a life of delicious independence, but into four years of dreadfully enforced social bondage as part of their pledge to join an animal house Greek letter organization, the better to botch their precious university days.

"Greek Life," a document published by the University of California at Santa Barbara, actively promotes communal life on campus by advocating that one's every act be in concert with others. There, to be sure, an individual takes a back seat — or no seat at all. The message is clear: if you're a loner, stay out. "Every member will be able to take part in organizational activities as officers, committee chairpersons or committee members," it advises. "Fraternities and sororities provide a wide-range of interesting activities." [Such as?] "You'll be able to get involved in planning a community service project, a dinner with another fraternity or sorority, a dance or step shoe, and new member recruitment." Best of all, it continues, "You are going to make many new friends. [Good. That's why we're here.] It will be exciting for you... electing new officers...planning socials...doing community service, ...studying with partners...going on retreats...learning fraternity or sorority history."

We are also assured that "hazing is absolutely forbidden." To the contrary, however, an anonymous ex-Greek letter man commented that in his fraternity pledges are "generally expected to have the Greek alphabet memorized utterly — to ensure this, they are expected to recite the entire alphabet no less than three times while holding a burning match. If they haven't finished, then their fingers get burned."

Despite their stalwart adherents who defend to the death the brotherhood and sisterhood of Greek letter societies, such mobs have none the less come under fire, and deservedly so. Hank Nuwer's *Wrongs of Passage: Fraternities, Sororities, Hazing and Binge Drinking* (Indiana University, 1991) addresses forced participation into such wholesome activities as servitude, intimidation, verbal abuse, degradation, nudity, physical coercion, paddling, electric shocks, beatings, forced calisthenics, sexually demeaning behavior, explicit songs, sexist, racist or anti-Semitic acts, sleep deprivation, branding, tattooing; chemical, cigarettes and cigar burning; dousing with dangerous or objectionable substances such as urine, human or animal feces, cleaning fluids, objects retrieved from toilets, partaking spoiled foods capable of causing or transmitting diseases or bacterial infection, eating objectionable, unusual or spicy concoctions, not to mention participation in boxing or wrestling matches, unauthorized swimming across lakes, ponds and rivers, degrading competitions; wearing silly or unusual clothing or objects, carrying spears, paddles, oars, bricks, concrete blocks, stuffed or live animals; performing dangerous stunts, demanding that pledges refrain from visiting parents or other non-group members, interfering with class time and other school-sponsored activities; participating in scavenger hunts, sleeping in closets and bathrooms. It is all, Newer reminds us, done in the name of "group identity," and "cult-like behavior."[1] One might add that it is splendid boot camp preparation for the humiliation of corporate life wherein one is obliged to surrender himself to the inanities of business culture, regardless of how preposterous those pursuits may be. The object is to subject oneself to any personal disgrace in the name of finding tribal identity.

Of particular alarm has been an array of problems associated with uncontrolled alcohol use in fraternities and sororities. Studies have demonstrated

---

1 Michigan's "House Legislative Analysis Section" reported in 2004 that in its state alone a Ferris State University student "died after participating in an unofficial hazing party that involved heavy drinking," and that at the University of Michigan the Sigma Chi chapter was "kicked off campus after a pledge suffered kidney failure...after being deprived of food and water and being forced to do calisthenics." In another case, a 12 year old team player at a middle school suffered "a serious broken leg from forced participation in an 'eighth grade hit day,' while athletic coaches looked on with laughter."

that heavy drinking particularly among young sparks during the college years' tends to abate markedly through about age 30; that heavy drinkers tend toward environments that support heavy drinking and the central role of alcohol in fraternity life; that students in Greek organizations averaged significantly more drinks per week, engaged in more often and suffered more ill effects from such consumption; that Greek organizations contribute to student drinking misbehavior; that students became more intoxicated at fraternity parties than at private residences; that alcohol is part of a "key component of a complex system that socializes pledges to the fraternity norms and values"; that "members of high drinking houses viewed their social reputations more positively and heavy drinking as more acceptable than did members in houses with reputations for less drinking"; that "students with a background of high-quantity drinking in school were more likely to join Greek associations than other students; that (as one study expressed it), "membership in a Greek association was shown to be both a facilitating and enhancing factor in alcohol use." Of particular interest has been the observation that college students have a tendency to overestimate the amount of alcohol their peers consume. Students of a more outer-directed disposition felt an obligation to consume more, the better to fit in, since fitting in is what one does best in Greek organizations.

Ex-fraternity men[1] are out there in great numbers, and of course have their views on what sort of organizational encounters they've endured as a result of living in a swarm. Some speak anonymously. Others disavow their fraternity days and say little about them. Recalls one: "rituals are not dissimilar to military induction, which are psychologically designed to break down the individual ego, and ensure allegiance to the organization. Without this bonding ritual, fraternities generally aren't cohesive. This is the real reason for hazing — and the real reason it'll continue despite efforts from the left to eradicate it." In an amusing corollary, *Science News* on March 27, 2001 carried an inconclusive note entitled "How Locust Loners Form a Swarm," observing that "although the word locust usually calls to mind plagues of biblical proportions, these insects actually start out as shy, solitary creatures. Yet within a matter of hours they can transform into the farmer's worst nightmare, joining forces to create a voracious, migrating swarm." It continues by noting, "researchers have known for some time that swarm formation results

---

1 Some live to regret their affiliations. *The New York Times* on August 4, 1992 reported that "three members of Sigma Nu fraternity at the University of Texas were sentenced to up to 30 days in jail" for having participated in "organizational hazing" after "a pledge was repeatedly beaten, humiliated and led nude by means of a claw hammer."

when locusts become crowded. But exactly what prompts the transformation to gregarious conduct has remained unclear," albeit new research that appeared in the *Proceedings of the National Academy of Sciences* "indicates that stimulation of the locust's hind legs sparks the behavioral revolution." The note concludes by suggesting that as locusts bump into each other in close quarters, "the process of behavioral gregarization is initiated, leading to the formation of local aggregations." Police (neither invited nor unexpected) who have nevertheless turned up at fraternity houses at embarrassing not so say incriminating times, also have a tendency to swarm, which is to say hover like bees out of a hive. But swarming and bumping into bodies inside of a supposedly secret organization is no way to approach four years of university education.

Writer John Marr in a piece called "Fatal Fraternities: A History of Deadly Hazing" published in the August 3, 1999 issue of *Whoa!* has noted that "one thing stands between the fraternity pledge and his Promised Land of keggers, bong hits, and gang rape: hazing." Indeed, "before learning the secret handshake, he must be beaten with paddles, zapped with cattle prods, and drenched in vomit — and survive." Marr cites a *U.S. News and World Report* estimate that "at least 65 students have died since 1978 as a result of fraternity hazing." Among what Marr calls "some of the Greeks [*sic*] greatest hits": is the Kappa Alpha Psi chapter at Southeast Missouri where, if caning pledges was not enough, the brotherhood expanded its violence to include "slapping, kicking and bodyslaming" to its repertoire, thereby beating one young man to death, for which seven of the brothers ended behind bars on manslaughter charges. At Maryland's Towson State University in 1982 in the midst of a "round-the-clock regimen of paddlings, forced calisthenics, binge/purge drinking and other less savory practices" one sleep-deprived Alpha Omega Lambda pledge, clad in a Playboy bunny costume, died behind the wheel of an automobile he was attempting to drive. Then at Alfred University in New York fun-loving Klan Alpine fratboys stuffed a pledge in a car trunk for as long as it might require for him to down a pint of Jack Daniels, a six pack of beer and a bottle of wine, something the poor chap accomplished within 40 minutes, after which he was ordered to engage in another drinking game that entailed more beer and a vomit-filled garbage can. The victim died from alcohol poisoning. The chairman of Alfred's board told *The New York Times* that, to put it mildly, "The Greek system is beyond repair." In 1956 the Delta Kappa Epsilon brothers at the Massachusetts Institute of Technology dumped a pledge in a snowy field at one in the morning, and ordered him to appear at the fraternity house by eight. After a week his body was discovered beneath the surface of an icy reservoir that he apparently had mistaken for an open field. Three years later at the University of Southern California seven pledges were confronted with a pig's head at a Kappa Sigma dinner table, and were ordered to consume brains and raw liver. Six of the sheep, desperately in need of fraternity membership, complied. The seventh choked to death, but it was all in the name of good fraternal fun that does wonders for an 18-year-old's self-esteem and his intellectual maturation.

In the face of such outrages, fraternities have occasionally attempted not only to save face, but also to advance the impression that their criminally uncivilized proclivities have been impossibly misunderstood and overemphasized. Consider, for example, the a young Interfraternity Council president's unconvincing response in the March 16, 2006 issue of *The University Daily Kansan* to a *Time* magazine article entitled "Taming the Toga." *Time*, it argued, "clearly misinterpreted the purpose and mission of the fraternities at the University of Kansas," arguing that the *Time* article was commenting on fraternities across America, not to local UK chapters. The letter asserts that "there has never been a focus on unhealthy behaviors in the [local] Greek [*sic*] community; rather, the focus has always been on building respectable men of character and value" through "activities that promote healthy living and self-respect," adding that "member fraternities are not aimed at modifying the behaviors of fraternity men, but act as a resource for men to use, reminding them of their continual pursuit of our Greek values: scholarship, service to others, brotherhood and leadership," to which a reader responded, "Amen, there has never been a problem...within the Fraternity Community. Except... when that pledge got thrown through a window."

A *Forbes* magazine article published on January 31, 2001 seemed to suggest that if one can avoid being hurled through a window, fatally poisoned by alcohol or choked to death by eating raw pig's brains or being left to drown in icy waters, one may live to enjoy a prosperous (if not civilized) life, provided that one has any modicum of civility left to do so. Fraternity boys have, through their wonderful fraternal memories and their degrees in things like "business administration," done surprisingly well, despite having enrolled in universities that looked the other way at the abject savagery going on under their very noses. "Don't be surprised if you see your company directors exchanging secret handshakes at the next board meeting," *Forbes* said cheerfully. "After all, about a quarter of all chief executives on the Forbes Super 500 list of America's largest corporations were members of college fraternities." Moreover, "despite what movies such as *Animal House* (1978) suggest, fraternities and sororities are more than just freshman rush and beer busts.

The social skills that help students gain admittance into the Greek system are the same aptitudes that can later give them a leg-up in corporate climbing." Good point. Are not college fraternities the boot camps of large corporations? "Plus," the article continues, "once they've [been] graduated, they can tap into the network of past fraternity brothers or sisters [The same ones who made them wallow in vomit, burn their fingers while reciting the Greek alphabet three times, eat pig brains, beat them with canes, left them to drown in icy waters and hurled them through windows maybe?] who litter [You can say that again.] all tiers of corporate America." *Forbes* presented an honor roll of old fraternity boys who became company CEOs, to wit: Sanford Weill (Alpha Epsilon Pi) at Citigroup that in its third quarter of 2008 reported $7.2 billions in asset write-offs and bad mortgages; Maurice Greenberg (Sigma Alpha Mu) at American International Group over which the American government seized control to prevent its falling into bankruptcy; William B. Harrison Jr. (Zeta Psi) at J. P. Morgan Chase that in 2008 blew $2.6 billion in bad debt and became bank holding company under the supervision of the Federal Reserve; Henry Paulson (Sigma Alpha Epsilon) at Goldman Sachs that in 2008 had its third quarter share price tumble by more than 70 percent, and thereby qualified Paulson to become Secretary of the Treasury thanks to a Skull and Bones fraternity brother in the person of George W. Bush; Alan Lafley (Psi Upsilon) at Procter & Gamble the shares of which fell 27 percent between December of 2007 and October of 2008; G. Kennedy Thompson (Beta Theta Pi) at Wachovia that by June of 2008 dropped $6.1 billion in asset valuation, $5.6 in loan loss reserves and a mere $500 million in auction rate securities; Warren Buffett (Alpha Sigma Phi) at Berkshire Hathaway that in the first half of 2008 saw its insurance premium revenue fall by $7.1 billion; Robert Nardelli (Tau Kappa Epsilon) at Home Depot (its 2008 second quarter fell by eight percent, and later at Daimler–Chrysler, the common shares of which plunged over 40 percent from the fall of 2007 to the summer of 2008; F. Duane Ackerman (Lamba Chi Alpha), now emeritus at BellSouth; and G. Richard Wagoner (Delta Tau Delta) at General Motors that recently all but disappeared after a $15.5 billion quarterly loss. It is safe to assume that such corporations are run like fraternities, and both, as one commentator suggested, could profit from "adult supervision." It was the investment banks that all but destroyed the American economy in the fall of 2008 and set off an economic chain reaction around the world. The North-American Interfraternity Conference claims that whereas an estimated 8.5 percent of "full-time" university graduates compromised themselves by joining phony Greek societies, that 8.5 percent has (predictably) "spawned" 48 percent of all American presidents, 42 percent of U.S. senators, 30 percent of congressmen and 40 percent of U.S. Supreme Court justices. This may be nothing to brag about. Presuming that these figures are even remotely accurate, the implications are sobering at the least, and ominous at the most. Considering the rampant abuse they've endured as young people, one cannot but wonder whether their corporate and "public service" roles have not been undertaken out of an urge for retaliation for they abuse they've been handed — and accepted. One can see why. Gallup reported in the summer of 2007 that Congress earned itself a 14 percent approval rating. One may wonder what ratings corporate CEOs might have elicited, had their employees been given the opportunity to rate them with impunity.

Circumstances are gradually changing, however. Back in 1931, the president of Swarthmore said that when he first arrived on campus in 1921, "there were 153 members of Women's fraternities, constituting just over 60 percent if the women then in the college," whereas currently there are 228 affiliated women, or 77 percent. The result, he said, "is a situation which tends to be uncomfortable for the minority left outside." By March of 1932, a board consisting of alumnae, fraternity members [ironically] and a team of women decreed that pledging women was to end, although they allowed fraternities to continue operating. A popular fraternity song that rang out in that era, asserted:

> I've got a little Phi Mu girl
> Way down in sunny Dixie land
> With eyes of snare me, dare me,
> Oh do you care for me blue.
> As long as Grecian frats shall stand
> She'll wear the golden heart and hand
> And maybe, some day a frat pin.
> I'll tell you that pin
> Will make a stunning guard for her little Phi Mu pin,
> Girls may come and girls may go
> But she's the only girl for me, I know,
> And when the children go to school
> They'll follow Dad and Mother's rule
> And wear the badge that makes some jolly Greeks of them, too.

Fortunately, however, times are changing. A publication called *Student Poll* in 1998 conducted interviews with 500 college-bound high school seniors with high scholastic aptitude performance. "The study," so the report notes, "was drawn and weighted to represent the national distribution of students with qualifying SAT scores by geography, gender, intended major, and income." The findings were encouraging, in that the report recommended that universities "develop and enforce policies that will reduce the influences of pledging, rush, and other rituals associated with Greek membership that reinforce social exclusivity and the creation of social castes and cliques." The report also advised universities not to "give excessive attention to fraternities and sororities or Greek life in admissions publications, web sites, campus tours or any other communications," inasmuch as "there is more to be lost than gained by doing so." It also urged that "if your campus has a dominant fraternity and sorority system, encourage the creation of strong social alternatives that will appeal to the majority of students who have no interest in Greek life and reduce the influence of the Greek social system on campus social values." Evidence indicated that whereas "fraternities and sororities will not have an unfavorable impact on recruitment," nonetheless "few students intend to participate in Greek life and fewer still to live in Greek housing," adding that "parents, on balance, disapprove of Greek membership" and apparently view such participation as an unimportant "part of a student's educational experience." The study also remarks that alumni interviews support essentially the same opinions. More precisely, 62 percent of students reported no desire for Greek membership, versus 18 percent who were of the opposing view. Some 68 percent said they could "take or leave" membership. Another 25 percent said that membership was "important but not critical." Still and all, a full 99 percent of respondents said they did not select a university on the basis of its presence or absence of Greek societies.

Mark Alden Branch, writing for the October 1998 *Yale Alumni Magazine*, noted that "For some alumni of a certain age, the words 'Yale' and 'fraternity' go together as naturally as 'blue' and 'blazer.' But for those undergraduates who came to Yale in the 1970s and 1980s, the sight of Greek letters on Lake Place houses and on posters advertising 'rush' events is disorienting and not a little alarming." Branch adds "today's Greek scene bears little resemblance to the one that expired 25 years ago." Even so, he continues, "the Yale administration and many students have watched the resurgence of fraternities warily. Nationwide, Greek-letter organization groups carry a reputation for excessive drinking and rowdy adolescent behavior. And, in an issue more particular to Yale, there is concern that fraternities — by establishing homogeneous social hubs off campus — could pose a threat to the democratic social structure of the residential colleges, which are one of Yale's most attractive selling points." In the meantime, Yale's Dean of Student Affairs has been fretting over the "balkanization of the student body," wary that students "go off into separate discreet units."

Colby College in Waterville, Maine (along with Bowdoin, Middlebury and Williams), as Ben Goes has written in the *Chronicle of Higher Education*, has taken a still harder line. Whereas it "has clubs for all types of students, including environmentalists, homosexuals, and Republicans," anyone presuming to establish a fraternity may well be "suspended for a year, or expelled." To the contrary, there are those who argue that "a ban on fraternities denies students the constitutional right to associate with whomever they choose," albeit courts have as a rule been on the side of university administrations. Colby and Middlebury, Goes reminds us, closed their fraternities in the middle 1980s. Bowdoin was to have shuttered its fraternities by 2000; Denison and Hamilton cleared them out in 1995. He also reported that "the four colleges say that they have been able to recruit a greater number of highly qualified students since phasing out the fraternities, and that there appears to be little interest in Greek life among currently enrolled students." Said one student leader, "The social life here is pretty good. We don't really need fraternities or sororities."

That is essentially how Dartmouth president James Wright and Board of Trustees felt back in 1999 (although they did not explicitly say so in public) when there had been fraternities on campus for over 158 years, and when there were currently one third of its undergraduates population affiliated with its 25 Greek cliques. There was, however, formidable resistance from students and alumni to whom the idea was, according to reports, "overwhelmingly negative." Today, Greek life at Dartmouth (whose motto is *vex clamant is indecent*, meaning "a voice crying out in the wilderness") is still in place, although certain problems persist. The Associated Press released an item called "Police Raid Dartmouth College Fraternity" on June 9, 2006, without specifically identifying the object of the raid that involved the seizure of "10 crates, a computer and other items." Ironically, the fraternity in question was Alpha Delta, of which 1964 Dartmouth graduate Chris Miller (one of the script writers for *Animal House*) was a member. The fraternity had been under police surveillance since October of 2004. "Frats and sororities are central to the social life on the rural [Hanover, New Hampshire] campus, and some of them have a reputation for hard drinking and raucous behavior," said *The New York Times*. One undergraduate told the AP "Alpha Delta can be "a pretty crazy house," but admitted that it was not the only one. The Theta Delta Chi fraternity had been indicted the year before on a charge of serving alcohol to minors. Back in 2001 Dartmouth banned the brotherhood of Zeta

Psi for making public "the sexual exploits of its members." Notwithstanding, recent Dartmouth press release naively claimed, "We have made progress toward...improving [the] 'Fraternity and Sorority system.' In the meantime, *The New York Times* reported that at Rider College in Lawrenceville, New Jersey, a freshman fraternity pledge died following a raucous party. An autopsy revealed that the victim had a blood alcohol content of 0.426 percent, allegedly more than five times the figure that establishes intoxication for drivers. *The Times* further noted that the county prosecutor's office had charged (and subsequently dropped those charges against) the school's dean of students and its director of Greek life but also charged three students with aggravated hazing.

In Arcadian Oxford, Ohio, home of bucolic Miami University, the Theta Chi fraternity earned a two year suspension after its members urged alcohol on an under aged student who lost consciousness and twice visited the town hospital for attention. The university's "director of ethics and student conflict resolution" declared that "such activities violate university policies and are also against state law," adding with extraordinary naiveté that "there are safety concerns involved with hazing," and that "hazing is counter to the stated goal of fraternal life." Then the university's "director of Greek affairs" asserted dubiously that whereas the organization has "the right to exist without affiliation with Miami," nevertheless "maintaining the chapter while it suspended from the university will present difficulties for the fraternity, since a suspended fraternity is not eligible to participate in any activity with Miami, on or off campus, and would not be able to use the university's name, logos, financial accounts or services provided by any university office." That said, the Greek affairs director seemed unaccountably to undercut his own severe edicts by claiming that "this is a fraternity with a proud tradition at Miami, and both the national organization and the university are eager to see Theta Chi as part of Miami's Greek community again."

Oh, brother. It bears mentioning that Miami University prides itself on being the "Mother of Fraternities," having provided a home to Beta Theta Phi (1839), Sigma Chi (1855), Delta Zeta (1902) and Phi Kappa Tau (1906). "As you wander around our beautiful campus," a university promotional blurb reads, "you will see much of the impact of our fraternities and sororities. The Beta Bells, the Phi Delt Gates, the Delta Delta Delta Sundial, The Phi Tau Circle, and the new Chi O Corner.... About a third of our undergraduate student population are members of our Fraternity/Sorority community." Later we're assured that "There are many programs and events sponsored by the governing councils and the individual fraternities and sororities. Greek Week is just one of these programs. Traditionally held in September, Greek Week is a celebration of the interfraternal spirit on campus." Said a recent graduate and former president of the Interfraternity Council, "It's definitely cool to know that you are a part of something that's bigger than yourself."

Clearly, Miami University is no place for troglodytes and isolants. Many a student of independent nature has been appalled by the Greek presence that undermined the vitality of his collegiate experience. One of the earliest negative reactions to Greek letter organizations came from the pen of George D. Budd (1843–1874), who was graduated from the University of Pennsylvania in 1862. Budd recalled that when he arrived at the university in 1858 there were four of what he called "Greek Letter" or "secret societies," the nature of which "stand for some word unknown to any but the initiated." His impression was that they have chapters in numerous universities and that they organize themselves in a way similar to Free Masons. Allowing that in some schools they may "have a literary character," at the University of Pennsylvania they were nothing but social clubs. "Besides being the cause of much waste of time," he said, "they are very detrimental to the morals of their members, as there generally is a great deal of dissipation connected with them." Budd continued by saying that they posed a threat to fellow students, and that they are condemned by the faculties. Even so, he believed that Greek societies were merely formed by social motives and encouraged the formation of "little cliques." He further believed that they controlled campus-wide elections by voting for their own men. Of Zeta Psi, he remarked, "They have a powerful chapter, but their members are almost all 'babyish' in their character. Of Delta Phi: "It is a very numerous and powerful society throughout the United States; and the chapter here is very aristocratic and rich. It is very exclusive, and is confined to the 'upper ten' of the college. They are very noisy in their rooms, much to the disgust of the Young Men's Christian Association which has its rooms in the second story of the same building." Of Phi Kappa Sigma: "It was fast declining, and finally gave up the ghost. It had some fine fellows in it, but many of them were hard cases; and were always the foremost in the college rows."

Alternate Orange was at Syracuse University the "alternate [read left of center] student newspaper" supposedly "funded by Syracuse University students" who in 2000 published a protracted diatribe against Greek societies called a "revision history." Some of their arguments are valid, others merely paranoid. Some of the more salient points of their case sound bromidic today, namely that the system is "sexist, racist and homophobic"; that it preserves "the oppressive social relations of late capitalism" through "class domination"; that it provides "a network of social relationships and contacts that will insure" its "privileged entry into and monopoly over commanding roles in the world of business, media, law and government"; that "sorority women are most likely to be victims of fraternity sexual assaults"; that it draws from "the already generally privileged population having access to four-year university education"; that it is "regulated by exclusion, internal differentiation, and suppression"; that it "monopolizes 8 to 10 times their fair share of the most lucrative and influential jobs in the country"; that it "actively work[s] to reproduce bourgeois society"; that it disciplines "through intimidation"; that it places "the needs of men" over "the needs of women"; that it helps "to insure that women will continue making less than men for equal work"; that it provides a place where 'boys will be boys': that it "supports "the university administration's aims and practices" in return for the university's providing "a general license for their activities and attitudes"; that it consists of "good –deed-doers" who contribute seven million dollars and one million 'man' hours to charities per year," albeit it "tends overwhelmingly to support the most conservative and inefficient charities"; that it uses charity as "an ideological screen that obscures" its "social function"; that it is no more humanitarian than Exxon and ITT"; that "give a small percentage of their wealth to charity to cover the fact that they have skinned their great fortunes off the thin hides of the rest of us."

What, then, did *Alternative Orange* propose? That fraternities be "stripped of their association from the university," albeit those same universities refrain for fear of losing "financial contributions from fraternity alumni"; that they be "forced to ban campus fraternities through public pressure, to wit: "'extreme' forms of 'guerrilla' activism" assuaged by "radical pedagogues"; that their host universities be "brought to recognize that their continued support of the fraternity system will cost them dearly in bad publicity and loss of revenue in times of severely diminishing resources." For the self-directed person, the best way to deal (albeit one need not deal with them in the first place) with Greek organizations is to ignore them in the way one ignores most other forms of infectious inanity in government and private enterprise. The solitary person is the one best situated to close his doors to the rampant stupidity he encounters in the outside world, and attend to his own business. Eliminating fraternities is more or less pointless, since fraternally-oriented people will merely join something else like the Moose or the Rotary Club the Daughters of the American Revolution or some sort of Masonic organization that no one besides its loyal followers seem to comprehend — or wish to. There is no harm in this, since society is amply populated with people who cannot survive without joining some sort of club, especially those with trick handshakes, arcane symbols, mysterious induction ceremonies and all such balderdash.

That said, some universities, in the realistic knowledge that ridding themselves of Greek "societies" is close to impossible, do what they can to defuse them by, so to speak, shutting off their beer. One theory is that if you remove the alcohol, you remove the fraternity as sure as one can halt ethanol-burning automobiles if you stop planting corn. Back in 1986 Penn State, then ridden with some 52 fraternities, decreed not that the drinking be ended, but that it be prohibited at recruiting functions where (to be on the safe side) guests be required to show some form of reliable form self-identification. A fellow acting as Interfraternity Council membership chairman, with the straightest of faces, told the press the he recommend "a lot more emphasis on recruiting of good members and a lot less emphasis on alcohol." Some of the fraternities, in turn, accused the local constabulary of "underhanded tactics." The police chief responded that "those of us in law enforcement were adamant that the drinking age is 21 and not 18 or somewhere in between." In 2005 the University of California at Berkeley addressed the same problem by going one step beyond Penn State. The plan was simply "to enact a ban on alcohol consumption at all events hosted by campus fraternities and sororities." The dean of students said that the university was somewhat alarmed by incidents of "alcohol abuse, hazing, fights, and badly managed parties at all types of Greek organizations." Berkeley at the time had an estimated 70 fraternities whose herds of followers were estimated at 2,500, more than enough to take prisoners and burn the university down. Current regulations decreed that hard liquor was prohibited, but that beer and wine were permitted for students of legal boozing age, as long as the beer did not originate from "kegs or other bulk containers," a suggestion that will do down in history as a damned fine idea. Writing for *The New York Times* in 2005, Benoit Denizet-Lewis recalled his own fraternity days, and how "backed into a backyard near the campus of Northwestern University in Evanston, Ill., there were some 100 drunken college students, beer spilling from paper cups, industrial-size ketchup bottles overturned on the grass near the grill and gaggles of hard-drinking sorority girls (including one self-described Phi Delt groupie) keeping pace with the boys." Two of Denizet-Lewis's wary fraternity brothers, by the way, cautioned him "not to mention their names in this article."

Another ineffective way of purging secret societies from university campuses is to cite the obvious: that they discriminate on the basis of race, color, religion, gender, social class and any other preposterous pretext. Discrimination is their middle name. A ludicrous *cause célèbre* broke out in 2007 at the College of Staten Island when the college sought to banish a Jewish fraternity that would not admit women [not to say gentiles], as *The New York Daily News* pointed out, "even as it was promoting mixed-gender outings to a karaoke bar and a strip club." A woman federal judge thought it was a perfectly good idea to escort undergraduate women to strip clubs, and signed off on it. Subsequently, an appeals court said that the judge erred, meaning that the fraternity would not have further access to college facilities, its name or its money. The fraternity, in the meantime, reminded all concerned that its high-minded purpose was to "foster and promote brotherly [but apparently not sisterly] love, to inaugurate a spirit of cooperation [as for example the women's agreeing to pass a gala evening at a strip bar] and helpfulness." You can't beat that as a guide to a fulfilling life. Moreover, as the fraternity's legal counsel cogently reminded everyone, "Admitting women would lead to romantic relationships [not to mention unwanted pregnancies]" causing "inevitable jealousies and other conflicts." Points well taken, illustrating once again that if one is in search of clear thinking, consult an attorney. In a triumph of obfuscation, the court held that "the group's mixed-gender outings mean it's not protected by the First Amendment in the same way as an organization that strictly limits its activities to a single gender." The frat house lawyer conceded that lucid point. As a further clarification, *The Daily News* pointedly mentioned that only four years before, the frat had "sponsored outings to laser tag, karaoke and a strip club" and that the judge agreed was an ideal place for the frat boys to check out prospective members [as well as naked ecdysiasts] — essentially the same opinion of the original federal judge held.

In a more learned commentary on discrimination in secret societies, Anthony W. James's "The College Social Fraternity Antidiscrimination Debate, 1945–1949" begins by saying that after World War II when some schools wrote racial and religious quotas into their admissions policies, some northern institutions did not, thereby offering minorities better access to collegiate life. James observes, "While the incorporation of racial and religious minorities into the extracurricular life of American campuses guaranteed fundamental civil rights, it also challenged accepted patterns of interpersonal relationships. Integrated dining, dancing, and other social relations were perceived as threatening to many whites who feared even greater intimacy, including intermarriage, might result," adding that "some whites connected anti-discriminatory activity with communism and feared undermining the democratic process." It remained to be seen how well or badly "blacks, whites, Protestants, Catholics and Jews would relate on the postwar campus." Meanwhile there had been considerable hand wringing on the part of those who saw fraternity life as emphatically undemocratic, as if those closed societies had ever been anything else. James also correctly points out that when most of the fraternities were established, the huge majority of students were white Protestants. Accordingly, some fraternities specifically wrote in clauses stipulating that, indeed, prospective members must be white Protestant males, and that there were "gentlemen's agreements" in place to bar the doors to blacks and Jews. When those fraternities formed an alliance, Jewish and African American fraternities were excluded again. Then it came to pass that Jewish and African fraternities began to fear that their organizations would come undone if they admitted wasps. James reminds us that at the time, blacks were struggling to overcome broad racial discrimination. It also happened that military service people lately returned from battle in World War II tended to be far less discriminatory, having fought shoulder to shoulder with people of all colors and ethnic origins. He cites one returned solder's conviction that "Many of us have served in the armed forces in the past three or four years and we came to know men of all types, races, creeds and colors. We learned to judge men for personality and character, and I think we should continue." Meanwhile, a young man of color pledged to the Delta Upsilon fraternity at Bowdoin in 1946 after having been "depledged" the previous year by Sigma Nu after the latter was apprised that no blacks could be admitted to its charmed circle. James also cites an Ohio State student's to integrating his fraternity chapter, saying, "if you're going to talk about niggers — count me out!" In the forties, by the way, one of the Swarthmore fraternity chapters caused itself to be disowned by its national organization for admitting young African American men. Today, Swarthmore rather apologetically explains that yes, it harbors fraternities, but no, they don't amount to much. "Swarthmore does not have a big frat scene," the college reports. "That's evident from the numbers: About 70 men — fewer ten percent of male students — belong to one of the College's two remaining houses."

Only three of the *U.S. New & World Report's* top 10 national liberal arts colleges — Swarthmore, Davidson and Pomona — still tolerate fraternities. Exclusionary policies, to be sure, also applied variously to Catholics, Orientals and persons believed to have come from the lower classes. Others continued to believe that anti discrimination policies were, as mentioned before, inspired by "communists" to destroy the fraternity system. James draws our attention to the opinion of another person of the discriminatory persuasion, who bluntly conceded, "I would surmise that the overwhelming majority of the men would violently oppose serious consideration of a Negro for membership, simply because they recognize that while he might be perfectly good fraternity material within the walls of the house, he cannot otherwise move in the same atmosphere as white members under the present attitude toward the Negro." Another frat boy opined that "pledging any student of Negro descent [would] be considered an unfraternal act."

Nevertheless, young men continue herd in to fraternities, quite prepared to be abused and badgered into a brand of conformity that might well stay with them for the rest of their lives. In 2006, *U.S. News* identified the 17 most fraternity-infiltrated schools in the United States, beginning with Washington and Lee (at 79 percent), DePauw (75 percent) Sewanee-University of the South and Wabash College (60 percent), Millsaps College (54 percent), Centre College and Westminster College (51 percent), Faulkner, Ohio Valley College and Transylvania University (50 percent), Rhodes College (49 percent), Birmingham-Southern College and Massachusetts Institute of Technology (48 percent), Washington and Jefferson College and William Woods University (47 percent). The 17 least fraternity-infested (among those that suffer fraternities on campus) were Gustavus Adolphus College and Kenyon College (27 percent), Allegheny College, Centenary College of Louisiana, and Mercer University (26 percent), followed by Stetson University, Albright College, Coe College, Elon University, Massachusetts College of Pharmacy and Health Science, Rockhurst College, South Carolina State University, Tristate University, University of Missouri-Rolla, University of Rochester, Valparaiso University and Washington University in St. Louis (all at 25 percent).

Even worse percentages turn up among schools that tolerate sororities. DePauw University and Washington and Lee crown the list at 74 percent, Sewanee-University of the South (68 percent), York College (66 percent), Birmingham-Southern College (65 percent), Wofford College (60 percent), Millsaps College (56 percent), Rhodes College and Wake Forest University (53 percent), Centre College, Faulkner University, Ohio Valley College, Transylvania University and Vanderbilt University (50 percent), Bethany College (49 percent), Pennsylvania State University-Erie and William Woods University (48 percent), Baker University and Harding University (47 percent), Albion College (46 percent), Hillsdale College, Lafayette College and University or Richmond (45 percent), Elon University and Washington and Jefferson College (44 percent), Rose-Hulman Institute (43 percent), Duke University and Westminster College (42 percent), Denison University, Furman

University, Georgetown College, Rollins College and Westminster College (40 percent). Even schools with the least sorority domination, show significant percentages, as for example Lambuth University, Pepperdine University, Willamette University, Wittenberg University (29 percent), Doane College, Allegheny College, Alma College, Centenary College of Louisiana, Creighton University, LaGrange College, Linfield College, Ohio Wesleyan University, Ursinus College, West Virginia Wesleyan College and Worcester Polytechnic Institute (28 percent), Augustana College, Lenoir-Rhyne College, Mercer University, Miami University, Spring Hill College, Trinity University, Union College, (27 percent) Bradley University, Dickinson College, Gettysburg College, Illinois Wesleyan University, Massachusetts Institute of Technology, Monmouth College and the University of Alabama (26 percent). With this much commitment to a collegiate social life, one may ask whether receiving an abundant education matters in the slightest, given the unceasing Greek emphasis upon anti-intellectualism, fitting in, obeying absurd requests, submitting to abject humiliation and slavishly following precisely those principles that deliberately undermine individuality, self-reliance, independence of mind and spirit.

What sort of collegiate life do independent students have at these divided institutions? Since there're generally not interested in excessive socializing, they devote their days to better, independent pursuits, among them studying, working, and maybe tipping a few pints with their mates on the weekend. At Greek-minded Miami University they were called GDIs, meaning God Damned Independents, signifying that they're damned for their independent ways, or perhaps they're too damned independent in the eyes of those late adolescents who flock toward secret societies where their social dependencies, possibly caused by low self esteem, require constant group support. There is, of course, a penalty on most college campuses for being too independent. Nonetheless, at the end of the day the unaffiliated usually retire in solitude like hermits to their hermitages, monks to their cells and scholars to their garrets. Since some undergraduate women date only frat boys and will socialize with no one else, lone males become all the more alone. Secret societies are barnacles on the bow of enlightenment. The result may be a serious social division that inevitably causes independents to feel that they are second-rate university citizens in schools that secret societies have all but poisoned. Maybe they are. Said one such male student, "Most people I knew in college were fairly normal types who focused on their grueling studies and had little time to go drinking and sleeping around." Independents (among them such despised minorities as geeks, English majors, lone wolves and other hermetically-inclined intellectually-engaged students who haunt the dim corners of libraries, keep their own company, become part of the campus's detested flotsam and jetsam) recoil at the proposition that they're not to rock a boat or rattle a cage; that they're to be obedient, compliant or consenting to some ridiculous authority; that they're to shut up and do as they're told; and that they are not, under any circumstances to think for themselves. This tablet of guidelines, long cherished by generations of pledges, of course, runs in direct opposition to the basic purposes of higher learning that encourage free expression, open exchange of ideas, critical evaluations of virtually everything academic. The high minded idea, in other words, is to populate American society with intelligently educated citizens.

Back in 1907 *The Sorority Handbook*[1] (authored by Ida Shaw Martin, aka Mrs. William Holmes Martin) through its relentless gibberish laced with a generous dollop of balderdash, did what it could do pressure young women into herd submission, arguing ludicrously "the sorority becomes one of life's great forces in teaching the beauty of self-sacrifice. [How so, we may wonder.] Leadership under the spell of this great power [To what "great power" do we refer?] must be magnetic. Self-confidence, then, is creative, self-control restrictive, self-sacrifice persuasive." Sorority, says Mrs. William Holmes Martin, means that a number of students have banded together and that a number pledge themselves to work unfalteringly and unflaggingly for high ideals, and for [unspecified] noble aims." She cites *in passim* the plight of a young college woman who "as one of a crowd...lost self-consciousness [but] within the chapter group the tension was relaxed and normal," meaning essentially that she must surrender herself to the authority of group-regimented social approval. This, she argues, leads one directly into the clutches of a sorority. "The oldest secret organization to enjoy an uninterrupted existence up to the present day," she proudly declares, "was Kappa Sigma, founded at Elmira College in 1856." Elmira College was in its second year in 1856. Since then, it has emerged from the Dark Ages. In response to a query on why it does not permit a "Greek system," the college's retort was that "students here do not want fraternities or sororities. Elmira students voted out the Greek System because it was too divisive for a friendly, small college environment. Instead, we sponsor college-wide dances and other social events."

---

1 *The Sorority Handbook* enjoyed a long literary life, having evolved into at least six editions. Its author Ida Shaw Martin of Roxbury, Mass. is credited for having been one of the Delta Delta Delta sorority's "founders," and who subsequently became its "Grand President," its "Grand Commissioner of Education" and finally its "Grand Historian." She died in 1940, and in 1976 was elected to the "Fraternity Hall of Fame."

A University of Georgia source explains, "A sorority is a sisterhood." The *OED* regards it primarily as "a body or company of women united for some common object, esp. for devotional purposes," suggesting also that it is "the female section of a church congregation." Phi Beta Kappa,[1] the oldest of American Greek letter societies, began in 1776 at the College of William and Mary. Its origins were purportedly religious or literary, but eventually deteriorated into adolescent cliques with, as we have seen, discriminating membership policies that infested even some public high schools. This led the State of Mississippi, for one, to prohibit their presence in secondary schools in 1972, but waffled, oddly enough, to grant exceptions to the "Order of DeMolay or similar organization sponsored by any branch of the Masonic Orders or a like fraternal organization." At the University of Georgia, however, folks refer to a sorority as "a diverse group of women who work and interact closely with each other to achieve goals," meaning essentially that instead of working singly, they function through "the interdependence of a group," in all likelihood not nearly as diverse as they seem to suggest. The undisclosed source that authored a blurb called "About Sororities" defined a sorority as "a group of women bound together by common principles, goals and experiences," being careful to say nothing about its being in any sense "diverse." It claimed to offer a "home away from home" for a young woman entering college, and seemed to guarantee that she will discover belonging in "a group of women who are interested in [her] and [her] well-being," being careful also to add the caveat that only at the time of initiation will this young woman be availed (through the dubious offices of some mystigogue) to what, precisely, the sorority's "highest ideals" and symbolic significations might be. Only then will the mysteries of the universe be epiphanously revealed. As a new recruit good standing, "You'll [read "you *will*"] attend dances, theme socials with other Greek groups, Parents' Weekend, and Greek Week." Eventually, it says, "You'll ["you *will*"] have the chance to meet sisters from all over the state and country," and "you'll participate in campus and regional Pan-Hellenic activities, where you'll work with other sororities to promote the Greek system." This, mind you, is all in the name of having a home away from home. But after all, the nonsense continues, "Sorority membership means friendships for a lifetime."

---

1 Phi Beta Kappa, as almost everyone knows, is a horse of another color, not to be confused with the social fraternities/sororities under discussion here. Its claim of endorsing "the principles of freedom of inquiry and liberty of thought and expression" is what it appears to be. Phi Beta Kappa still publishes *The American Scholar* quarterly.

But don't count on it. One sorority member told investigative writer Alexandra Robbins that when "a group of pledges who don't know each other have joined a sorority whose members have probably met them no more than twice — and have been strictly prohibited from making contact with them personally up to this time — everyone's supposed to bond and become a cohesive unit. Logic says it won't happen, and it usually doesn't. The sorority houses are so big (usually in excess of 150 members) that cliques form right off the bat." Continuing, she comments, "After about a year (after all that "sisterhood" and "togetherness" indoctrination crap caused by ineffectual hazing led by the girls wears off) all you're left with are multiple groups of five to ten friends that happened to live in the same place as everyone else in the sorority but rarely, if ever, associate with them at all — if downright not hate them all. You say sorority, we say big cathouse there for the taking. That's the reputation they have, and deservedly so."

Indeed, there is a dark side to all this, an abundance of which was made excruciatingly public by Robbins's *Pledged: The Secret Life of Sororities* (2004) that rather blew the lid off of what everyone but the most naïve of us had long suspected: that sororities foster the worst side of women's undergraduate years, what with their clandestine ritualism; their anachronistic secret knocks and secret passwords; their silly songs and silly ceremonial séances, their "fake feminism"; their bogus claims of public service; their interference with the education process for which these women allegedly enrolled at universities in the first place; their mania for social acceptance; their yielding to absurd peer pressure; their shallowness; their superficiality; their outright stupidity. The object of Robbins's inquiry was ostensibly to investigate four questions: 1) "Why are twenty-first century women still so eager to participate in such seemingly outdated, groups and activities? 2) "What is the purpose of sororities and what does membership truly require of the sisters? 3) "How does a sisterhood change the way a girl thinks about herself? and 4) Do sororities cause women to fall further behind in the gender wars or are they instead women's secret weapon?" Robbins herself has described sororities as a "popular group of girls from high school — cooler, prettier, wealthier, multiplied by ten, living under one roof, and recognized by their college as a clique" characterized by the creation of "a world of High Priestesses, Temples, and secret handshakes" where pettiness and petulance combine to foster a "herd mentality" that "can encourage conformity, cliquishness and compromising morals."

It can, and does, get worse. "The urge to fit in can be so petrifying, especially at the start of the year, that the new girls often go to great lengths to blend in as quickly and seamlessly as possible," the same thing that military recruits tend to do. "If they don't make every effort to conform, [they] worry that even after being invited to join a sorority, [that] they could be deemed unsuitable sister material and subsequently be cast out of the group." Needless to say, Robbins (then a 26-year-old able to pass for 19), encountered every sort of resistance to her infiltrating sorority life, if life it can be called. Every source had something to hide: the National Panhellenic Organization, the various paranoid sorority national headquarters, and the local sorority gatekeepers. One of them put Robbins on notice, saying "All of the national sororities have decided on a blanket policy not to cooperate with any members of the media." She cut through the static by "going undercover," engaging the cooperation of four sorority women (each of them scrupulously protected from editorial exposure by concealing their school's identity, their sorority's name and any other giveaway information) who became surprisingly forthcoming, confirming what Robbins had merely suspected about "loyalty, sex, conformity, drugs, violence, verbal abuse, mind games, prostitution, racism, forced binge drinking, eating disorders, rituals, 'mean girls' [whatever those may be] and secrecy." On "Squeal Day when the humble candidates receive their sorority bids at Southern Methodist the young women, all dressed in white shirts and denim, are herded like sheep inside an auditorium, handed their sorority bids and ordered to sit on them until some mystic voice informs them that that they may open those envelopes at which time the react by "crying, laughing, screaming, hugging each other in groups, or slipping away to a corner to weep alone." Later, "they are jostled [again, like sheep] through a mob of fraternity brothers who" attack the women "with water guns and hoses, drenching the sisters until long after the mandatory white shirts are transparent. The girls who do not get into the house of their choice run regardless, crushed and sobbing." Wrote one Indiana University student in *College News*: "I just sat and watched all my friends get accepted into the sororities of their choice. Next year, they'd all move into new homes and build new friendships and start new lives. What about me? Where would I live? Who would my new friends be? The most intense pain was the ache of rejection. Wasn't I pretty enough? Smart enough? Did I not own the right clothes? I felt humiliated, like all my bad traits and unattractive qualities had been nit-picked and put on display for everyone to see. I spent 19 years trying to build my self-esteem and in one instant, it plummeted....things don't always go as planned."

You bet they don't. *The New York Times* in February of 2007 reported that on DePauw University's Greek-saturated campus some of Delta Zeta's "national officers" showed up with the intention of determining why the local sorority house was only half occupied. They interviewed 35 members and ordered 23 of them to pack up and get out, the reason being that they were deemed "insufficiently committed" to snaring new members. Those 23, *The Times* reported, "included every woman who was overweight," as well as the "black, Korean and Vietnamese members." The few who remained, it reported, "were slender and popular with fraternity men — conventionally pretty women the sorority hoped could attract new recruits." Then six of the 12 quit. One is put in mind of that procedural note handed out to members during rush week, saying, "NOTE: Seat your least desirable rush guests near the door so they are escorted out first." The commotion that followed burgeoned across campus, precipitating student protests, angry letters from parents and faculty, and a two-page letter from its apparently Greek-friendly president who said (according to *The Times*) "that he had been stunned by the sorority's insensitivity." Back in Oxford, Ohio, the president of Delta Zeta explained that the sorority had not evicted the 23 women, but rather had tempered the blow by telling them that "the membership review team has recommended you for alumna status," meaning that "members receiving alumnae status should plan to relocate from the chapter house" within 30 days. Then the sorority said that its actions were designed to support the "enrichment of student life at DePauw." This wasn't the first time that Delta Zeta had enriched student life at DePauw, however. In 1967 it had refused a candidate with a black father and a white mother. In 1982, an uproar developed when a black woman was denied membership in its cozy sisterly circle. One "unintended consequence" of this deplorable dilemma, may have been to encourage a more independent life free from comprehensive socialization.

Running in packs, after all, has its down side. Kazimierz Janowski, who produced a BBC program called "One Planet: Rats," reminds us that in urban life, rats are seldom "12 feet from doing what they like best: eating, playing, sleeping and having lots of sex — a bit like humans, really." They're pack rats, and "They live alongside us in drains, sewers, cellars and burrows. They feed on our leftovers and share with us the title of the most successful mammal on the planet," albeit "they bring out feelings of fear and revulsion in people. It's a common fear that rats bite people, even though statistics show that you are 10 times more likely to be bitten by a fellow human being." Several human beings formed a rat pack in the 1960s, among them Sammy Davis, Jr. (whom Gerald Nachman of the *San Francisco Chronicle* accurately referred to as "a one-eyed black Jew"), Frank Sinatra, Joey Bishop, and Dean Martin, all of whom transformed rat packery into a temporarily popular nightclub act.

Sinatra: "Do you have a fairy godmother?" Martin: "No, but I got an uncle we keep a close eye on."

In America there is a fraternal organization for nearly every purpose. Some merit keeping a close eye on, others not. There can be no question that Americans are and have been fraternally addicted, even obsessed. Many are so excessively arcane that they preclude any rational comprehension. All such organizations apparently exist to accommodate some real or perceived need, such as the irresistible desire for belonging, possibly arising from a deficiency of self-actualization and self-reliance. It is small wonder that American universities have been all but taken hostage by them. There was once even a fraternity of fraternities. Had you joined it, you would have joined damned near most of what was joinable. It was called the Associated Fraternities of America, organized on March 22, 1902, and represented by some 42 "societies" who laudably set out "to unite all reputable fraternal beneficiary orders of America for concert of action in all matters of mutual interest, and for mutual benefit and improvement of all things tending to growth, permanency and usefulness, and for the prevention of all things tending to injure their progress." It sounded positively, comprehensively, wonderful. Its leadership fell to no less a statesman than C. H. Robinson of the Brotherhood of American Yeoman, and Edmund Jackson of the Mystic Workers of the World. Desiring to become even more fraternally comprehensive, they set out to unite themselves with the National Fraternal Congress. Out in the wide open spaces, The Anti Horse Thief Association (circa 1863) described itself as "all that name implied and much more," the much more being "an association of law-abiding, peaceable and liberty loving citizens, banded together for mutual protection and fraternal assistance, to make the commission of crime more difficult, and the capture of criminals more certain." By George, you can't do appreciably better than that. The AHTA later became a fraternal lodge, and even founded its own *de rigueur* Ladies Auxiliary. The organization boasted that even "courts recognize its value and approve it, ministers praise it, and all good people recognize it as a great exponent of right, justice and honesty."

Well said. The American Krusaders, on the other hand, was a splinter group of the Ku Klux Klan intended for white Protestant foreign-born American citizens. On the lighter side, the Ancient Mystic Order of Bagmen of Bagdad [*sic*] (1895) began in Ohio, calling itself the "fun" and burial insurance arms of the Order of United Commercial Travelers of America, wherein members dressed in "pseudo-Arab costume[s] and fesses [*sic*] for parades." It indeed sounded like fun. Others thought so too, expanding its membership to 6,000 by the 1980s. The Ancient Order of Free Gardeners, supposedly founded in Scotland in the 18th century, consisted of various affiliated lodges whose members were classified by any of three arcane degrees: 1) the Apprentice (predicated upon the Adam of Genesis), 2) the Journeyman (somehow related to the narrative of Noah's ark), and 3) the Master Gardener (identified with King Solomon). Ceremonies related thereto included solemn obligations, passwords, secret signs and a catechism. Failing of anything else, the Free Gardeners were listed on the Register of Friendly Societies, meaning that the group was more or less benignant. Not so The American Order of Clansmen (not affiliated with the KKK) that judiciously limited itself to "English-speaking white males" in San Francisco, circa 1915-20 and became in more enlightened times an "insurance benefit society." Meanwhile, the Ancient Order of Froth Blowers (1924-31), founded by a chap named Bert Temple in gratitude to Sir Alfred Fripp, who had supposedly operated upon his stomach, was largely a fund-raiser for the Invalid Children's Association. It's hard to quarrel with that. Out of the AOFB came the Angelic Order of Fairy Belles and the Amiable Order of Faithful Bow-Wows. There's something for everyone. The Ancient Order of Druids in America, says that occult organization, "is a Druid church of nature spirituality rooted in the Druid Revival of the eighteenth and nineteenth centuries, and offering an opportunity for modern people to experience the teachings and practices of traditional Druidry in today's world." The "Ancient Order of the Knights of the Mystic Chain," on the other hand, is probably a derivation of the Knights of Pythias (celebrated in the old American vaudeville gag about how "Damon went out and got Pythias drunk"), what with its calling its lodges "castles," and its degrees of purification: "Page," "Esquire" and "Knight." The AOKMC may have originated in Reading, Pennsylvania, in about 1870, but (according to reports) failed to survive the Depression of the 1930s. These days, the Alliance of Transylvanian Saxons is an insurance and annuity outfit. Other than that, it puts its might and main into singing societies, dance groups, brass bands and traveling bowlers. We have no objection to that. To become a member, however, one had to purchase one of its financial products. The Black Legion, besides being the name of a 1937 Humphrey Bogart film, was a Detroit faction of the KKK. The Associated Press described it as "a group of loosely federated night-riding bands operating in several states without central discipline or common purpose beyond the enforcement by lash and pistol of individual leaders' notions of 'Americanism.'" The Benevolent Order of Monkeys" describes itself as "an ancient society, a fraternal order of primates, both hairy and hairless, whose history dates back long before the dawn of man. Before Atlantis, before Mu, we met under cover of night in the darkest jungles of the world." The Daughters of the Eastern Star is "designed for the wives, daughters and female relatives of men affiliated with Masonry," with emphasis upon "the god of Masons, secrecy and oath," combined with "character building to obtain salvations by works," and "a claim to obey the Bible, although salvation by faith in Jesus Christ is a prerequisite to salvation." The aforementioned Order of DeMolay describes itself as "an organization dedicated to preparing young men to live successful, happy and productive lives," DeMolay refers to Jacques DeMolay, who at the age of 21 joined the Order of the Knights Templar, an organization sanctioned by the Roman Catholic Church. A Catholic women's group known as the Daughters of Isabella has as part of its mission, "to know one another...and better help one another" for the purpose of "uniting all Catholic women in a sisterhood," whereas the "Daughters of Mokanna" has as its divine mission "to provide a social meeting place for the ladies of El Jaala Grotto. One of the women is designated as the "Mighty Chosen One." They are not to be mistaken for "The Daughters of Penelope" who are affiliated with the Greek Orthodox Church and who sponsor antique shows. Nor are they to be confused for the "Degree of Pocahontas," an American Indian group whose officers bear such weighty titles as "Great Pocahontas," "Great Wenonah," "Great Minnehaha," Great Prophetess," "Great Keeper of Records," "Great Keeper of Wampum," "Great Guard of Tepee," "Great Guard of Forest," "Great Trustee" and so forth. The Daughters of Rebekah, "on the other hand "made their first appearance in Pembrokeshire in May 1839, when a group of men, disguised in women's clothes, attacked the tollgate at Efailwen." Which of us does not crave high-minded social living? "The Dames of Malta," we are assured, is a "secret fraternal Order, also known as Ladies of the Knights Hospitallers of St. John of Jerusalem," and "are an auxiliary of the Ancient and Illustrious Order Knights of Malta." They call their governing body "Zenodacia," that is "under the jurisdiction of the Supreme Grant Commandery of the A&IOKM," if that signifies anything.

Shopping for a fraternal home? There are copious possibilities, provided that you will be permitted inside. Try "The Ancient and Honorable Order of E Clampus Vitus," aka "E Clampus Vitus," aka "Clampers," that in the middle nineteenth century was a parody of other fraternal orders. This one fell under the alleged stewardship of folks such as the "Noble Grand Humbug," and the "Grand Imperturbable Hangman." For the more sober among us, there is always the "Eternal and Universal Brotherhood of Mystics," open to "those who may wish to join this Occult Organization which exists here and in the Astral or unseen world." The "Fraternal Order of Beavers" merited honorable mention in Sinclair Lewis's *Main Street* (1920), where he wrote that "Beavers, human Beavers, were everywhere; thirty-second degree Beavers in gray sack suits and decent derbies, more flippant Beavers in shirtsleeves and frayed suspenders," albeit "whatever his caste-symbols, every Beaver was distinguished by an enormous shrimp-colored ribbon lettered in silver [reading], 'Sir Knight and Brother, U.F.O.B Annual State Convention.'" Persons of more mystic inclination may investigate the "Fifth Order Melchizedek and the Egyptian Sphinx," alleged to have been a secret society for both men and woman, although its last known appearance was in Boston in 1894. Lest there be any fraternal confusion, the FOME preferred at times to call itself "The Solar Spiritual Order of the Silver Head and Golden Star" that it claimed to have organized "several thousand years B.C." Another option is the "Fraternity of United Friars," whose select membership claimed to emulate "only the love of learning, the scientific attainments, the charity and benevolence professed by all the religious orders of the Romish Church." The "Girls of the Golden Court," a Masonic "appendant body," is presumably yet available to "young ladies between the ages of 12 and 18" under the auspices of the "Order of the Golden Chain." For "fun and good fellowship," give the "Mystic Order of Veiled Prophets of the Enchanted Realm of North America" an attempt, inasmuch as it pledges to dispel "the gloom and fret and worry and gives a brighter outlook and kindlier feeling, while it strengthens the fiber for real serious work and so brings true blessings and beautifies the fellowship of the Prophets." That is probably more than can be said on behalf of the "Hermetic Brotherhood of Luxor," more popularly known as the H B of L, the best informational source for which is Thomas Burgoyne (aka "Thomas Dalton"), in his book entitled *Light of Egypt* (apparently out of print). "The Hooded Ladies of the Mystic Den" was an auxiliary of the Ku Klux Klan intended to keep the girls occupied while the boys were nocturnally hiding behind white hoods (Sinclair Lewis called them "high dunces' caps") keeping America safe for cowardly racist barbarism. Since 1910, those committed to keeping America commercially safe for trees have been free to join "The International Concatenated Order of Hoo-Hoo."

Other hoo-hoos inclined join cults, clubs and fraternities, their denials to the contrary, are probably not the most independent folks out there, and yet their organizations ironically carry the words "Independent Order of" in their titles, examples being "Owls," "Alhambra," "Chosen Friends," "Deer," "the Empire," "Good Samaritans & Daughters of Samaria," "Immaculates of the United States of America," "Knights of Phythias," "Muscovites," "Mechanics," "Mystic Brothers," "Odd Fellows," "Puritans," "Rebeckahs," "Rechabites," "Rainbow Girls," "Red Men," "Shepherds," and "Svithoid." Possibly too, you may qualify as one of the "sons of," as in "Sons of Abraham," "St. Luke," "Twelve Knights & Daughters of Tabor," and "Vikings." Of these, the Rechabites are of particular interest, if only for their "agenda" (as people today are fond of calling such things) that rendered them a teetotal sect that consigned its women and children to tents in the name of decency. In fact, people who form themselves into sects have a tendency to call themselves "knights of" or "of the" something grand and outrageously uplifting, such as "Knights of the Altar," the "Apocalypse," "Ancient Essenic Order," "Blue Cross of the World," "Holy City," "Columbus," "Cork," "Dunamis," "Father Matthew," "Globe," "St. George," "Golden Circle," "Golden Eagle," "Grand Legion," "Golden Rule," Honor," "Holy Cross," "Holy Sepulchre," "Invisible Kingdom," "Invisible Colored Kingdom," "Immaculate Movement," "Jericho," "St. John," "Labor," "Sword," "Maccabees," "St. Wenceslas," "Pythias," "Peter Claver," "Royal Arch," "Red Cross," "Red Cross of Constantine," "Relief," "Round Table," "St. Andrew," "St. Columcille," "Southern Cross," "Sherwood Forest," "St. John," "St. Lawrence," "Square Table," "St. George," "St. Ignatius," "St. Joseph," "St. Martin," "St. Patrick," "St. Paul," "St. Peter," "St. Richards," "St. Thomas," "Tabor," "Templar," "Malta," "White Cross," "Wise Men," "York Cross of Honor" and such like. *Knighthood* is therefore the last word in clan life. If they haven't elected themselves into knighthood, they can at least qualify as "Sons of" something, such as "Benjamin," "Bethlehem," "Italy," "Pericles," "St. George," "Temperance," "Veterans," and so forth. Failing of all that, they can count themselves members of numerous "fraternals," like the "Fraternal Aid Union," "Brotherhood," "Mystic Circle," "Mystic Legion," "Order of Alaskan State Troopers," "Order of Bears," "Order of Beavers," "Colonials," "Clover Leaves," "Eagles," "Firefighters," "Orioles," "Police," "Pineapples," "Americans," and so on.

Indeed, in America alone there are undoubtedly more herds of people than herds of animals. Affiliative women like to band together as "Ladies of," or "of the" something appropriately cabalistic, as for instance, "Abraham Lincoln," "Ancient Order of Hibernians," "Grand Army of the Republic," "Golden Eagle," "Order of Reindeer," "Royal Arcanum," "Maccabees of the World," "Orange Benevolent Association," "Beer Buffalo," "Oriental Shrine," "Pennsylvania Slovak Catholic Union," or "American Liberty." There are, of course plenty of daughters out there, to wit: daughters of "Hope," "America," "Duke Richard," "Isabella," "Isis," "Liberty," "Mokanna," "Nile," "Norway," "Penelope," "Pocahontas," "Rebekah," "Scotia," "Scotland," St. Richards," "Veterans,"

"Republic of Texas," "Union Civil War Veterans," and any other cause to which one could possibly attach oneself, such as "The Michigan Cock Fanciers Association" — for which there is fortunately little to no information to be had. Had there been, odds are that the group would have been besieged with applicants who might otherwise turn to the "Order of the Mystic Star," the "Order of Pink Goats" or the P.E.O. Sisterhood, still taking applications in Des Moines, Iowa. The P.E.O. even owns and operates Cottey College, described as "a two-year, independent, liberal arts college for women, by women, and about women," located in Nevada, Missouri. The group invites travelers to visit Iowa Wesleyan College, Mount Pleasant, Iowa, to visit its "P.E.O. [allegedly meaning "protect each other"] Memory Rooms."

If even the P.E.O. won't let you in, try "The Military Order of the Cootie," but only if you belong to the Veterans of Foreign Wars — who have been known to don red pants with a white stripe down each side, as well as a lace-trimmed red vest with a gold-outlined bug-like creature with flashing light bulb eyes. We regret to say that the "Mystical 7," once alleged to be one of the "most ambitious college societies in the world," is no longer with us, although "The Order of Good Times" ("L'Ordre de Bon Temps") may still be taking applications, having reported that "nous passames cet hiver fort joyeusement & bonne chair," which is more than most people can say, especially the "Polish Falcons of America," whose motto, after 110 years, is still "A Healthy Spirit in a Healthy Body," and whose lodges are still called "nests." The "Ancient, Honorable and Fragrant Order of the Pink Goat" was invented by a gaggle of drunken Rotarians at a Buffalo convention and is no longer accepting new members. We doubt whether "The Perfect Initiates of Asia" continues to thrive, having limited their numbers to African architects. We are reliably informed that whereas the PIA touted such elevated ideals as religious tolerance, equality, and the brotherhood of man, its "influence has always been debatable." We have long recommended that the respectable women we know strongly consider membership in the "Rathbone Sisters of the World," an auxiliary of the "Knights of Pythias" that, the last we knew, "permitted members of the masculine parent to join," but "in the usual fashion," the precise implication of which we are not altogether qualified to judge. Persons in or near Rockford, Illinois might give strong consideration to the "St. Ambroglio Society" that is, quite frankly, receptive to persons of Italian heritage, having let it be known that "if you want to do business with a paesano, this is the place to find them [sic]."

Failing of all that, there is always Yale's "Skull and Bones," whose membership has included such politicians as William Howard Taft, George W.

Bush, W. Averell Harriman and John Kerry — bonesmen all — and all of whom have been sworn to secrecy. Reported CBS News's "Sixty Minutes," Skull and Bones "is as essential to Yale as the Whiffenpoofs, the tables down at a pub called Mory's, and the Yale mascot — that ever-slobbering mascot" about whom Yale student Cole Porter in 1910 wrote the "Bingo Eli Yale" football fight song:

> Bull dog! Bull dog! Bow wow wow.
> Eli Yale!
> Bull dog! Bull dog! Bow wow, wow.
> Our team can never fail.[1]

"Sixty Minutes" further reported that the fraternity "with all its ritual and macabre relics [allegedly among them: the skull of Apache chief Geronimo that] dates as far back as 1832 when it became a new world version of secret student societies common in Germany at that time. Since then, it has chosen or 'tapped' only 15 senior students a year who become patriarchs when they graduate — lifetime members of the ultimate old boys' club." An eavesdropper once videotaped a solemn Skull and Bones initiation ceremony, wherein initiates are "supposed to recount their entire sexual histories. The other 14 members are sitting on plush couches, and the lights are dimmed...and there's a fire roaring and...this activity is supposed to last from between one to three hours." Said another commentator, "you take these young strivers, you put them in this weird castle; they spill their guts with each other[;]they learn a commitment to the community." Perhaps so. One can easily get the impression that hazing is a masochistic reprisal that at least subconsciously sets out to punish its inductees for their capital stupidity Additionally, initiatory rites are largely designed with the intention of assessing a candidate's desperation for group membership. Some neophytes, as we have also seen, are so inexorably bent upon group approval that they are quite willing to endure any embarrassment, any indignity, any humiliation — as long as the group eventually accepts them as one of their own, after which the former neophytes initiate other candidates, reducing them to beggarly grovelers. Loners and other hermetic types are especially puzzled about what motivates someone to surrender so much for so little, specifically trading his self-

---

1 Charles Schwartz in his *Cole Porter: A Biography* (1977) reminds us that "Bingo Eli Yale," that Porter submitted in a 1910 Yale song competition, "quickly became the rage of that football season" and "helped make Cole a big musical man on campus," supplemented later by his "Fla De Dah," and "Beware Yale" that are now "considered Yale classics."

hood and self-esteem for what amounts to the anonymity that arises from herd mentality.

Military life, for example, has always been a fertile ground of initiatory brutality. Indeed, it is a monstrous fighting fraternity that, when it is not taking aim on the enemy, is at war with itself. Richard Henry Dana's *Two Years Before the Mast* (1840) had as one of its purposes the exposure of naval brutality typified by a sadistic captain's savagely flogging two sailors, saying, "If you want to know what I flog you for, I'll tell you. It is because I like to do it! — Because I like to do it! — It suits me! That's what I do it for!"[1] He is not alone. Others like it, too. In our own day, NBC's "Dateline" obtained 1991 and 1993 video footage from an ex-marine showing a Camp Lejeune North Carolina initiatory rite called "blood pinning," wherein 30 or so marines wielding Gold Wing pins with half inch posts attached (awarded after 10 successful parachute jumps) that they were pressing into the chests of new recruits. The U.S. Department of Defense released details of the victims who were, in the words of writer Linda Kozaryn, "screaming, wincing and squirming in pain, [trying] to pull away as blood streamed through their T-shirts." Kozaryn remarked, "Hazing is forbidden in the Marine Corps, but it remains an insidious problem because it is secretive." Suzy Hansen of salon.com. cited "military rituals — like fraternity rituals — [that] take the initiate into this dark underworld where they're [*sic*] deprived of sleep, infanticized and feminized. Often there's a good deal of homoeroticism. Simulated sex is not unusual." She adds, "The problem is, what we're talking about are secret practices in a very closed institution and there's typically not a lot of scrutiny." Widespread incidents of torture — some of it at the hands of women — at the Abu Ghraib prison in Iraq have been linked to the torturers themselves having been tortured as part of military ritual.

"The problem is," of course, not limited to American military practices. James. K. Wither, writing in the *Journal of Power Institutions in Post-Soviet Societies*, has noted that the military "has struggled to eliminate incidents of bullying from the ranks, which have tarnished the image of the British Army," citing as one example from a British infantry regiment "a 20 year old private [who] testified that his initiation consisted of being burned on the genitals, sexually assaulted with a broomstick, forced to march in place with a string tied to his genitals and ankles and dropped from a window." Elsewhere he concedes, "It is perhaps not surprising that problems associated with the

---

1 In the *Uncollected Prose, Dial Essays* (1840), Emerson remarked that Dana's book "will open the eyes of many to the condition of the sailor, to the fearful waste of man, by whom the luxuries of foreign climes are made to increase the amount of commercial wealth."

mistreatment of soldiers in basic training were comparatively overlooked. However, some measures introduced to combat racial and sexual abuse and harassment undoubtedly assisted the victims of other forms of bullying," albeit those measures were often prompted by "media reports of bullying and harassment and the unexplained suicides of young soldiers in training." Indeed, the *London Independent* reported in November of 2005 that criminal investigations were ongoing in reports of initiatory "violent bullying" in the Royal Navy, including an account of "a newly qualified member of the navy's Royal Marines, beaten unconscious by someone who is said to be one of the man's senior officers." Another marine confirms "that initiation rituals involving the sadistic use of violence were commonplace," and that in this case "wounds inflicted were so severe as to be life-threatening." Elsewhere, *The News of the World* reported "newly qualified marines breaking their legs after being made to jump out of windows," and having "electric pads, taken from massage machines, attached to their testicles and head." Military organizations have a curious habit, therefore of discrediting, even humiliating themselves by condoning acts that will elicit near unanimous public outrage, something that they evidently believe they deserve. Two such incidents occurred in 2007, one of them involving two junior NCOs affiliated with the Royal Green Jackets who fabricated reasons for tormenting two 19-year-old soldiers who they insisted drop to their knees and lick urine from the floor, something that a military spokesman claimed that the recruits had "chosen" to do. The Green Jackets again found the publicity they were seeking when a video containing footage of a soldier who was subjected to having a vacuum cleaner placed on his private parts, to having been chained to an upright bed, to having cigarettes snuffed out on his chest and to having beer poured over him." The teenagers had allegedly been understandably absent without leave. This time a spokeswoman said, "The Army has a zero tolerance policy on bullying. These sorts of incidents are very rare."

They are not unusual among participants in team athletics, however. In an article appropriately called "Athletes Abusing Athletes" published by ESPN, Tom Farrey writes, "In Vermont, hockey players grab each others' genitalia and parade around in a freshman initiation ceremony. In Connecticut, a high school wrestler is hog-tied and sodomized with the blunt end of a plastic knife. In Oklahoma, a football player suffers a head injury after being humped by teammates." Athletic hazing customarily takes the form of physical abuse and alcohol consumption. Team players being team players, they are willing to accept manifest indignities good-naturedly for the right to participate with others on American playing fields. The only comprehensive study of athletic hazing has come from Alfred University (the same university that invited a goodly amount of bad press from its fraternity hazing), which defines hazing as "any activity expected of someone joining the group that humiliates, degrades, abuses or endangers, regardless of the person's willingness to participates." The report also cites the 41 states that carry anti-hazing laws on their books, although some are "specifically targeted to fraternity hazing and do not cover athletic or high school hazing," and notes that state laws also "vary on whether or not consent of the person hazed is included in the definitions of hazing." Universities themselves seem to condone it, since they look the other way when they allow Greek organizations to get away with anything they can get away with, and try to ignore the antics of Big Ten university athletic coaches who tacitly, even openly, abuse athletes. Speaking of looking the other way, Farrey notes, "The executive director of the National Federation of State High School Associations [claimed] that hazing is all new to him."

The Alfred report determined the percentage of male athletes engaged in questionable activities who participated in at least one unacceptable act, revealing that 81 percent had been subjected to "being yelled, cursed, or sworn at"; that another 81 percent has been subjected to "tattooing, piercing, head shaving or branding"; that 85 percent had been forced to wear "embarrassing clothing"; that 98 percent has been forced to participate in "calisthenics not related to a sport"; that another 98 percent had been ordered to associate only with certain people; that 99 percent had been deprived of "food, sleep or hygiene"; that 100 percent has been forced to act as "personal servant" to players off the field; and that another 100 percent had been forced to consume "extremely spicy/disgusting concoctions." More than half (males and female athletes, both) had been pushed into alcohol-related initiatory activities such as participation in "drinking contests." Eight percent reported that they had been" tied up, taped, or confined in small spaces," seven percent said they had been forced to simulate "sexual acts," 11 percent said they had been ordered to steal or destroy property, and 12 percent said that they had been required to make "prank calls," or engage in harassing others. The Alfred study concluded that those "most at risk of being hazed to join a team" were males who had no Greek affiliation, most likely swimmers, divers, soccer players and lacrosse players, were registered on a rural campus in the east or south, and who come from a state with no anti-hazing law." Female athletes, the study said, "were much less likely than men to be subjected to unacceptable acts such as destroying or stealing property, beating up others, being tied up or taped, being confined in small places, being paddled, beaten, kidnapped or transported and abandoned."

A vaguely amusing document called "Preventing Hazing at Harvard," apparently authored by one or more undergraduates, claimed that hazing male athletes was with the laudable intention of developing or demonstrating masculinity, making "boys/men tougher," and denouncing homosexuality. It would seem, on the face of it, that if one had those motives, he could develop them himself. The Harvard statement is predicated upon a platform of dubious assumptions predicated upon two obvious fallacies: 1) "that one can only succeed in a group environment," and 2) that acceptance in that group entails a "rite of passage" that apparently doesn't rule hazing out. This, it advises, has its downside, to wit: that "when hazing is involved in the process of affiliating with an organization or team, the costs of holding membership in the group may end up outweighing the benefits." Ergo, it's best not to disrespect newcomers in an organization, nor is it a good idea to alienate them. Besides that, it may interfere with some sort of "meaningful initiation" (without disclosing what the meaningful initiation might be). Might it involve eating pig brains? In addition, it warns that such activities might damage his sense of self-worth, and thus tread on his civil liberties and interfere with the "trust and unity" one is attempting to foster, and quite possibly lead to problems between the group and some (heaven help us) alumni, "constitute a form of violence, and "pose criminal and civil liability issues." By Jove, spoken like Harvard men. Worst still, the white paper advises, it could "lead to the canceling of an athletic season" (we hadn't considered that possibility) and (perish the thought) "create risks of disbanding an organization or losing members." That we concede would be altogether unthinkable in a setting that thrives on groups, committees, cliques, teams and regiments. Northwestern University, however, doesn't altogether view hazing in the same light. It seems that a year or so ago some unsavory photographs surfaced that show the women's soccer team humiliating some of its members, or maybe prospective members. One of the pictures revealed women in their underwear in compromising circumstances, namely being blindfolded and having their hands bound. Another shows a woman "drinking what appears to be beer" and another one catches two of the women kissing. Even worse, two other photographs clearly illustrated the women performing "lap dances" for the benefit of the men's soccer team. It goes on to say that a message left at the office of the women's' soccer coach "was not immediately returned." We don't like the sound of that. The entire university, we understand, was in a dither. A bureaucratic university source eventually replied sternly that "if the investigation shows that there has been a violation of Northwestern's policies, appropriate sanctions will be imposed and the athletic department may take additional action, as well." In the end, the university suspended its women's soccer team.

Hence we have been hastily availed to what might be called "the joy of joining" in some of its multifarious manifestations. Joining is mostly about joining a team, playing with the guys, learning to take orders, fitting in, craving group approval, putting everyone on notice that yes, you are perfectly normal. That sort of thing. In its numerous definitions of "join," the *OED* suggests any of several related things, such as "to put (things) together so that they becomes united or continuous; to fasten, attach, connect, unite; also, to connect by means of something intervening or attached to each, e.g. two islands by a bridge;" and elsewhere "to link or unite (persons, etc. together) in marriage, friendship or any kind of association, alliance or relationship; to unite, associate, ally." Others, including some of the more cliché-bitten among us, have suggested other familiar uses of the word, such as to "be joined at the hip," "joining forces," "join the fun," join the Marines" (as we are about to see) "join the fray," "join them (if you can't beat them,)" "join the club," "join the ranks," "join hands," "join in," or "join up" and simply "be a joiner," which is to say a woodworker, or a person who joins every possible thing that can be joined and who has a predisposition to connect everything that is connectable. What prompts people to join is something of a mystery, since it necessarily diminishes the joiner who apparently believes that his selfhood can be (as it were) amplified by aligning with others to create a larger, more imposing self, in the sense that "two heads are better than one, two hundred heads are better still than one and so forth. It further assumes that one is a mere insignificant particle whose potency (if indeed he has any) can be uncorked only through association, even if it means receiving a sound thrashing as part of the admission price for associating with a hoard of folks who also do not hold themselves in particularly elevated esteem. If the group wins a rugby game or a belching contest, the joiner nonetheless remains a miniscule part of a larger, bigger, more imposing order of idiots to whom he reports. Had he remained unaffiliated, he would at least have had a shot at doing some attention-getting thing such making his own acquaintance. One ought to be not only his best friend, but (conceivably) his *only* friend. Joining interferes and probably prevents this coming to terms with one's identity.

Historian Dale Boudreau has speculated that by 1865 there developed what he calls "the golden age of fraternity," if that not be another oxymoron, when something like "150 secret societies were in full blossom," estimating that "out of an adult male population of 19 million, 5.4 million [roughly 28 percent] belonged to fraternal orders." Commenting three decades later, Ronald Grimes, another historian, believed it was even higher. This begs the question of how 28 to 40 percent of American men (let's say one out of three) were somehow or another affiliated. How was it possible for so many to take such rites seriously? His response was "fraternity," meaning "a sense of solidarity among middle class Protestant men uncompromised by the presence of others — women and Indians, but also uninitiated men," probably "inspired" and "patterned" after Freemasonry. Part of the result, he wrote, was that "men were able to make business contacts and maintain a web of social connections." He then introduced another question: "is it that young men found in the rites solace and psychological guidance for negotiating the troubling passage into manhood?"

Possibly so, but it makes a difficult process inestimably more difficult. As we have seen, joiners (be they masochistic young men or women) are virtually unconcerned about their being deprived, beaten and dumped on, so long as it leads to the membership they're craving. Accordingly they will present themselves in huge numbers to those two unequaled headquarters of punishment, the Marine Corps recruit (boot camp) training depots. The one at Parris Island[1] near Beaufort, South Carolina graduates over 17,000 marines a year. The average daily male recruit population is about 3,786, whereas the average female recruit population is about 600. The one at San Diego graduates about 21,000 men and women, the average age being 19.1 for males and 19.3 for females. The Corps concedes, up front, that its Marine boot camp is more challenging — both physically and mentally — than the basic training programs of other military services, since recruits are required to commit "a startling amount of information" to memory. The abuse toward, and reconstitution of, recruits continues for more than 13 weeks. Upon arrival they receive instruction in military history, "customs and courtesies," basic first aid, uniforms, and leadership core values. Then it's four levels of swimming qualification. Then marksmanship, Basic Warrior training, combat endurance, written tests. The Corps also concedes that even former Marines regard those 13 weeks as "the most difficult thing they ever had to do in their entire lives." "The Crucible," that is "A Rite of Passage for all Marines," consists of 42-foot miles and 29 "problem-solving" exercises. Recruits are required to carry ammunition cans up to 50 pounds and dummies up to 100 pounds

---

1 Parris Island rather gingerly markets all 12.2 square miles of itself to the tourist trade, inviting the curious to visit the barracks and Leatherneck Square followed by cocktails at the Brig-n-Brew and dinner at Traditions.

in addition to 782 gear, uniform and M16 A2 service rifle weight. They will spend some of their happiest hours crossing two horizontal cable-supported logs, demonstrating their knowledge of hand-to-hand combat skills, climbing over an eight foot high horizontal log, recovering a downed pilot and transporting him through a mile of wooded terrain, swinging like Tarzan on ropes, retrieving a wounded dummy from an 18-foot tower, moving two ammunition cans over the top of a 36-foot ladder obstacle, resupplying water and ammunition, embarking on nine-mile hikes, and receiving for their trouble a Warrior's Breakfast consisting of steak, eggs and potatoes.

Suppose you want desperately to become a Marine. What do you do besides signing your life away? It's easy. Begin by running three miles a day, and taking rather long (up to ten mile) marches. Perfect your sit-ups and your pull-ups. If they give you any problem, join a Physical Conditioning Platoon for 21 days. As they say, "once you're in, you don't get out until you can do three pull-ups and 40 sit-ups in two minutes, and run three miles in less than 28 minutes." When you arrive at Parris you will be allowed one telephone call and be assigned a "diet tray" if you're overweight, and "double rations" if you're under weight. You will memorize "11 General Orders for a Sentry," the "Marine's Hymn, "USMC Core Values," the characteristics of the Ml 16 A4 Rifle, and the "Code of Conduct." Bring nothing but your driver's license, Social Security card and check book. Nothing else. Non-issue items will come out of your pay. No over-the-counter medicines are permitted. If you bring them, they will be confiscated. All prescription medicines will be re-evaluated by a military physician then either confiscated or re-issued by the military pharmacy. Women will be issued birth control pills "to ensure their systems maintain their regular cycle" although Marine Corps contraband includes birth control methods, weapons, pornography, playing cards, alcohol, tobacco, drugs, cameras, radios, civilian clothing and email. Recruits receive one hour of free time every evening and four hours on Sunday mornings. Visitors are prohibited. Withal, it is a marvelous regimentation for those who cannot regiment themselves, illustrating once again that if one cannot discipline oneself from within, then some other party will accomplish it from without. It is not without its inevitable excesses, however. *The San Diego Union Tribune* on November 16, 2007 published an article headlined "Marine is given 6 months for abuse," calling it "perhaps the biggest recruit-abuse scandal in Marine Corps history" that ended with a drill instructor's being sentenced to six prison months (out of a possible nine and a half years) for having hit "recruits with a tent pole and flashlight to making them drink water until they threw up, then making them wallow in their vomit." Said the defendant's father, "Marine officials have their heads in the sand if they don't think this is happening every day."

It probably is. In January of 2008 *The New York Times* reported that a Jacksonville, North Carolina Marine corporal was believed to have murdered his pregnant Marine girlfriend, "whose burnt remains were excavated from a fire pit in his back yard." It continued, "Authorities have described a violent confrontation inside his home that left blood spatters on the ceiling and a massive amount of blood on the wall." The victim's uncle told reporters that "she was raped" and that "the Marines did nothing to protect her." As the Czech poet, playwright and president Vaclav Havel has written: "If every day a man takes orders in silence from an incompetent superior, if every day he solemnly performs rituals acts which he privately finds ridiculous, if he unhesitatingly gives answers to questionnaires which are contrary to his real opinions and is prepared to deny his own self in public, if he sees no difficulty in feigning sympathy or even affections where, in fact, he feels only indifference or aversion, it still does not mean that he has entirely lost the use of one of the basic human senses, namely, the sense of humiliation."[1] Of course, the victims willingly surrender themselves to a multitude of indignities when they enter a fraternity house or a military training depot, since they have surrendered themselves to tyrants who presume to control their lives absolutely. Nor do they seem to mind. They may even think that they have it coming. This is the *reductio ad absurdum* of herd mentality without which we would have no punks to mistreat young undergraduates, or marines to fight our wars.

So too, Michael Schirber writing for *Live Science* has observed that "Bees do it, Birds do it. So do fish and wildebeests." The "it" to which he refers is the human tendency to follow blindly. "Human beings," he reminds us, "tend to follow each other with a herd mentality," seeming to follow "some complex communication that goes on between the informed and the uninformed," adding "that the entire group will tend to settle on the direction with the greater number of informed individuals." Stephen Dubner, also writing for the *Times*, has noticed that in grocery stores, customers avoid non-existent lines in favor of cueing up behind other people. An anonymous online blogger reported to his annoyance that, having carried his lunch to a remote section of a restaurant; other people invariably followed him and sat nearby with theirs. Said he, "They weren't quiet eaters, either. They coughed, sneezed, blew their noses, slurped and in general sounded like a herd of pigs

---

1 Havel took advantage of the anti-communist support from the West especially after that regime banned his plays and seized his passport.

feeding at the trough," commenting also that "I am definitely not a herd animal and prefer to eat my lunch or dinner in the peace and quiet of the home I call my cave."

Another person commenting on post-Thanksgiving shoppers reported, "Not only do they have to be prepared to engage in physical violence to that last discounted flat-screen television, but they also have to contend with hideous traffic. The wild-eyed consumerism that infects people after Thanksgiving is a little creepy." In another *New York Times* article, this one dealing with the initial retail availability of the fabled iPhone, reporter Jeremy Peters noted that for days customers had camped outside the Apple flagship store at Fifth Avenue near 59th Street in New York, because owning an iPhone was one of those things one must do, even if one did not really want an iPhone nor understand how to operate it. They became deservedly known as "converts who did not know much about the phone [then retailing between $500 and $700] other than that they had to have it." One such person "got in line outside the Fifth Avenue store around 7 p.m. on Thursday and slept all night in a folding chair." He later "used words like 'elegant' and 'beautiful' to describe the iPhone, which at that point he had only seen in pictures." Other customers hired people to wait outside the store on their behalf. Another customer was offering his place in line for $160. One man stood outside for six hours waiting for the doors to be flung open. Twenty-one days later, *The Times* also dispatched a reporter to greet the long awaited 12:01 retail reception of J. K. Rowling's *Harry Potter and the Deathly Hallows*. Of course, everyone had to possess a copy, if not read it. At a Manhattan Barnes & Noble store, "lines snaked around the block as police officers ordered fans off the street." Some customers turned up in Harry Potter costumes. At another store on Columbus Circle, bookstore managers shouted, "Are we ready for Harry Potter?" A crowd screamed its hurrah. In London, meanwhile, a 15-year-old Netherlands girl waiting for Harry Potter staked herself outside Waterstones for two days — in the rain. By eight that evening, 500 others "wrapped around several city blocks."

Herd mentality obviously affects highway traffic, usually by obstructing its flow. One recent traffic snarl developed when drivers slowed to view some newly posted graffiti. In Chicago, it is not unusual for traffic unaccountably to reach a complete halt, pause for a few minutes, and then unaccountably resume at full speed, the object being for the herd to detain and thereby control other motorists. A recent item on sheep dogs in Salt Lake City's *Desert News* tells us that "as long as there have been domesticated sheep, there have been dogs to help herd them," observing too that "ducks have the same flock instinct as sheep. If we used chickens, they'd go every which way. But dogs can round up ducks and herd them into pens just as they do with sheep." Quipped Kinkos founder Paul Orfalea, "We're raising sheep in our educational system, not independent thinkers and doers." Thinkers and doers, however, are obviously unwelcome in a collectivist, team-oriented society. In a related note, *National Geographic News* reported that "Chimps can be team players," adding that "The researchers believe both children and chimps are willing to help but that they differ in their abilities to interpret when help is needed."

Adolescents are particularly at risk of submitting to peer pressure. A publication underwritten by the Palo Alto Medical Foundation and intended for teenagers actually recommends herd life. "It is important to all of us that we feel like we fit in with other people," it advises. "Having friends, or peers, that are like you, and who you can count on to listen to you is important, too," noting, however, that one should avoid persons "who criticize you, make fun of how you feel, and dare you to do things." Another source of teen counsel also recommends interdependence, asserting "your best friend is possibly the most important person in your life. What would you do without someone you can tell all to?" On a considerably different note, The BNET Research Center has published a 2000 document called "Fitting In: Exploring the Emotional Dimension of Adolescent Peer Pressure," suggesting that teens conform out of a sense of shame. Relying upon data collected from a dozen college students, the paper argues "that negative emotions pay a role in peer influence, particularly feelings of inadequacy and isolation, as well as feeling ridiculed, all of which may be indicative of shame. Thus, shame-related feelings may be instrumental in motivating individuals to conform," to which one might also infer that the conformity may also begin to explain why older teens are willing tolerate the sometimes extreme abuse (for some real or imagined offences or other failures) pursuant to that conformity.

The infinite and manifest joys of lone wolfery begin by obliterating ("root and branch," as they say) all obstacles to perfectly wonderful virtues such as self-acceptance, self-adulation, self advancement, self-affirmation, self-analysis, self-assertion, self-confidence, self-containment, self-control, self-dependence, self-determination, self-direction, self-discipline, self-emancipation, self evaluation, self-healing, self-hood, self-management, self-policing, self-promotion, self-protection, self-renewal, self-restraint, self-selection, self-sufficiency, self-trust, self-worth and self anything else that may be necessary not merely to cope, but to prevail. Odds are that, if successfully done, one will live a life moons away from badgering fratboys and haranguing drill sergeants who purport to furnish a place of benevolently fraternal belonging. Granted, this psychological rebuild is well beyond the reach of all but the most irretrievably narcissistic, which is to say those with an appropriately strong sense of selfhood inappropriately and unfortunately taken to be a personality disorder characterized by an extraordinary sociopathic self-preoccupation. It is instead a life driven, as it should properly be, from within rather than without. This may well become cause for skepticism. Matt Welch, author of a book called *McCain: The Myth of a Maverick*, has called John McCain's supposed "stubborn individualism" into question, citing his subject's public assertion that "we are fast becoming a nation of alienating individualists, unwilling to put the unifying values of patriots ahead of narrow self-interests."

Nevertheless, James H. Douglas (Harvard law graduate, and later Air Force Secretary) reminds us that "our forebears worked hard in this difficult land, and their reward was the freedom and independence of self sufficiency." So too, the repressively aphoristic, defiantly homoerotic Quentin Crisp held that "the consuming desire of most human beings is deliberately to plant their whole life in the hands of some other person. I would describe this method of searching for happiness as immature. Development of characters consists solely in moving toward self-sufficiency." America celebrates its Independence every July 4, and honors the 56 men who courageously signed it into law. Louis Brandeis has rightly referred to them as "those who won our independence...valued liberty as an end and as a means. They believed liberty to be the secret of happiness and courage to be the secret of liberty." Out in the American mid-continent, Missouri, Ohio, Kentucky and Minnesota each named a settlement "Independence" presuming it to be a virtue. Walt Disney, of all people, said that Mickey Mouse, of all mice, "is, to me, a symbol of independence," which he undoubtedly is. It is altogether fitting that America's citizens, be they mice or men, prevail as independent beings and conduct their lives accordingly a certain originality of mind and spirit, despite Tocqueville's ominous observation that he knew of no country where there is "so little independence of mind and real freedom of discussion as in America."

All the same, one has little choice but to strike out alone, taking his own chances, assuming his own risks, finding his own identity. The Grecian hero Odysseus, without membership in any fraternal or even military society, prevails by his cunning and intellect in the development of *The Odyssey*, while one by one his men perish largely because of their collective stupidity and ineptitude. Rascals like Odysseus, on the other hand, move more adroitly, more astutely and far more quickly than any army or bulbous corporate colossus. The free thinking rascal and New Yorker Robert Green Ingersoll, possibly the best recognized orator of the American 19th Century, Civil War combatant, attorney, secular humanist and favorite of Mark Twain, wrote in 1873 of how "at every hand, are the enemies of individuality and mental freedom. Custom meets us at the cradle and leaves us only at the tomb," commenting later, "In my judgment, every human being should take a road of his own. Every mind should be true to itself — should think, investigate and conclude for itself." Ingersoll, with his strangely persuasive abilities and rhetorical sleight of hand, also wrote an amusingly didactic dialog:

> "A monarch said to a hermit, 'Come with me and I will give you power.'
> 'I have all the power I know how to use," replied the hermit.
> 'Come,' said the king, 'I will give you wealth.'
> 'I have no wants that money can supply,' said the hermit.
> 'I will give you honor,' said the monarch.
>   'Ah, honor cannot be given. It must be earned,' was the hermit's answer.
> 'Come,' said the king, making a last appeal, "and I will give you happiness.'
> 'No,' said the man of solitude. 'There is no happiness without liberty, and he who follows cannot be free.'
> 'You shall have liberty too,' said the king. 'Then I will stay where I am, said the old man.
> And all the king's courtiers thought the hermit a fool."

Hence we are succinctly introduced to a contemplative figure at once a hermit, a man of solitude, and (ironically) a "fool," who illustrates the merits of solitude and maturity that predictably strike the rabble as foolish. This stray fragment of 19th century popular homespun philosophy nevertheless embraces the virtues of a life led outside the mainstream wherein a person of moral substance rises above the commonality of king and courtiers. Its exemplary moralistic anecdote puts one in mind of New Testament moral authority through which Ingersoll, this secular prophet and popular entertainer, easily gathered a bumptious audience. Even the much maligned and much publicized atheist Madalyn Murray O'Hair had a soft spot for Ingersoll and his work. "He was far from being a saint," she wrote. "Except for the issue of abolition, into which he was indoctrinated by both of his parents. He was on the 'wrong' side of every human issue." She mentions too that he was a ruthless attorney for the railroads; that he spoke against Lincoln until the war broke out; that he vigorously defended corrupt politicians; that he opposed suffrage for black males; that he was drawing what today would be up to $50,000 a lecture; that he participated in more than one bar-room brawl; and that, were he with us today, "he would probably be a Reaganite." Ingersoll, withal, was very big in Peoria, and at the very least had a fertile medicine-show mind of his own that did indeed with mostly-concealed misanthropy bring in the sheep.

Chapter 5. The Intellectual as Loner

> The hero acts alone, without encouragement, relying solely on conviction and his own inner resources. Shame does not discourage him; neither does obloquy. Indifferent to approval, reputation, wealth, or love, he cherishes only his personal sense of honor, which he permits no one else to judge.
> — William Manchester, *A World Lit Only by Fire* (1992)

Circumstances such as we have painfully described in the previous four chapters oblige the intellectual, sometimes out of desperation, to find an exilic refuge amid the generally inhospitable social climate into which he finds himself unfortunately consigned. Since intellectuals thrive on the life of the mind, it follows therefore that the only suitable shelter is precisely there: a Platonic world of ideas that he regards as home, because it can only be his refuge. He opts for this because it is the place he prefers to be, and also the place to which he is driven by a primarily mundane environment (to borrow Wordsworth's expression) of "getting and spending." An intellectual has difficulty coming to terms with other people, even when those people happen also to be intellectuals who in turn have their own "relational" (shall we say) difficulties. The relentless pursuit of learning, metamorphosizes him into what the rest of the world views as every bit freak and monster (of which he is all too fully aware) possessed of possibly subversive ideas that demand he stay to himself because there is no one left with whom to communicate acceptably on any level. If there were, it still would not repay his time to communicate at all, because (quite frankly) too many others have too little to say to him. Nor is his merely a place to which he can escape, but it is the only environment suited to his hermetic requirements. Certain aquatic animals, after all, inhabit the bottom of the sea; certain winged beasts take wing to the serenity and peril of their aeries. Consider it ascetic withdrawal, meaning the self-discipline of hermetic detachment for purposes of systematic inquiry and cogitation, yes, but not for purposes of escape. To the contrary, it is a deeper engagement in this world of ideas that leads one into a higher and fuller independence. These are not pipedreams; they're intellectual journeys.

This is why the popular expression "public intellectuals" (delivered especially into common parlance by Richard Posner's 2001 book of the same name) is an oxymoron in that one cannot very well be an intellectual and remain passionately connected to the world of common streetwise affairs at the same time. Michael White in his biography of C. S. Lewis says in passing that "For those lucky enough to live the life of an Oxford don it has always been very easy to seal oneself off from the world, to ascend the clichéd ivory tower." Adding, "Many of those who become dons are by nature uninterested in most mundane matters and prefer the realm of pure intellect to the prosaic world of what most people would consider normal life." Public intellectual might be construed to mean theorists such as Charles Darwin, Albert Einstein or Sigmund Freud who are widely recognized (but not read) by the general public. Posner also distinguishes between the independent and the affiliated intellectual, whereas no true intellectual could be affiliated with much of anything because he is far too much the private, independent, cerebral investigator who is thereby worlds removed from much else. He prefers it that way, and enjoys a particularly active mental life as cogitator and theorist, set impossibly apart from the society's mainstream that is in turn seldom subjected to public judgment because the public is incapable of judgment. It is also because the public is unaware that intellectuals are lurking somewhere out there in some attic or beneath some manhole cover of their own devising. The University of Chicago anthropologist Michel-Rolph Trouillot has said the role of the intellectual is "to question over and over again what is postulated as self-evident, to disturb people's mental habits" and "to dissipate what is familiar and accepted." This contentious role all the more widens the gulf between intellectuals and the public, resulting of course in the intellectual's further disengagement and alienation from the common run of public life.

This is perhaps just as well, since the two are likely to be irreconcilable. The public is still grappling with dead-and-buried controversies surrounding Darwin's work. The best course of action is for intellectuals to continue being intellectuals without soiling their hands with any further public controversies. Not to do so merely re-ignites a tendency toward misanthropy, something easy enough for intellectuals to acquire. Accordingly, intellectuals have no geographic place to hide and precious few to protect them. Edward Bulwer-Lytton, the all-but forgotten nineteenth century satirist and public dandy, wrote in his *Pelham, or Adventures of a Gentleman* (1828) that "Genius did not save Milton from poverty and blindness — nor Tasso from the madhouse — nor Galileo from the inquisition; they were the sufferers; but posterity the gainers." They and their intellectual successors have learned to use anonymity and reclusiveness as merely another shield from the added threat of public outrage. In other words, it's one more reason to remain resolutely in life's shadows. Public life has variously ignored and deserted him anyway, so he has no better place to travel with his intellectual baggage but into the solitude that breeds still more alienation. So it is that intellectuals, had they not enough on their hands, are constantly targets of intellectual jealousy. The American novelist Nelson Algren remarked "the avocation of assessing the failures of better men can be turned into a comfortable livelihood, providing you back it up with a Ph.D." The popular Scottish children's writer Kenneth Grahame (1859–1932), we are reliably told, passed up an Oxford education thanks to an uncle who had assumed the role of his guardian. Grahame later wrote with a certain acerbic mockery that "The clever men at Oxford/ Know all that there is to be knowed./ But they none of them know one half as much/ As intelligent Mr. Toad." So too, the American poet e.e. cummings wrote, "Humanity I love you because/ when you're hard up you pawn your/ intelligence to buy a drink."

Then too, intellectualism is self-alienating, since others are easily, sometimes too easily, intimidated. The result is all the more likely to separate intellectuals from everyone else, although it must be reemphasized that intellectuals thrive on their sense of separateness. It causes them to renounce societal superficiality and pettiness all the more. Aside from the ever rising tide of American anti-intellectualism that will be discussed presently, there seems to be almost unanimous confidence that intellectualism is a rare, expensive and exclusive commodity consigned to relatively few hands in American society. Maybe it is. This, for reasons not entirely clear, fails to motivate the rank and file of American citizenry who might early have embarked upon a life of solitary inquiry, but did not. They might have used their learning to cash out later, as one might cash handsomely out of some huge casino. Learning seems instead to be hastened in such a way that shortens the time and distance between mind and mouth. The intention is to learn something quickly and as a result earn quickly. One might for example apprentice to the bricklayer's trade and thereby learn and earn: acquaint oneself with bricks and mortar with sufficient speed to keep oneself employed, sheltered and fed thereafter. But this process has not the slightest similarity to an intellectual's life of continuous study, mental application and lifelong curiosity. Each life plays out in its own way. The British novelist Angus Wilson, another Oxford man, suggested that one might just as well keep it that way. There are "quite cultivated people," he said, "who would argue that you had no right to impose...any sort of cultivation upon a population which preferred to remain philistine and to use its money in philistine ways."

Intellectuals are less likely to feel the pangs (should there be any) associated with solitude, since they cannot very well be punished for enjoying the same blessed seclusion they themselves have sought and jealously protected. "My solitude," John Keats said, "is sublime." So it is, therefore, that the intelligentsia lives a life substantially different from the rest of American society. Furthermore, their paths seldom intersect, their minds seldom meet, their times never coincide. Intellectuals have a tendency to view their intellectuality as "normal," and therefore find non-intellectuals strangely limited. This circumstance, of course, occasions even more distance between intellectuals and the rest of the world, and causes them to make a career (so to speak) out of alienation.

Intellectuals, almost always, *de rigueur*, acquire a Doctor of Philosophy degree, a Ph.D., that ordinarily has little or no formal connection to the systematic study of philosophy but which is rather a scholar's public certification. Whereas you don't need to be Jewish to enjoy Levy's Kosher Rye, it helps. Whereas you don't need to arm yourself with a Ph.D. to pass yourself off as an intellectual, it helps. You don't have to be especially bright, but that helps, too. Obviously, not all Ph.D.s are intellectuals, nor care to be, nor are able to be. Furthermore, Ph.D.s are unknown quantities and qualities, meaning that they're all the more difficult to evaluate, since the breadth and depth of their learning remains a puzzle. We presume that any M.D. understands certain principles of medicine; any J.D. certain principles of jurisprudence. One can't be altogether certain that every Ph.D. can find his way to the mens' room, however. We once encountered a chap with a Ph.D. in philosophy to whom we raised a rather commonplace question about Plato. He responded by saying that he had never read Plato, which caused us to wonder what in blazes he had studied. Ph.D.s in "education" are generally understood to be appallingly substandard, as are Ed.D.s, something that, Mencken wrote, "American schools of pedagogics dispense to their inmates too inept for a Ph.D., even in 'Education.'"

Truman Capote said that whereas some people are born bastards, others earn it on their own. Likewise, some Ph.D.s were loners before they acquired the degree; others became loners as a result of it since, as we know, what we might call "extreme studies" have the potential to drive a person mad or into hermetic seclusion or both. Pursuing the degree is what one might call a "personal experience," in that most of the work is a private undertaking and to be sure hermetic in nature, probably thrashed out alone in huge book-saturated academic libraries. This is a strangely satisfying experience for loners, since rather little socializing happens inside libraries, and since one does not normally speak to anyone. Of course one does, in the course of human events, register for courses, but in graduate schools the attention is upon the subject at hand rather than upon the person in the next classroom seat who, chances are, is not of a pronouncedly social disposition anyway. Since academic courses have their limitations, one tends gradually to take charge of his own education, which is probably one of the earliest definitive gestures toward becoming an "intellectual."

There are extremely unforeseen and unfortunate sides to intellectual adventuring, one being that acquiring a doctorate can easily cascade into a political morass involving the various personalities and predispositions. Some of the professoriat may happen to like certain students and wish them well, others not. Quite often they don't care for each other, a circumstance that can have serious implications for a student's academic prospects. There is also a certain amount of hazing (yes, hazing) that takes the form of someone's earnestly telling students after a couple of graduate school years that they know nothing, and that they're not to forget that they know nothing. True, any intelligent person, except a few with fragile egos, will with humility candidly admit the obvious: that even by his own estimate he knows virtually nothing. In the midst of this studying students may be told that if they can't perform better, they may consider some other line of work. It is, one would suppose, rather like a Marine drill sergeant's in-your-face message that you'll never be a Marine. The intention is to discourage and dishearten, to cause students to develop self-doubt and a diminished sense of self-esteem. With that much understood, there is the customary university insistence upon a demonstrated reading comprehension of two, sometimes three, "foreign" languages such as German, French and Latin. The benefits are civilizing, although a candidate may be required to spend a year learning how to assume some control over those languages, the better now and again to pepper his prose with cunningly appropriate Latin phrases. One learns along the way that he can on occasion trust his intuition over the things he reads. Emerson,

with characteristic irony, warned in "The American Scholar" against over in-
dulgence in books, reminding us that, "Meek young men grow up in libraries,
believing it their duty to accept the views which Cicero, which Locke, which
Bacon, have given; forgetful that Cicero, Locke and Bacon were only young
men in libraries when they wrote these books." One of the more threatening
sides to acquiring a Ph.D. is that the success or failure of these four to six
years spent with Cicero, Locke, Bacon and a few hundred other young men
in libraries finds its climax in four or five days of examinations, the outcome
of which determines whether one measures up for the doctorate—or not. It
sometimes happens that a person fails his examinations simply because he
is perceived by the faculty to be too arrogantly confident. At this juncture,
many students, including the stronger ones, become disheartened and leave
the university without the degree. Others register at a different university
to complete their work. There is no reliable way to estimate how many dis-
continue their studies, although it's been estimated at 50 percent, about the
same percentage as failed American marriages. Others force themselves to
reconstitute, return in six months or so, and retry the examinations. They
may perform less well this time but are nonetheless deemed to have per-
formed sufficiently well. They are probably living on a shoestring by now,
and therefore doing without many of life's amenities. Their friends (should
they have any) and relatives are wondering when they're going to leave universities behind and find the kind of normal employment that normal people
normally find.

It's a little late for that. They are also under obligation to submit a more
or less publishable book-sized manuscript, sometimes in more than one volume, although probably no one will publish it because it is likely to be too
impossibly abstruse and too irrelevant. Dissertations are written under du-
ress and there is no way to avoid them. One's mentors read them, or say they
do, and request certain alterations in its content as part of the doctoral rite
of passage. There is a high probability that years later the doctoral recipient
cannot to save his soul recall precisely what his dissertation had to say. It
is also probable that whatever it said could just as well be distilled into a
brief article and published in some middlebrow journal that almost nobody
reads. A chap named James Dobie quipped that "The average Ph.D. thesis
is nothing but there transference of bones from one graveyard to another."
The next thing to do is "defend" those sere bones before a panel of university
professors, not all of whom come from the candidate's discipline. In reality,
the defense is not so awfully difficult, since no one knows (or cares) more
about that arcane subject under scrutiny than does its author. Nevertheless,

the doctoral candidate finds himself ambushed with questions intended to undermine whatever he has written, and to push the candidate off balance, possibly unprepared to respond lucidly to much of anything. But the ritual is not yet over. He will be requested to leave the room, quietly closing the door behind him, while university dons debate whether or not to recommend to the university president and the board of university trustees that the candidate be awarded a Doctor of Philosophy. Meanwhile, he paces alone (as he customarily is, and most probably shall remain) in the corridor of an old university building. Maybe 20 minutes pass and then the door opens, and out steps some scholarly-appearing chap who offers congratulations. The former candidate is now a member of the club and suddenly not anywhere near as blockheaded and incompetent as they first surmised. By this time he has had quite enough of universities. In a peevishly Parthian affront, he does not show up for graduation ceremonies. Someone calls his name, but he doesn't respond to the call. His diploma arrives in the mail, two weeks or so later, by which time he has returned to his solitary life.

Doctoral degrees invite odd and unanticipated consequences. They are especially useful for securing dinner reservations, but the heft of that much study in those four to six years, however, does not altogether fall into place for years, more likely decades. As one holder of the degree correctly said, it demands years for a doctorate to "cure," which is to say mellow and mature. Now the newly minted Ph.D. is irrevocably in a world of his own, and there is no turning back. Learning, after all is surrendering one's innocence. He is somehow "different," "apart," "estranged," "odd," "anti-social," but he's always been that way. Now it's more pronounced. There's almost nobody with whom he can converse easily, but there is also nothing new about this. Some civilians have heard about Ph.D.s, but they are unfamiliar with them, what they signify, and how one might acquire one. Ph.D.s are also common targets of jealousy, usually from people who don't have them. They're the same people who cannot distinguish M.D.s from chiropractors. Paradoxically, our new Ph.D. meanwhile begins to realize that he was not taught much in graduate school, after all. At the same time, however, his family and acquaintances, grow uneasy in his presence, and attempt to contradict every utterance he makes, the object being to illustrate that he is not as "smart" as he appears. In the next twenty years he will have learned five times more than he knew at the graduation ceremonies he did not bother to attend. He is every inch the odd duck that he is taken to be.

Where do doctorates go? Ordinarily, it remains for other universities to "take them in," which is to say provide a source of income and give them pointless work to accomplish. A Ph.D. has traditionally and ominously been referred to as the "terminal" degree, and the "union card" necessary for admission to a university faculty. While that may solve a financial problem, it raises a variety of other difficulties. One hears reports of their being an oversupply of Ph.D.s, whereas there is an undersupply of people who can afford their services. Junior and community colleges tend remorselessly toward anti-intellectualism and therefore generally rely upon persons whose education ended at the master's level, if that. Sometimes they load up on high school teaching retreads and thereby endorse some of the academic atrocities committed in those places. Meanwhile, universities expect a return on intellectual investment, and therefore place certain awkward demands upon intellectuals, such as luring them out of their monkish seclusion and placing them in the middle of what might be considered a fortress of collective intelligence. This can present problems, among them that it's necessary to be more or less civil and sociable if one is to survive from day to day in a university setting. The obstacle here is to metamorphose a loner into an affably loquacious member of a faculty. In some cases this can be accomplished; other times not. Faculty people work in the midst of other intellectual loners and misfits. There are, of course, cliques and groupers among the faculty, some of whom pass most of their campus lives exchanging leftist political opinions, gossiping, indoctrinating the naïve, and performing like nightclub comics. There are also students of various stripes and colors to shepherd through their studies and other perplexities. One is never sure how to take them. Michael White has mentioned that when C.S. Lewis encountered first year students at Oxford, his "verbal onslaughts were unnerving" because he initially "expected too much from his young charges," although he "later tended to accept them with ironic reservation." By whatever the means, teaching needs to be properly accomplished, but it's also time consuming and unconscionably inefficient. Intellectuals don't react well to having their time wasted, meaning among other things that they resent pressure to lend their support to inconsequential committees and irrelevant meetings that dot the days of must faculty types. Universities are also hotbeds of mental and emotional maladies, and other behavioral instabilities that come with being a late adolescent, as most students are. Hence the intellectual soon finds that he has temporarily rented out his body and soul to some supposedly greater good, that being the education of a new generation of Americans. Nevertheless, the intellectual is left to do the best he can in what are basically impossible conditions, such as turn up for receptions and faculty get-togethers, social things that he is quite obviously unable and therefore unwilling to perform ably. His plan therefore is to manage his courses (as few as possible), keep a few office hours and disappear. There was once a professor at the University of Iowa who occupied a small office with a large window that opened at ground level. On one occasion he was hotly pursued by a gaggle of students that he temporarily eluded by hurriedly repairing to that office, securing the door, hoisting the window and vanishing over the campus lawn. When the students discovered that his office door was secured and that no one responded from within, they inquired of another faculty person what had become of Professor X. "He has made," the faculty person responded with feigned dignity, "a fenestral escape."

Precisely. Many an intellectual would have made his fenestral escape had there been a fenestra from which it could be accomplished. Many of the professorate secretly believe, but never say, that if it were not for the students, university life could become rather pleasant. There is something to be said for that, inasmuch as not all of those who appear to be students are actually worthy of that name. This is not so much a reflection upon their mentality as it is their disarming lack of commitment to a life devoted to learning that reaches well beyond university walls and campuses and continues for as long as they shall survive. The ideal circumstance is to manage no courses at all but to hole up inconspicuously in a seldom-visited *sanctum sanctorum* of a library, culling notes and other essentials for that next book he has been deliciously contemplating. To do this he would need to pull the plug on provosts, deans, department chairs who — never having taught very well, nor published anything, nor conceived of an original idea — are now supervising and policing a few faculty who have handily accomplished all of that. The next step toward the improvement of university life will be to end all remnants of unsolicited social activity. Universities, after all, are not social clubs; therefore one need not participate in anything remotely construed as merely convivial. In the meantime, it may be remotely possible that a faculty person may, however unwittingly, have accomplished something that would justify his presence there in the first place, such as playing some crucial role in developing the outcasts of tomorrow, the freaks of the future, the geeks of the great divide that separates the intellectuals from the intellectual pretenders.

Universities have other pernicious problems with which true intellectuals emphatically want no involvement. One of them is the ephebic presence of secret societies to which we have referred earlier, in that (say what they will) such groups have done nothing to foster intellectual life in a setting ostensibly committed to the life of the mind. To the contrary, it is astonishing that any of its adolescent members can grope their way to a baccalaureate. Another is the trend toward indoctrination rather than responsible instruction, a problem to which we have referred. Worst of all is discovering a place to park an automobile, assuming that one has something with which to park. The denial of a parking place may be interpreted as a university's saying that it does not solicit your presence, and will not, therefore, make it possible to enter its mighty fortress that consists of endless roadblocks, real and symbolic. In some places faculty members are accorded the best of what little parking may exist, followed by graduate students, seniors, juniors, sophomores, freshman and what roving interlopers may show up. The general impression is that guests are not especially welcome except of course tinhorn politicians (another redundancy), corporations and other wealthy parties willing to leave large sums of money to be wasted by the incompetent types who mismanage most universities by layering them with large numbers of committee-loving dolts who are not only unnecessary, but counterproductive.

The long and the short of all this is that intellectuals ordinarily want no involvement with the nemeses universities are, mostly because of less than ideal circumstances enumerated here. To be sure, there is not an abundance of intellectuals in universities. They would much prefer not to be one of the so called "public intellectuals" to which we have referred, but "private intellectuals," the meaning of which is anything one wants it to mean, most likely that one is, as the words say clearly, to be privately intellectual without being trapped in a bustling university or packed off a mental hospital devoted to the rehabilitation of persons with politically unpopular views. The true intellectual continues to exhibit unmistakable Platonic characteristics, chief among them what has been called "the harmony of the human soul with the universe of ideas," a more than rhapsodic expression meaning that one prefers living more in the realm of pure ideas than in the mundanity of life as it is ordinarily lived on bustling university campuses. This may sound suspiciously like an impossibly high-toned way through life, but it does aspire, at the very least, to apply the mind toward the best and highest of aims of contemplation. "The safest general characterization of the European philosophical tradition," Alfred North Whitehead long ago observed, "is that it consists of a series of footnotes to Plato." Whitehead, we need hardly say, was a highly contemplative university man himself, having taught both mathematics and philosophy at Harvard.

Be it in Cambridge or anywhere else, there is the problem of perpetual assignment to tasks that are bound to rub the intellectuals the wrong way. Many of them detest university life, which is entirely understandable, and yet university life provides a decent income and other amenities that make it perhaps at times too comfortable. Russell Jacoby reminds us in *The Last Intellectuals: American Culture in the Age of Academe* (1987) that "intellectuals born at the turn of the century — Lewis Mumford (1895-), Dwight Macdonald (1906-82), Edmund Wilson, (1895-1972) — represent classical American intellectuals [who] never or rarely taught in universities." Compared to other kinds of employment, it's quite easy and it requires relatively little time — once you're safely inside the system and have developed durable sets of lecture notes. The tribulations attached to earning the union card of acceptability, however, do not mark the end of other problems attached to university survival. Those in a position to hire candidates waste no time asking how many learned books and papers one has published in the six months since receiving the degree and thereby "joining the club." Loners, obviously, don't join clubs, but nonetheless find themselves obliged to appear, at least, like the team players they aren't. Jeffrey Theis noted recently that "social exchanges, or the lack of thereof, in the department mail room are an apt metaphor for the state of collegiality in academic." One might be well advised to turn up at every cocktail party just to be on the safe side. Not to do this will eventually show up on one's paycheck. In the absence of tenure, one's employment is always tenuous. Some universities used to hire three candidates with the intention of retaining one. Retention has mostly to do with tenure, an outdated but cherished custom in academic life that awards what amounts to lifetime employment in one's academic department, i.e., one's fraternity. Tenure is durable. One may even be discovered in an erotically compromising position with the dean's wife — and get away with it. Stranger things have happened. Over the years, tenured people have somehow gotten away with some embarrassingly nefarious activities. Over the decades, on the other hand, many an excellent prospect has been denied tenure, while just as many thoroughly improbable (variously disagreeable, overbearing, lazy, obsequious, pretentious, posturing and outright stupid) blowhards have received tenure, subsequent promotions, accolades and money. Receiving tenure rests upon being liked, or even "well-liked," to borrow a silly expression from Arthur Miller's emphatically not silly American classic *Death of a Salesman*. The whole system invites comparison with the insidious and superannuated undergraduate fraternity mentality located perhaps a precarious block or two from one's academic department.

Make no mistake: universities are for professors, just as hospitals are for physicians. They have become corporations, something that intellectuals seem instinctively to despise. But caught they are, in spite of their sometimes highly independent ways, in the web of a corporation, although they can still retire to their offices and off-campus garrets. Many of them perform the best they can in classrooms, but those classrooms introduce problems and liabilities of their own. Students complain frequently and even claim to understand more about the academic subjects at hand than does the professoriat. True, the content of coursework, and the evaluation of it, is subjective and therefore always open to question. Salary increases, absurdly enough, are often tied to student approval/disapproval ratings, but this has been known to cut two ways, depending upon whether one is liked or well liked, or neither one, by those incompetents who parcel money (usually public money) out. Suppose a certain professor has overwhelmingly high student ratings. This may be interpreted to mean that he's doing an outstanding job, and therefore deserves a ten percent raise in salary, mostly because he's well liked. It may also be interpreted to mean that he has compromised standards and handed out absurdly liberal grades, and therefore deserves no wage increase at all. This signifies that he's not liked.

Traditionally, students (what relatively few there are) enter collegiate life at about the age of 18, and receive their diplomas at about the age of 22 when they are still cursed with relatively late childhood, something that potentially causes problems for everyone in the academy. That is entirely to be expected, and there's nothing to be done about it. They may have to wait well beyond the age of 30 to exhibit incipient signals of maturity. In the meantime, universities may rightly be viewed a huge babysitting organizations. Therefore, the newly-minted Ph.D. becomes not only part of a fraternity; he is also babysitter to the eternal immaturity of undergraduates, many of whom are fond of passionate flag-brandishing causes, most of them a little left of center, that are apt to result in public demonstrations that invariably surface in April. Ergo, should you notice students storming the president's stately mansion beneath the watchful eyes of riot police, and you don't happen to possess a calendar, you know that it must be spring. There are not demonstrations in say, September, October and November when the heated *causes célèbres* of the previous April have vanished like the snows of yesteryear.

Schools of "education" have given teaching an irretrievably bad name, and therefore certain members of the intelligentsia bristle if they hear themselves called "teacher," since it is a pejorative term that belittles serious scholarship and research and seems to infer that one spends his times showing people how to dot their i's. To them a teacher is a teacher. Only that. He's an imbecile who believes he can teach people things despite his knowing nothing.

Scholars, if the truth were known, would rather not bother with that, inasmuch as one can just as well learn fundamentals by reading the right books. If these scholars happen to be the loner-intellectuals to whom we have been referring, they will be especially disinclined to address crowded classrooms. "Coaching" is quite another thing. Suppose a student wants to perfect his skill at playing the violin. When he has problems or questions, he takes them up with a virtuoso who can respond person to person. Loners and other solitary, inner-directed types generally understand that one teaches oneself and that sitting in classrooms is no match for sitting in libraries or, as we have said, resolving troublesome questions by consulting a scholar or some other authority who actually understands what he is talking about.

Somewhere out there in the gathering clouds of the horizon is the ongoing menace of anti intellectualism (a term made popular in the 1950s) in American culture. It is a problem excellently examined by historian Richard Hofstadter in his *Anti-Intellectualism in American Life* (1966) a timeless volume that should be read by nearly everyone, particularly social and cultural historians, sociologists, academicians and other intellectuals. Anti-intellectualism has a long, interesting and complicated history that still courses menacingly through American culture. Anti-intellectuals place more credence upon dunces than dons, so much so that in 1936 University of Chicago president Robert Hutchins predicted the high demand for vocational schools would result in anti-intellectual universities, something that makes about as much sense as anti-religious houses of worship, although such places probably exist. Hofstadter notes that some of the so-called "inspirational cults" have even "eliminated doctrine." Paradox that it is, anti-intellectual universities are indeed with us, pandering more to the practical than the philosophical. This has largely come about through perceived public demand that has little or no commitment to intellectual discovery. If the public wants a bachelor's degree in dogfood technology, by George it shall have it. Hofstadter said that "Whenever intellectuals 'become absorbed into the accredited institutions of society," they gradually relinquish what he calls the "cult of alienation," Moreover, Hofstadter wrote, "they not only lose their traditional rebelliousness but to one extent or another *they cease to function as intellectuals.*" In other words, intellectuals have been known to back down, something toward which Loren Baritz angrily responded, "Any intellectual who accepts and approves of his society prostitutes his skills and is a traitor to his heritage."

What we discover today is public hostility toward anything even loosely associated with the intellect: grammar schools, high schools, vocational schools, colleges, universities, scholars, professors, libraries, writers, intellectuals, academic degrees, caps, gowns and so forth. In southern Ohio recently, folks gathered to celebrate the destruction of an elementary school. Nearby, a university built a regional campus over what had been a landfill, then systematically destroyed it from within through indiscriminate admission policies and decades of egregious mismanagement. The public likes diplomas but detests studies. Most people read no books, speak badly, write not at all, drop out of educational programs, evade studies, do whatever they can to avoid learning anything, even conspire to derail courses of study. Intellectuals, particularly reclusive ones, obviously want no part of them, and devise ways of urging them out of classrooms where they are tuition-paying dead weight. There are relatively subtle ways of hastening their departure. If ten percent among his enrollees are students, one can nudge the other 90 percent of enrollees out the door — which is perfectly all right, provided they leave their tuition money and close the door gently. Meanwhile, absenteeism in university classrooms is epidemic; resistance to learning is prevalent. Henry Bauer, in a 1996 paper entitled "The New Generations: Students Who Don't Study," reports that "A T-shirt sold at Duke University proudly announces, 'You can lead me to college, but you can't make me think.'" One recent graduate from a California university boasted that he had spent four years there "without cracking a book." Thus, conditions are more than anti-intellectual; they, like Greek letter organizations, constitute an attempt to turn university campuses into playgrounds. Enrollees (we can't call them students) drop out, flunk out, wander away and disappear. While this is happening, the better university professors are busily educating themselves, which is something that they would far more prefer to do. They read more; they write more. This is perhaps the best aspect of university involvement, granting that the university involvement is emphatically where a private intellectual wants to find himself as solitary private intellectual. You teach yourself and are paid for it. No one else seems to want learning. Thus it is that Ph.D.s contentedly continue practicing the study habits they have acquired. Adolescent rioters, meanwhile, pursue whatever happens to be the riot-worthy adolescent passion of the day.

In another paper, this one authored by Paul Trout at Montana State University and titled "Student Anti-intellectualism and the Dumbing Down of the University" (1997), Trout cites numerous manifestations of anti-intellectual behavior among enrollees, to wit: not reading, not contributing, not attending, not preparing, not consulting material placed on library reserve or received as handouts, not doing more than the minimum, not learning more than the minimum, not observing academic requirements, not respect-

ing real students, not respecting anything that smacks of "higher education." Trout correctly observes that "Nobody can say precisely how many
anti-intellectual students [sic] now sit in college classrooms, but the number
appears to be growing and in some contexts seems to have reached a critical
mass," whatever that may mean. He also cites a Virginia Polytechnic philosophy professor who reports, "A majority of students is more or less dis-
affected and an alarming number (10 percent? 15 percent?) seem positively
alienated," claiming that "unprecedented numbers [of enrollees] rarely come
to class, have not read the material and have scant interest in learning it." A
former English professor in the eastern sector of the country commented,
"Most students nowadays are reluctant to learn and to think and resent being
awakened from their stupor." Lawrence Steinberg has written that campus
anti-intellectualism carries with it "enormous implications and profound
consequences." Another philosophy professor, this one at Syracuse University, asked how many of his 280 students had prepared for class. When 18
said they had, he walked out of class and paid $111 for an advertisement in
the school newspaper, complaining that they had displayed "more indifference than I would have thought possible."

Trout himself feels that "American colleges could follow the same path
as American high schools and become warehouses of anti-intellectual and
anti-educational slackers," suggesting that in the future, "a battle will be
waged between institutions where enrollees meet their prescribed performance challenges, and those that will instead dumb down to accomodate the
lowest common denominator." Speaking of slackers, a fellow named Mark
Noble in Peterborough, Ontario defines the slacker as "someone who wants
to succeed, and has every intention of doing so, but due to the mitigating
circumstances of life and a combination of counter-productive personality
traits, they [sic] rarely meet the goals they set out." The *OED* calls it "a person
who shirks work, or avoids exertion, exercise." Trout also reminds us, as if
we need reminding, that large numbers of bodies mean large numbers of dollars and large numbers of salaries paid to large numbers of people. J.E. Stone,
in an essay called "Inflated Grades, Inflated enrollment, and Inflated Budgets: An Analysis and Call for Review at the State Level" (1995), notes that
managerial types keep track of credit hours, but not how much (if anything)
enrollees learn, simply because there is "no economic incentive to do so,"
concluding that "enrollment-driven funding weakens commitment to high
academic standards." Stone also mentions, ominously, that "there is great
incentive for faculty collectively to support the administrative emphasis on
growth," i.e., the insidious practice of dumbing down.

Consequently, bureaucracies and herd mentalities have captured and de-filed universities, as if anti-intellectual secret societies and armies of dunces have not left anything behind to ruin. The private intellectual finds no benev-olent reception in them and is all the more alienated. But, on the other hand, since alienation is his stock-in-trade, a convenient excuse for him to vanish into possibly arcane intellectual pursuits all the more, forswearing any al-legiance to these failed bastions of supposedly higher learning. Hofstadter reminds us that "a self-conscious concern with alienation, far from being peculiar to American intellectuals of our time, has been a major theme in the life of the intellectual communities of the Western world for almost two centuries," saying also that various circumstances have led them "into a sharp and often uncomfortable confrontation with the mind of the middle class." Robert Hutchens was not only correct in predicting that the anti-intellectual university was looming, but that — to take the brighter view — for the enlightened, a liberal education "frees a man from the prison-house of his class, race, time place, background and even his nation."

All this is undeniably so. We might add that whereas the intellectual as creative loner has been undermined by insufferable university and social life, he has little choice to break from the prison-house of his condition and allow his life to assume its own shape. Numerous intellectuals of different times, talents and circumstances have reasonably well managed to evade banality altogether, among them Marcel Proust who, though he circulated freely in, and wrote freely about, the some of the more select salons of French society, nonetheless retired behind the famous cork-lined walls of his Parisian apart-ment to compose himself. Proust's eccentricities are legend. His biographer Jean-Yves Tadié has written that his subject "was a recluse in his [fumigat-ed] bedroom most of the time, used to wear long-johns and socks and shawls knitted from Pyrenean wool." He directed that, as partial protection from the asthma attacks that tormented him, his clothing be heated in an oven. "At his feet," Tadié notes, "were small jugs of boiling water." Fearing drafts, "he had a sheet nailed to his bedroom wall." He is believed to have worked by night, retired at around eight in the morning, and slept fully dressed, some-times attired in gloves. His breakfasts were the same: "three croissants, café au lait boiling hot and steaming, eggs in béchamel sauce, fried potatoes and stewed fruit." Proust visited male brothels to witness men flogged at their own request and survived a procession of alluring mistresses. His astonish-ing seven-volume *Remembrance of Things Past*, arguably the finest experiment in 20th century fiction (at the beginning of which he devotes 50 pages to recounting his difficulty falling asleep without first having his mother kiss him) has been so exquisitely rendered as to be "uncriticizable." Not surprisingly, he had difficulty securing publishers, as had independently-inclined Flaubert and Joyce, and ended by underwriting his own publications.

Asserting one's identity obviously has its penalties, but to do so is infinitely greater than proceeding to one's grave without having achieved the fullest of self-realization. As an extraordinary American lyric poet, arguably the best at her art, Emily Dickinson created an enduring place for herself not only in American letters but in world literature. Notwithstanding, her grave is behind a Mobil filling station in Amherst, Massachusetts. She deserved better. Her weather-ravaged headstone reads:

Emily Dickinson
Born
Dec. 10. 1830
Called Back
May 15, 1886

Like Proust, Dickinson survives as one of the most public of intensely private, inner-motivated, literary personalities, this one at best indifferent to the publishing of her work. She and Whitman, different as they are in virtually every poetical aspect, survive as the two wild cards, the two shining beacons in 19th century American verse. As someone said, in her day women were supposed to inspire poems, not write them. Some of the Emily Dickinson legend is less than accurate, although it bears repeating because it captures at least an essence of truth. Her world, infinite thought it assuredly was, was at the same time limited to what she could view from her bedroom window. Another popular notion was that she could not tell time. And when Dickinson attended a seminary overseen by the formidable women's education advocate Mary Lyon, Emily refused to "rise" on an occasion when Miss Lyon requested that all young women in her charge who wished to be Christians identify themselves by stepping forward. She held her ground. Her biographer Richard B. Sewall comments that she was known there as "all intellect" and "always first in her class," and has usually been regarded as outwardly obedient and inwardly rebellious. Dickinson ended her formal studies, recording in a letter that she was "cheered by the thought that I am not to return another year," after having embraced "many of the girls" she encountered there. Later in life Dickinson invited guests to perform musical recitals, but listened to that music while concealed behind a door set ajar in the upper rooms of the Dickinson family home in Amherst. Under the care of her sister Lavinia, she became evermore reclusive with age. On one celebrated occasion she allegedly dressed in bridal white and stepped out, at night, to view a church then under construction. A family friend reported that Dickinson "shut herself away from her race as a mark of her separation from the mass of minds." She viewed herself as "standing alone in rebellion," referring to herself as "the cow-lily," and claiming to be mentally "as quick as a trout." Much of her verse is captured, with a gentle cynicism, and partly for mnemonic reasons, in "hymn meters" (any of three or so metrical combinations used in popular Protestant songbooks). The result is a new secular series of poetical signals and messages packaged in old shells. Sewall prefaces his biography with certain caveats about Dickinson's personal nature, especially questioning whether her extraordinary privacy was the result of "deliberate planning" or other "compulsive forces," matters that little concern most literary critics but hold some interest for psychological inquiry. Thomas Wentworth Higginson, a Civil War military figure closely implicated in the poet's life, remarked after meeting her that "she was much too enigmatical a being for me to solve in an hour's interview, and an instinct told me that the slightest attempt at direct cross examination would make her withdraw into her shell."

"Each age," Emerson wrote, "must write its own books." A new wave of American writers, some of whom share some of the reclusively inward habits of Dickinson and Proust, have composed some of those books. America's professional literary recluse from the 1950s has been Jerome David Salinger, whose solitary habits found a place for him in the pages of *The New Yorker*, *The New York Times*, *Esquire*, *Newsweek*, *Life* and on the cover of *Time*, primarily for having published five remarkable books: *The Catcher in the Rye* (1951), *Nine Stories* (1953), *Franny and Zooey* (1961), *Raise High the Roof Beam, Carpenters* and *Seymour: An Introduction* (1963). Salinger has determinedly fought off his wives and his once worldwide readership in a long series of nasty incidents apparently intended jealously to protect his privacy, something that he has every right to protect. He had, however, passed some extremely non-private years at Valley Forge Military Academy, New York University (a year), and Ursinus College in Pennsylvania (a semester). His 1941 fling with Oona O'Neill, the debutante daughter of playwright Eugene O'Neill had, however, not nudged him into anonymity, either, nor had his years with the US 12th Infantry with which he confronted the enemy at the Battle of the Bulge and at Utah Beach on D-Day. Asked by a civilian what his initials, J.D., signified, he replied, "juvenile delinquent." Salinger had his generous share of regimented life, and did not care for it, so much so that he has since become more or less invisible — the proper thing for a person absorbed in his work which at its best centers upon young people and other innocents.

It appeared for a time that *The Catcher in the Rye* would make Salinger a one-book solitary celebrity, something that may have happened to Nelle Harper Lee, an intellectually emancipated product (like her childhood friend Truman Capote) of Monroeville, Alabama. Lee enrolled at the University of Alabama's law college, became an exchange student at Oxford University, and in time wrote three particularly seminal sentences: "Mockingbirds don't do one thing but make music for us to enjoy. They don't eat up people's gardens, don't nest in corncribs, they don't do one thing but sing their hearts out for us. That's why it's a sin to kill a mockingbird." One is tempted to say that Harper Lee didn't do one thing except to author, at age 34, *To Kill a Mockingbird* (1961). That would not be fair to say, however, since the book won a Pulitzer in 1961, sold an estimated 10,000,000 copies in numerous languages, and also provided a Southern narrative that allowed Gregory Peck to portray the character of Atticus Finch on the screen. She, in the meantime, satisfied the hearts and minds of Hollywood with a passage that would warm the hearts of inner-directed, independently-minded people everywhere: "But there is one way in this country in which all men are created equal — there is one human institution that makes a pauper the equal of a Rockefeller, the stupid man the equal of an Einstein." She continued, "That institution, gentlemen, is a court. It can be the Supreme Court of the United States or the humblest J.P. court in the land, or this honorable court which you serve. Our courts have their faults, as does any human institution, but in this country our courts are the great levelers, and in our courts all men are created equal."

One of Miss Lee's endearing qualities is, according to reports, her apparent self-effacing refusal to say much of anything to anybody these days. On the occasion of a reception at the president's mansion at the University of Alabama, *The New York Times* referred to her as "one of the most reclusive writers in the history of American letters." *The Times* reported that during a book signing, "a little girl in a velvet dress approached Ms. Lee with a hardback copy of 'To Kill a Mockingbird,' announcing that her name was Harper. 'Well, that's my name too,' Ms. Lee said. The girl's mother, LaDonnah Roberts, said that she had decided to make her daughter Ms. Lee's namesake during her pregnancy." This was on the occasion of a children's essay contest that Miss Lee had stipulated would be limited to those who were (interestingly enough) home-schooled. In January 2007, at the age of 80, she did make an appearance at a high school in Montgomery, Alabama, on the occasion of a theatrical rendering of her novel. The primary role in the play fell to a young man named Joseph Williams, possibly the only black student at Fairfield High Preparatory School, who accepted the assignment with some hesitancy and profited from what has been described as a "life-changing experience." Following the performance, Miss Lee accepted a piece of pottery designated as a "unity vessel" on behalf of the Alabama State Council of the Arts. She then posed with the cast and crew, received what was reported to be a "standing ovation," but had nothing to say except to some of the students, with whom she met privately. The performance had taken place at the Davis Theater that, also according to locals, is across a street from a bus stop where Rosa Parks refused to surrender her seat to a white man 51 years before. The following November Miss Lee, then 81, received America's highest civilian honor, the Presidential Medal of Freedom bestowed by President Bush *pere*, and thereafter returned to Monroeville where she has been living with her 90-something year old sister Alice, also an attorney.

Possibly the King Kong of reclusive American literary figures is the greater than mysterious Thomas Ruggles Pynchon author of such better known (among *literati*) pieces as *V* (1963), *The Crying of Lot 49* (1966), *Gravity's Rainbow* (1973), *Slow Learner* (1984), *Vineland* (1990), *Mason & Dixon* (1997) and *Against the Day* (2006). Believed to have been born in 1937 at Glen Cove, New York. Pynchon went to extraordinary lengths to conceal his whereabouts (rumored to be in Mexico at times, northern California at others) and jealously secure his privacy. He has been the object of reckless and sometimes ludicrous speculations, as for example rumors of his being the elusive Unibomber or even J.D. Salinger. These frivolous investigations, have been encouraged further by his refusal to be photographed, interviewed, questioned and so forth. There is reason to assumed that he is a recovering joiner, as evidenced by his having been in the U.S. Navy (a photograph of him at around the age of 20 has him, if it is indeed he, in a sailor's suit); by having enrolled at Cornell and Berkeley; by his employment at Boeing; and by his participation in the sixties west coast countercultural movement. Notwithstanding, Pyncheon has, over the years, collected serious literary accolades such as a MacArthur Fellowship, National Book Award, William Dean Howells Medal from the American Academy of Arts and Letters, Richard and Hilda Rosenthal Foundation Award of the National Institute of Arts and Letters, a John D. and Catherine T. MacArthur Fellowship (believed to be worth $330,000 over five years), and consideration for a Nobel Prize, although Nobel Prizes, political in the worst sense of the word, have been "awarded" to more than a few ridiculous recipients. CNN called him (with Churchillian revival rhetoric), "an enigma shrouded in mystery veiled in anonymity," that qualified him as "the Greta Garbo of American Letters." Writer Andrew Gordon, who knew Pynchon at Berkeley, has written that according to Pynchon's friend Jules Siegel, "When Pynchon lived in Mexico in the sixties, the Mexicans laughed at his mustache and called him Pancho Villa." Continuing, "There's a hoary old joke whose punch line goes, 'Did I know Pancho Villa? Hombre, we had lunch together!' Mine goes, 'Did I know Thomas Pynchon? Man, we smoked dope together!' Except it's no joke; it really happened." As recently as November 2006, Adam Kirsch of *The New York Sun* remarked, "Thomas Pynchon is known as the most seductively difficult of living novelists. He has the kind of following that only a bearer of esoteric knowledge can attract — not just readers, but disciples."

Such are eccentric examples of free-spirited creative loners at their free spirited, creative and productive best. One could, as we have seen, do far worse, and become like most of the people one encounters, morphed into outer-directed dead souls merely scratching directionless from one day to the next as if trapped in a darkened closet. But excellent freedom arises out of certain inner radar and a profound belief in oneself that one need not much more than speak to anyone else. Joseph Wood Krutch once remarked, "To have passed though life and never experienced solitude is never to have known oneself. To have never known oneself is to have never known anyone." We have been looking into writers and their craft because theirs, like a painter's, is executed alone in splendid seclusion, without committees. There are no layers of phony authority, no meetings, no walk-throughs, no performance reviews, no water fountain politics, no clock-punching hours, no jammed highways and parking meters. Mati Unt in *Things in the Night* has observed that Kierkegaard "did not care for large public events because every crowd is in itself an untruth. The only way is isolation, aloofness, Only the individual is a reality and only the individual is true," continuing, "Is not the whole point of this world for people to separate and become individuals?" Picasso, who apparently thought so, said, "without great solitude no serious work is possible."

This is not necessarily to suggest that behind high-flown rhetoric praising individuality's cult there are not distressing consequences, among them mental and emotional problems and, of course, alcohol. In 1988 there appeared a particularly informative small volume entitled *Alcohol and the Writer* composed by Donald Goodwin, M.D., then chairman of the University of Kansas Medical Center's Department of Psychiatry. Dr. Goodwin, as it turned out, knew a thing or two about medicine and about literature, having been an undergraduate "English" major close to those who wrote literary criticism and poetry, having studied with none other than the critic Lionel Trilling and the poet W.H. Auden. Not until the age of 29 did he enter medical school. His hypothesis is that among well-recognized American writers in the first half of the 20th century, an alarming proportion was in the clutches of alcoholism. The inevitable reaction to this hypothesis is the assertion that hard drinking pervades all occupations. Goodwin argued, in turn, that after bartenders, writers most often die from cirrhosis of the liver, the disease most often linked to alcoholism, than any other occupations, with postmen ranking last. Anecdotally, Goodwin points out that 70 percent of Americans who won a Nobel Prize in literature were alcoholics. In his own words, "first there was Sinclair Lewis — very alcoholic. Then came Eugene O'Neill — very alcoholic. Next was Pearl Buck, who hardly drank. Then followed William Faulkner — very alcoholic. Then Ernest Hemingway — alcoholic ('Drinking is a way of ending the day,' said Ernest). John Steinbeck comes next — a 'two-fisted' drinker by some accounts, alcoholic by others." As to Saul Bellow, Goodwin comments, "Jews, like women, are 'protected' against alcoholism...for reasons one can only guess at." He continues by presenting a list of putatively alcoholic American writers, namely Poe, Edwin Arlington Robinson, Ambrose Bierce, Theodore Dreiser, Hart Crane, Sinclair Lewis, Eugene O'Neill, Edna St. Vincent Millay, Dorothy Parker, F. Scott Fitzgerald, Ring Lardner, Hemingway, John O'Hara, Faulkner, Steinbeck, Dashiell Hammett, Thomas Wolfe, John Berryman, J.P. Marquand, Wallace Stevens, e.e. cummings, Theodore Roethke, Edmund Wilson, James Thurber, Jack London, Tennessee Williams, Truman Capote, William Inge, Robert Benchley, Jack Kerouac, O. Henry (William Sydney Porter), Finley Peter Dunne, John Cheever, Conrad Aiken, Robert Ruark, William Saroyan, Irwin Shaw, Delmore Schwartz, Robert Lowell, Randall Jarrell, Jean Stafford, James Agee, Ralph Maloney, Raymond Chandler," and according to its nonalcoholic drama critic Brendan Gill, "almost every writer for the *The New Yorker* during the thirties." Dr. Goodwin also cited one of his medical colleagues who assembled a gallery of some 150 American writers whom he regarded as "alcoholics or very heavy drinkers." One wag theorized that if the percentage of alcoholic great plumbers equaled the percentage of alcoholic great writers, "the drains of America would be constantly clogged." In the end, Goodwin submits, the circumstance that cause alcoholism to flourish among writers may be unexplainable, although a number of possibilities have been advanced, among them *The Loner Theory*, the work of an historian named Gilman Ostrander (himself not a loner) who posited the notion that "Alcoholism is basically a disease of individualism. It affects people who from early childhood develop a strong sense of being psychologically alone and on his own in the world." Ostrander continues, "This solitary outlook prevents them from gaining emotional release through associations with other people, but they find they can get this emotional release by drinking. So they become dependent on alcohol in the way other people are dependent on their social relationships with friends and relatives." Goodwin, in turn, suggested that writers write because they are loners. It is, he speculated, "a profession which allows the individual to be tremendously convivial all by himself," adding that "writing and drinking are two forms of companionship," ergo Jews and Japanese enjoy a lower alcoholism rate because they rather expect their children to be more socially responsible. Goodwin advanced other curious theories, among them that to be a loner means that one "may facilitate trancelike states when it is time to write[,] and encourage drinking to overcome the shyness and isolation when it is time to relax."

Another school of non-thought has it that, to prevent your stumbling into more seclusion than you presently are in, the best way to write is in groups, a supposedly encouraging environment that we emphatically do not recommend. This communal process begins when you post a notice at your local English department or bookstore. When interested parties turn up, you do what is necessary to entrap them by letting them understand that writing cannot be accomplished alone. It requires old fashioned teamwork. Ask Shakespeare; he never thought of a good dramatic subject on his own. Neither did Chaucer. One anonymous writing organizer warns that to keep writing groups together is not easy, since "writers are a solitary lot and they tend to show up once and decide it is not for them." The problem? "They think writing is for loners." We cannot imagine how anyone could form that impression. Begin, then, by "instilling everyone in the group with a sense of community." That should help. So should assembling a socially aggressive loner club, attending public readings, book signings and barbecues. One source reminds us that "Even writers need a night out from time to time," a point, as one might say, well taken. Writers should ease out of their high-vaulted chambers, as Goethe's Faust did (with disastrous results), tip a few pints and acquire some new mates with literary inclinations. Elizabeth Svoboda has written in *Psychology Today* that whereas "In our society loners are pegged as creepy or pathetic," still and all, "outgoing people savor the nuances of social interactions, [whereas] loners tend to focus more on their own ideas." We don't like the sound of that. Within his comprehensive "Fates Worse than Death" listing, Brian St. Claire-King includes, in the "Eccentrics" category: "Unfavorable Stereotypes — Intellectual loners, odd[balls], extremists, [those] incapable of being part of a social unit." Svoboda, in turn, cites no less an authority than Jonathan Cheek, a Wellesley College psychologist who warily warns us that "some people simply have a low need for affiliation." Quite true, but mainly they do not wish to be inconvenienced by well-intentioned people who organize and participate in writing groups. Svoboda also directs our attention to a chap in Cleveland who, if he writes alone, also dines alone, including on Thanksgiving, so as to be spared visiting his brother-in-law's. When intellectuals consume coffee, chances are it's the *intelligentsia* blend, the precise content of which we are forbidden to disclose. We might, however, take the liberty to recommend a Hong Kong restaurant called *Mizu* that, according to more or less reliable eyewitnesses, "is a pleasure to visit, with scrumptious fusion food, both Asian and Western, a moody atmosphere with custom-made lanterns, and some real cute waitresses." There, at least, "You will see youngsters, intellectual loners (who love to be left alone) and expats." Moreover, "You will never forget the dining experience here, more so, because you have to enter the place bare footed." We have no problem with that, nor with the woman who, though divorced, is still "open to romantic relationships," with the proviso that she will continue to devote at least one day a week to locking herself in a room, the better to "stick feathers on a sculpture," which is more or less how writers of the solitary persuasion pass their choicer hours.

Loner-intellectuals are, as a rule, sufficiently equipped to function without anyone except professionals such as accountants, physicians, attorneys and so forth. The rest they can handle themselves. Politically, for example, the most likely place to hide, if any, is the 37-year-old Libertarian Party — which might conceivably get your vote, but not your application for membership, if indeed there is anything that merits joining. It advertises itself as the third largest political party in America but you usually can't find it, a sign that it represents something the two major parties don't want you to know about. As the Party itself says, "Many state governments place every imaginable roadblock in our path to keep our candidates off the ballot and deprive voters of a real choice," that choice being essentially smaller government, lower taxes and more freedom. Responds one unidentified source on why he is a Libertarian, "I'm a loner. This has two effects. First, it gives me a preference for liberty — leave me alone — over the community. Second, it means my political beliefs have not been shaped much by the opinion of other people." Interestingly enough, *The Washington Times* in December 2007 published an article claiming that whereas "card-carrying Libertarians are few and far between," nonetheless "libertarianism is palpably gathering steam," suggesting that the $8.5 million collected in support of Republican Ron Paul's quest for a 2008 run at the presidency has originated from "libertarian networks." It also cites Terry Teachout's recent *National Review* article suggesting that "small-L libertarianism has now attained a measure of cultural and intellectual respectability not far removed" from Reagan Era conservatism. Teachout mentions the Cato Institute's Brink Lindsay, who has argued that over the last half century that "the country has unconsciously arrived at a vaguely libertarian-ish consensus," namely something that is "culturally tolerant and yet demands personal responsibility for socioeconomic success." The Cato Institute itself explains that it is named "for Cato's letters, a series of libertarian pamphlets that helped lay the philosophical foundation for the American Revolution." The Cato to whom it refers is Marcus Porcius (95–46 BC), revered according to one source as "a man of unbending character, and absolute integrity, narrow, short-sighted, impervious to reason as to bribery." The same Cato (there were two in antiquity) was the subject of Addison's 1713 tragedy appropriately titled *Cato*. The Institute's having adopted Cato is perhaps an expression of the political right's intellectual tendencies. In any event, its "mission" is to "allow consideration of the traditional American principles of limited government, individual liberty, free markets, and peace," which on the surface sounds appealing enough. A Cato Institute "Policy Analysis" prepared by David Boaz and David Kirby argues "that some 10 to 20 percent of voting-age American are libertarian, tending to agree with conservatives on economic issues and with liberals on personal freedom," noting also that "Libertarians preferred George Bush over Al Gore by 72 to 20 percent," albeit "Bush's margin dropped in 2004 to 59-38 over John Kerry." They conclude by saying that "the libertarian vote is in play. At some 13 percent of the electorate, it is sizable enough to swing elections. Polsters, political strategists, candidates and the media should take note of it."

We hasten to add that for intellectuals to be associated with politics — or universities — is to soil their hands. Politics, for its part, has received especially well-deserved thumpingly bad reviews. "There is a holy, mistaken zeal in politics as well as religion," said the poet we remember only as *Junius*. "By persuading others, we convince ourselves." Remarked the Reverend Francis Cary, "Confound their politics/ Frustrate their knavish tricks." Henry Adams advised, "Practical politics consists in ignoring facts." Albert Camus once growled, quite spitefully, that "Ceux qui ont une grandeur en eux ne font pas de politique." (Those who have greatness within them do not go in for politics.) R. A. Butler attempts to assure us with counterfeit self-confidence that "Politics is the art of the Possible." Not so, said John Kenneth

Galbraith, who advised Jack Kennedy in a letter that "politics is not the art of the possible," but that it "consists in choosing between the disastrous and the unpalatable." So odious is it that Harold Wilson said that "a week is a long time in politics," something that one can easily imagine. Of particular interest to loners is C. Northcote Parkinson's jocular quip that men "enter local politics solely as a result of being unhappily married." Even the American journalist James Reston has assured his readers that "All politics...are based on the indifference of the majority." The point is that politics is a filthy, disreputable calling, so much so that it sullies whoever so much as touches it. The British man-at-large Matthew Pearce has written with unusual conviction that "Politics in America is mired in filth. When desperate men want to win the vote they will resort to almost anything."

The only safe quarter for a deeply reclusive intellectual is to be found in an ivory tower sufficiently elevated and fortified to keep him from harm's way. To leave that tower is to court disaster. That myth is best paradigmatically played out, as noted *in passim* (and with certain obvious omissions here) in Goethe's *Faust*, where (in the Kaufmann English translation) Faust the reclusive scholar is socked away, not precisely in an ivory tower but nonetheless in a "high-vaulted, narrow Gothic den," bitterly complaining that the intellectual life has played him dismally false despite his having presumably mastered philosophy, jurisprudence, medicine "and worst of all" theology — only to be left "the wretched fool I was before." Having renounced the scholar's life, he believes now that his scholarly energies have led nowhere. Faust then resorts to magic to assuage his torment while "Confined with books...every tome/ Is gnawed by worms, covered with dust." He resolves to leave his chamber to mix with ordinary folks in the streets. A cynical, rather comical spirit arrives to taunt him, as does the figure of Wagner, rather in the role of a sententious graduate student who is sufficiently shallow and pedantic and who searches naively for knowledge. "I've studied matters great and small;/Though I know much, I should like to know all," he declares, referring to the same futile quest for universal knowledge that Faust has shortly before denounced as altogether pointless. Faust in his spiritual desperation is on the verge of suicide by poison when at this critical moment the atmosphere rings out with Easter chimes that manage to rescue his spirit. In the next section he does indeed depart his high-vaulted chamber to take to the streets amid the common people who are with joyous abandon celebrating Easter as an advent of spring. Faust too experiences a sense of relief, proclaiming that "Released from the ice are river and creek,/ Warmed by the spring's fair quickening eye;/The Valley is green with hope and joy." He returns to his scholar's study fatigued but elated ("The love of man stirs in us deep,/ The love of God is stirring now"), until he opens an Old Testament he is attempting to translate into his "beloved German," only to be frustrated by insurmountable problems in the translative process.

The cynical Mephistopheles, "dressed as a traveling scholar," then appears from behind a stove. Faust immediately sees behind his guise that he is a devil whom one may identify as "the Liar, Destroyer, God of the Flies." Mephisto confirms that he is "the spirit that negates," and that he furthermore represents "everything that your terms sin,/Destruction, evil represent — / That is my proper element." Faust dozes off, whereupon Mephisto enlists help from airy spirits to "dazzle him with dream shapes, sweet and vast,/ Plunge him into an ocean of untruth." In the following scene, Faust concedes that he is at once "too old to be content to play,/Too young to be without desire," whereupon he again wishes to die. Mephisto reappears to strike that famous pact, or wager as it is sometimes called, between himself and Faust, the gist of which is that in this life Faust will be the master, Mephisto the "bond" (slave); whereas in the life to come, those roles will be reversed. Faust agrees and, having renounced the scholar's life, begins a quest for sensual pleasure, proclaiming, "I loathe the knowledge I once sought./In sensuality's abysmal land/ Let our passions drink their fill!" Another student visits him, only to have Faust deliberately mislead him with cynical advice that concludes with the student's reading in Latin "Eritis sicut Deus, scientes bonum et malum," lifted from *Genesis* 3:5 ("You will be like God, knowing good and evil") — the words with which the serpent temps Eve to eat the forbidden fruit. In the section called the "Witch's Kitchen," Faust, whose age has magically been reduced by 30 years to about the age of 20, sees, or believes he sees, a blissful womanly image in a mirror. Faust assumes that he's fallen in love, and orders Mephisto, per their pact, to procure her. The woman who corresponds to the figure in the mirror is Margaret, familiarly known as Gretchen, who, when we first encounter her, has just returned from her confessional in unassailable purity (Mephisto says that "She saw her priest just now,/And he pronounced her free of sin," adding that "She's so blemishless/ That there was nothing to confess"). In the section called simply "Street" we discover Faust in the process of winning Gretchen's heart as a first step toward seducing her, although Faust has not only developed an ever-intensifying enmity between himself and Mephisto but changed in a way that troubles even himself, saying, "Poor Faust! I do not know you anymore," while also conceding that his lust has turned to love. In preparation for the seduction, Gretchen attempts to evade her mother's discovery of the tryst by causing her mother to ingest a substance that will bring slumber; instead, it brings death. When we reach the scene entitled "At the Well," we learn that Gretchen is pregnant and humiliated. Her arrogant brother tells her that she has disgraced him, and soon after dies at the hands of Mephisto. When we reach the scene entitled "Dismal Day" we discover that that not only has Faust recovered his moral nature, but that he now cares more for Gretchen than for himself, although Mephisto reminds Faust that if he wishes to transcend morality he must forsake the luxury of a conscience. In the meantime, Gretchen is imprisoned at the gallows where she faces beheading for drowning her child. When Faust appears before her, the chains fall from her body. The first part of Goethe's *Faust* ends ambiguously. Gretchen remarks that this was to have been her wedding day, although Faust, cad that he is, has never intended to marry her. As Mephisto awaits her, evidently with the intention of carrying her off to Hell, Gretchen cries aloud, "Thine I am, father. Save me!" Mephisto cries out that "She is judged," whereupon a voice from above says simply, "Is saved," the meaning of which is clear enough: she has found redemption. Faust, however, disappears with Mephistopheles while Gretchen calls out his name in seeming desperation. Faust too is eventually saved, but not until the end of the drama's second part and with the intervention of what's usually called the *eternal feminine*.

Goethe's *Faust*, itself the product of a half century's work, is endlessly rich in irony and thematic implication which repeated textual examination can scarcely begin to elucidate. Let us posit for our own purposes that only a painstaking examination of the drama treats (among an array of other matters) the tortured plight of the reclusive but still restless scholar who in this instance is as learned as he is profoundly troubled by the failure of that leaning to address the most basic of life's dilemmas and metaphysical longings. At the beginning we are confronted with the conflict between the scholar's life and the life of the street; the life of the mind and the life of the senses; the life of discipline and the life of undisciplined freedom; the life of the spirit and the life of the body, the life of damnation and the life of redemption. It might be appropriate, if simplistic, to infer that had Faust known his place and stayed in it, the misery of what then subsequently transpired would never have come to pass. It indeed suggests to us that while the scholar's existence is less than ideal, it still preferable, although when we first encounter Faust the scholar we find that inasmuch as he has attempted to learn all, he has unwittingly (if perhaps unintentionally) attempted to mimic God. He even asks, "Am I a god? when he first appears in the drama. He has attempted to possess universal knowledge and understanding — a foolhardy quest wherein the scholar undermines himself. One is consequently put in mind once more of the stern admonition that the Lord God sets down in *Genesis*, namely that in the Eden, "You may eat from every tree in the garden, but not from the tree of the knowledge of good and evil; for on the day that you eat from it, you will certainly die." Having later transgressed against this very prohibition, Adam later claims that Eve made him do it. Maybe she did. Faust, on the other hand, has no one to blame but himself, having made that ill-considered pact with Mephisto, and having been disloyal to his own calling as scholar. In doing so set off a series of catastrophes that include three deaths and his bargaining away eternity as manservant to a devil. The problem is his self-abandonment among the common folks in whose company he is plainly ill-suited. He now seems a somewhat bored middle-aged loner-turned-rake, given to chasing the inaccessible. Out on the streets he chances to encounter a grateful old peasant who recalls the days when the young Faust practiced medicine with his father and thereby preserved the lives of many, some of whom "stand here, still alive,/ Whom your good father toiled to wrest/ From the hot fever's burning rage/ When he prevailed over the pest." Faust moves on, cynically advising the old peasant, in effect, to keep the faith. Shortly after, Faust tells Wagner that his father was nothing more than a fraud, as is Faust himself, and that "though the patients died,/ Nobody questioned: who got well." Indeed, outside of his high vaulted chamber, Faust does not mix well with people, and confronts himself as fallen scholar and opportunistic imposter.

Goethe's version of the Faust myth underscores the scholar-intellectual's "predicament" in the modern world, in that Faust's inquiring mind has left him profoundly dissatisfied in and out of his high chamber, the result being that he is spiritually homeless. Solitude does not altogether satisfy his longing, nor does the presence of others. Faust is insufficiently committed to live harmoniously among his books and papers, since his years of study have raised more questions than they have settled, leaving him in a rage. On at least two occasions he rails at the futility of academic inquiry. "Called Master if Arts, and Doctor to boot," he says on his first appearance, "For ten years almost I confute/ And up and down, wherever it goes,/ I drag my students by the nose — / And see that for all out science and art/ We can know nothing." By contrast, the pedantic Wagner says that he is not only content, be eager to charge ahead with his studies. "Most zealously I've studied matters great and small," he tells Faust, "Though I know much, I should like to know all." Later in the drama Faust reiterates, "I loathe the knowledge I once sought," and a few lines later claims that he has been "cured from the craving to know all." Mephisto voices essentially the same view in the "Study" scene when he dons Faust's academic cap and gown to masquerade as a scholar, the better to mislead a young student who arrives seeking academic counsel. Mephisto claims to have "contempt for reason and for science," at the moment the student arrives, and proclaims, as Wagner had done, that he aspires to universal knowledge. He even echoes Faust's impatience with the cloistered life, saying that "I should like to run away./ I cannot say I like these walls,/ These gloomy rooms and somber halls." From this point forward Mephisto clouds the student's mind with cynical views on the glories of learning, something that he will seize as if from a mother's breast and "drink each day with greater zest." The student, wanting a leave the correct impression, says that it is erudition he seeks, and that "nature and science is what I need." Mephisto urges him "to start with Logic," and later "give metaphysics your attention." After telling the poor fellow to select "a field of concentration," the student declares that "I almost think that theology would pay," something that of course rubs Mephisto the wrong way. "When it comes to this discipline," he replies, "wrong roads abound." Impatient, Mephiso then (in an aside) declares that he is going to stop the pedantry and play the devil that he is. He proceeds to advise the student to consider medicine because it is "easy to know," and because he can someday give women patients preferential attention, since "Their everlasting sighs and groans/ In thousand tones/ Are cured at *one* point everywhere." Moreover, he continues to recommend, "Right at the start, remove her clothes and touch her bust," should he want "Things for which others wait for years and years." The student, seeing the light of learning now burning bright, replies, "That looks much better, sir."

By this time, Faust has fallen from his ivory tower, where he seems to have self-quarantined so as not to harm anyone. A *tour d'ivoire* is a suggestive image that brings to mind the purity that whiteness often denotes. In 1956, a popular Eisenhower-era singer named Cathy Carr made herself a little more popular by singing, "come down, come down, from your ivory tower." The expression *to tower* suggests rising high, surpassing, and be imposing. The *OED* takes the term *ivory tower* generally to suggest "a condition of seclusion or separation from the world," and more generally "protection or shelter from the harsh realities of life." It is, in other words, a retreat especially suited to most of the intelligentsia, the better to clear their minds of the clutter, mindless disruption and vulgarity that life attends. It calls to mind nuns in their convents, monks in their monasteries, hermits in their hermitages. These are also places to hide from television, a goodly part of the population, the Internal Revenue Service, rappers, televangelists, politicians and car salesmen.

Whether hermitages of this sort are intellectually private is difficult to say. It is conceivable that "ivory tower" may be read as a euphemism for madhouse to harbor unreconstructed mavericks. They also put us in mind of light (in the sense of enlightenment) houses where estrangement may be elevated to a high art. In 1892, Henry James published a short piece called *The Private Life*, containing a character named Clare Vawdrey who achieves his privacy through his double, his doppelgänger. While one of them is out in public, the other is stashed away in his room. One is the public self; the other is his reclusive alter-ego. James also undertook a novel called *The Ivory Tower* that, by reason of his death, was never completed but left in a fragmentary state and published posthumously in 1917. In it is a passage that reads with characteristically Jamesian whimsy, "Doesn't living in an ivory tower mean the most distinguished retirement?" The remark reminds one of James's purported last words: "So here is at last, the distinguished thing." Faust fails to do anything distinguish himself except to destroy an innocent girl. As Logan Pearsall Smith (the same one who acerbically observed that "a best-seller is the gilded tomb of a mediocre talent") has written, "When they come downstairs from their ivory towers, idealists are very apt to walk straight into the gutter."

One would hope not, although intellectuals, even real ones, can become a menace (or at the very least a nuisance) to themselves as well as to society. Willa Cather's *The Professor's House* (1925) has as its vulnerable protagonist a certain Godfrey St. Peter, the introverted historian whose ivory tower is the attic of his old home in the comfort of his library and papers, although a series of personal problems motivate him to attempt suicide. The great and still underappreciated butterfly chaser Vladimir Nabokov first published his seriocomic novel of academe [1] entitled *Pnin* in 1953. He writes early in

---

1 The so-called "novel of academe" or "academic novel" is the ideal place to uncover portraiture of the intellectual-as-loner, since this sort of personality usually receives what we might call literary top billing in this ever-expanding sub-genre. Novels of academe are usually — but not always — satiric and wryly comic, and are often written by those who know academia best: the disgruntled academics who in turn write for other disgruntled academics. Here are some representative titles: Max Beerbohm, *Zuleika Dobson* (1911); F. Scott Fitzgerald, *This Side of Paradise* (1920), Willa Cather, *The Professor's House* (1925); Dorothy Sayers, *Gaudy Night* (1936); Kingsley Amis, *Lucky Jim* (1953); Mary McCarthy, *Groves of Academe* (1953); Randell Jarrell, *Pictures from an Institution* ((1954); Malcolm Bradbury, *Eating People is Wrong* (1959), *Stepping Westward* (1965) and *The History Man* (1975); Bernard Malamud, *A New Life* (1961); Tom Sharpe, *Porterhouse Blue* (1974); David Lodge, *Changing Places* (1975), *Small World* (1984) and *Nice Work* (1988); Armanda Cross, *Death in a Tenured Position* (1981); Robertson Davies, *The Rebel Angels* (1982); Don Delillo, *White Noise* (1985); Bret Easton Ellis, *The Rules of Attraction* (1987); Barbara Pym, *An Academic Question* (1986); Anne Bernays, *Professor Romeo* (1989); A. S. Byatt, *Possession: A Romance* (1990); John Kenneth Galbraith, *A Tenured Professor* (1990); Robert Grudin, *Book: A Novel* (1992); Jon Hassler, *Rookery Blues* (1995) and *The Dean's List* (1997); Carl Djerassi, *The Bourbaki Gambit: A Novel* (1994); Michael Chabon, *Wonder Boys*

the novel "Man exists only insofar as he is separated from his surroundings." The novel's outcast and protagonist is a 52-year-old potato-nosed anti-hero named Professor Timofey Pnin, aka "Mr. Tim," an escapee from "Leninized Russia" now teaching Russian to one student at Waindell College. Pnin has "an apish upper lip...a tightish tweed coat...a pair of spindly legs...almost feminine feet" attired in "sloppy socks," a "flamboyant goon tie" and long underwear. We discover him first as a railway passenger, but he happens to be aboard the wrong train. No passengers seat themselves either next to him or across from him. We are told that that "his life was a constant war with insensate objects that fell apart, or attacked him, or refused to function, or variously got lost as soon as they entered his company." He is, as we can hardly overlook, "inept with his hands to a rare degree." Moreover, Pnin becomes the campus's person most likely to be mimicked. One faculty fop carries the mimicry for over two hours, depicting Pnin teaching, Pnin eating, Pnin ogling a coed, Pnin narrating the epic of the electric fan, Pnin attempting to convince a colleague that they were "old pals." It was, says the narrator, "all built around the Pninian gesture and the Pninian wild English." As Nabokov's biographer Brian Boyd correctly asserts, "Pnin soon becomes an object of pathos as an exile, and ex-husband, a man alone, mocked and misunderstood...constantly at war with objects (alarm clocks, eyeglasses, zippers), a parody of the solitary intellectual as much lost among the philistines as a trinket trader among the savages." If, as Nabokov writes, "genius is non-conformity," then Pnin is an exemplary genius. "I don't care much for football," he says in passing. "In fact, I hate football. I'm not good at any game, really." Pnin fails his driving test "mainly because he started an argument with the examiner in an ill-timed effort to prove that nothing could be more humiliating to a rational creature than being required to stop at a red light when there was not an earthly soul around, heeled or wheeled." Pnin unwittingly becomes embroiled in campus politics and loses his job, commenting simply, "So they have fired me," then "clasping his hands and nodding his head." In the end, Pnin is one more wise fool, one more alienated intellectual, one more impractical buffoon, one more homeless scholar, alone and abandoned, this time at the whim of a small, petty, insignificant university. Waindell is little more than a ship of fools: a "somewhat provincial institution aptly characterized by an artificial lake in the middle of a landscaped

---

(1995); James Hynes, *Publish and Perish* (1997) and *The Lecturer's Tale* (2001); Jonathan Lethem, *As She Climbed Across the Table* (1997); Richard Russo, *Straight Man* (1997); J. M. Coetzee, *Disgrace* (1999) and *Elizabeth Costello* (2003); Francine Prose, *Blue Angel* (2000); Philip Roth, *The Human Strain* (200); and Elaine Showalter, *Faculty Towers* (2005).

campus, by ivied galleries connecting the various halls, by murals displaying recognizable members of the faculty in the act of passing the torch of knowledge from Aristotle, Shakespeare and Pasteur to a lot of monstrously built farm boys and girls." The chief casualty in all this is the intellectual, properly defanged and socialized to act as a cog in the wheel of the education industry, a bewildered intellectual on the wrong train in the wrong week and (as we're told in the novel's final sentence) carrying "the wrong lecture."

Goethe, as we know, placed universities and their supposedly intellectual wares in a defensive light. A more sanguine John Henry Newman in 1852 published *The Idea of a University*, calling such an institution simplistically, "the assemblage of strangers from all parts *in one spot*; — from all parts; else how will you find professors and students for every department of knowledge? And *in one spot*; else, how can there be any school at all?" He continues by calling a university "a school of knowledge of every kind," consisting of "teachers and learners from every quarter." It was, in other words, a vital convergence for education: teaching as much as learning.

Hence we encounter the intellectual as comedian. To find comedy, one must find something toward which he can feel superior. The unlettered Mark Twain transformed his honorary academic degrees into deprecating humor. So did Robert Frost who, after receiving Litt.Ds from Dartmouth, Harvard Amherst, Durham (England), Oxford and Cambridge, in addition to an LL.D from the University of Michigan, has been accused of anti-intellectualism, and who declared once that he had never earned an "honest" academic degree. Of course, it is one thing to joke about oneself, another thing to aim humor at someone else. Hollywood, itself anti-intellectual, has long depicted intellectuals as foppish crackpots. Beside the aforementioned *Animal House*, other titles in that genre are *Revenge of the Nerds* (1984), *Back to School* (1986), *Van Wilder* (2002) and *Old School* (2003), not to mention numerous campus films from the 1930s that seem always to involve a goofy, distracted professoriat and an immense institutional preoccupation with "the big Saturday football game with State." Among the celluloid favorites: *College Hounds*, and *College Lovers* (1930), *Huddle* (1932), *College Humor* (1933), *Hold 'Em Yale* (1928 and 1935), *We Went to College* (1936), *Hold 'Em Navy* (1937), *Hold That Co-Ed* (1938) and *$1,000 a Touchdown* (1939). There are old jokes, lots of them, about campus politics, as for example why Socrates could not be a candidate for a philosophy professorship, the response being that he has no Ph.D., no publications, no teaching experience. He admits to knowing nothing, he spends too much time partying, he wears a bed sheet and no shoes, he lets anyone into his classes, he doesn't charge tuition, he has no syllabus, he's a pedophile with suicidal tendencies, he has an arrest record and worst of all, he's past retirement age. Next? There is another old canard about why God is ineligible for tenure. He may have created the world, *but what has he done recently?* He has only one publication, it wasn't in a refereed journal, and we're not sure he wrote it himself. He rarely shows up in class. He dumped his first two students because they knew too much. Finally, how many full professors does it take to screw in a light bulb? Answer: One. He holds the bulb up to the socket and waits for the world to turn.

Pnin floats somewhere in this comedic soup, but as with most humor a serious undercurrent runs through the story and transcends the comedy because it speaks to the role of the intellectual in American culture. He is an old-world scholar. Henry Jacoby, who confesses his weakness for "university libraries, endless bookstacks [and] giant periodical rooms," has written that intellectuals who were "raised in city streets and cafes before the age of massive universities," are the "last" of their kind who "wrote for the educated reader." He also cites one survey that reveals that close to 40 percent of college and university faculty members are so "deeply troubled" that they are "willing to leave the academy." Pnin, for one, is a benignant, rather endearing soul, the ideal target for victimization: an alien academic drifter who has survived in a succession of rented rooms, vaguely in the tradition of the Wandering Jew, a figure who suffers perpetual exile. He also suggests one rooted in the tradition of the wandering scholar of the 12th and 13th centuries. Pnin is such a peregrinator, alienated by his intellect, inasmuch as that intellect remains a threatening, subversive figure bearing secrets and dangerous ideas that, like some vile disease, threatens to poison the populace at large. It is the mere gathering of those dangerous thoughts that cause him to become, despite his benignity, a public menace. As Patricia Owen-Smith has written, "It sometimes appears as if alienation is an imperative for scholarly research," which it assuredly is; the more one engages in the travels of the mind, the more alienated he necessarily is. Thoreau, as John Aldrich Christie emphasized thirty-five years ago, advised us to "live at home like a traveler," while at the same time he showed "all the signs of a global traveler" even if he actually "traveled a good deal in Concord." That does not change the perception of Thoreau's being any less dangerous, however, since in 1848 it was he who proclaimed, in the pages of "Civil Disobedience" (originally called "Resistance to Civil Government"), "That government is best which governs least," shortly amended to read, "government is best which governs not at all." He also had the audacity to suggest "Law never made a man a whit more just," and that "all voting is a sort of gaming," and most damning of all, if one is placed in the position of doing an injustice to another, then by all means, "break the law. Let your life be a counter-friction to stop the machine," mindful that "the true place for a just man is also a prison." It shamed him that his government was also a slave's government. No less than Mahatma Gandhi acknowledged that it was Thoreau who had influenced his doctrine of passive resistance that later made itself felt in the American civil rights struggles of the 1960s. Henry remains in some respects the prototype of the modern subversive intellectual in America, always casting his confidence on the side of fabled American rugged individualism and the primacy of the single man versus the mob. Lawrence Buell commented, "Thoreau has become the closest approximation to a folk hero that American literary history has ever seen." His foot-high gravestone in Concord's Sleepy Hollow Cemetery carries the single name: *Henry*.

It is telling that most of Henry's travels were incubated in his fertile intellect after his having consumed goodly numbers of published travel accounts. Although Henry traveled far more than is generally known, he never felt exiled to the point that he departed American shores. Other writer-intellectuals of his stature have been variously driven and alienated like so many vagabonds and wastrels out of their native countries. James Augustine Aloysius Joyce, the stunningly brilliant Dubliner whose highly controversial *Ulysses* (1922) became without question the premier novel in the English language in the 20th century, left Ireland ("an old sow that eats her farrow") on December 1, 1902, referring to his birthplace as "dear dirty Dublin" and his culture as "a race of clodhoppers." Joyce endured the dilemma that artist-intellectuals have always confronted, namely unremitting rejection. When, for example, *Ulysses* first appeared, Harvard's Irving Babbitt disparaged the book as something composed "in an advanced stage of psychic disintegration." Dismissed like Nabokov's *Lolita* (1955) as mere pornography, *Ulysses* first appeared in American bookshops thanks to inept legal fumbling that ended in the Supreme Court (it had been banned not only in America, but also in England and Ireland). Morris Ernst noted that "the first week of December 1933 will go down in history for two repeals, that of Prohibition and that of the legal compulsion for squeamishness in literature." John M. Woolsey, a none-too-bright United States District judge, claimed to have read the novel and judiciously decided that he "did not detect anywhere the leer of the sensualist," and although he found the reading experience "somewhat emetic, nowhere does it tend to be an aphrodisiac." Thank heaven.

The stylized record of Joyce's youth to about the age of 20 is captured in *A Portrait of the Artist as a Young Man* that he began in 1904 but did not publish until 1916. In this *Bildungsroman*,[1] more properly *Kunstlerroman*,[2] he appears as Stephen Dedalus (alluding to both St. Stephen, the first Christian martyr, and to Daedalus, the legendary Athenian smith whom Athena taught), although in the novel he tends to come across as a rather irascible youth and an invincible loner. His school friend (of which he has quite few) Davin tells him toward the end of the novel, "You're a terrible man, Stevie...Always alone." In the climactic end of the narrative, Stephen fantasizes upon what he believes awaits him: "The spell of arms and voices: the white arms of roads, their promise of close embraces and the black arms of tall ships that stand against the moon, their tale of distant nations. They are held out so to say: We are alone. Come." His mother, while putting his second-hand clothes together for his voyage, prays "that I [Stephen] may learn in my own life and away from home and friends what the heart is and what it feels." In the final sentence he alludes to his mythic counterpart Daedalus, saying, "Old father, old artificer, stand me now and ever in good stead." His departure represents a startlingly final separation from his county, his church and his family, the influence of all three of which permeate the novel. Perhaps nowhere in literary annals is there a more powerfully poignant rendering of the intellectual's separation from the menace of the philistinism of which Joyce, as a scholar and solitary talent, was all too well aware. In a letter to Bennett Cerf at Random House, he wrote that "Publishers and printers alike seemed to agree among themselves, no matter how divergent their points of view were in other matters, not to publish anything of mine as I wrote it." He continued, "No less than twenty-two publishers and printers read the manuscript of *Dubliners* and when at last it was printed some very nice person bought out the edition and had it burnt in Dublin — a new and private auto-da-fe."

American literati have long been inclined to expatriate themselves on real or imagined pretexts. Most of them repaired to Europe, preferring its immensely richer historical heritage. Most of them are to be regarded as "young men from the provinces," to borrow a phrase from Lionel Trilling that refers to naïve young fictional questers like Stephen Daedalus who bravely leave their homelands to discover more congenial environments elsewhere. Poe was not one of them, although he felt the misfortune of the artist in an

---

1 A Bildungsroman is a coming-of-age novel that treats a young man's (more often than a young woman's) arduous transition from childhood and adolescence into adulthood, as in Goethe's *Wilhelm Meister*, Dickens' *Great Expectations*, Joyce's *A Portrait of the Artist as a Young Man* and Salinger's *The Catcher in the Rye*.

2 A Kunstleroman is an apprenticeship novel that centers upon a young artist's aesthetic coming of age, as for example James's *Roderick Hudson*, Lawrence's *Sons and Lovers*, Maugham's *Of Human Bondage* and Atwood's *Cat's Eye*.

uncongenial atmosphere fostered in part by American anti-intellectualism. Hawthorne was not one, either; but he too complained in the Custom House preface to *The Scarlet Letter* about there never having been "the genial atmosphere which a literary man requires, in order to ripen the best harvest of his mind." He later accepted some governmental posts in Europe, and traveled widely there, but never considered himself an expatriate, although his wife Sophia moved to Germany and London after his 1864 death, and died in London despite having maintained a sort of honorary resting place near Thoreau and next to her husband back in Concord. She remained buried at Kensal Green Cemetery between 1877 and 2006, after which her remains were transported (using the same horse-drawn carriage believed to have carried Hawthorne to his grave) next to her husband's some 142 years later. She, by the way, viewed him as a strangely hermetic person, commenting "To the last he was in a measure to me a divine mystery; for he was so to himself."

The young novelist Joseph Conrad not only left his native Poland to become a commercial sailor, but also composed in English and became a British subject whose authorship never earned him the acclaim he deserved during his lifetime. Henry James and T. S. Eliot, to the contrary, not only took up residence in England, but also became British subjects. Although James counseled American writers to remain in America, he confessed in 1915 "about a twelvemonth hence I shall have been domiciled uninterruptedly in English for forty years, and there is not the least possibility...of my ever returning to the U. S. or taking up any relation with it as a country." Leon Edel records that on July 28, "accompanied by his solicitor, Henry James took the oath of allegiance to King George V.," saying "*Civis Britannicu sum*," then proudly announcing, "I don't feel a bit different." Eliot became a British subject in 1927, partly for the same reasons that Henry James (who had been tagged as an alien by the police, and had his whereabouts traced) also changed citizenship. Nevertheless, Tom Eliot believed that James had become more European than any European could have possibly been. Eliot, recently having been confirmed into the Anglican Church, said, "I don't like being a squatter. I might just as well take full responsibility." Some say that London was the cause of his death in 1965, since his smoking and his breathing the damp air allegedly encouraged the emphysema that carried him off, although Peter Ackroyd has noted that Eliot did not, in spite of his St. Louis birth, "believe himself to be an American at all," and that because he had worked assiduously to erase his American heritage, "There was nothing, either in his speech, his dress or his demeanor, that proclaimed the former middle-westerner."

No middle westerner, Ezra Weston Loomis Pound came from Idaho (where Hemingway died), an even less likely place for a world class litterateur and virulently anti-Semitic American expatriate of the fascist far right. Benjamin T. Spenser reminds us that Pound's longtime cohort Wyndham Lewis insisted that Pound "is — was always — must always remain, violently American," viewing him as an admixture of "Tom Sawyer, Whitman, Hemingway and Theodore Roosevelt." Others have placed Pound at the forefront of the precise and hard-edged American 20th century poets, although he rather got in his own way as an artist, delivering anti-American broadcasts from Italy between January of 1941 until July of 1943, often blaming Jews for international economic turmoil. That ended when American forces arrested him and penned him in a cage at an Army base near Pisa, after which he was judged mentally incompetent to face any kind of trial for 19 counts of treasonous activity, and warehoused at St. Elizabeth's mental hospital in Washington — from which he was released after 12 years through the poetic interventions of Eliot, MacLeish and Frost, the last of whom accepted most of the credit for having visited the Eisenhower White House expressly to make a case for "this difficult individual." In a sort of Parthian exchange, the hospital superintendent issued a statement saying that Pound was "permanently and incurably insane." That was in April, soon after which Pound was seen delivering some sort of poetical message on a hot afternoon while bundled in winter clothing. Expatriate to the end, he managed to qualify for a passport that permitted his return to Italy — partly financed by Ernest Hemingway, a fellow expatriate, to the extent of $1,000, a sum that was later returned to him as compensation for war wounds in World War I. Pound, in the meantime retorted that "I do not know how it would be possible to live in America outside a madhouse." There is a 1958 photograph of his delivering a fascist salute in Naples, although his death notice in *Time* ended by calling him "the man who never found a home."

Neither, for that matter, did Hemingway, another brazen young man exiled from the provinces, and literary bad boy with a mouth the rivaled Ezra Pound's. Ernest's ticket out of Oak Park, Illinois was, after having supposedly been rejected for military duty by reason of defective vision, as a volunteer ambulance driver for the Red Cross in Italy where the definitively crossed the line into manhood by having been severely wounded under mortar fire at Fossalta di Piave in July of 1918, 13 days before his 19th birthday. "I was an awful dope when I went to the last war," he wrote to his Scribner editor Max Perkins. "I can remember just thinking that we were the home team and the Austrians were the visiting team." He subsequently joined the Italian infantry until the end of World War I, then represented *The Toronto Star* for war coverage in the Near East, after which assumed residence in Paris where he became identified with other figures associated with the mostly English speaking "expatriate group" consisting of "Lost Generation" personalities such as Robert McAlmon, Gertrude Stein, Sylvia Beach, Malcolm Cowley, Wyndham Lewis, Max Eastman, William Carlos Williams, Joyce, Fitzgerald, Pound, not to mention Picasso, Matisse, and Leopold Stravinsky. Stein said, "Paris was where the 20th century was." Cowley's biographer Hans Bak called it "the intellectual capital of the United States," almost a "necessary 'second' country." Hemingway, of course, was to be identified with other places to which he could escape America, such as Spain, Africa, Cuba, Key West and finally Ketchum Idaho. To avoid becoming snared in American anti-intellectualism and philistinism, the *boobus Americanus* (as Mencken called them) or avoid having to suffer such Sinclair Lewis's not so glamorous Gopher Prairie types such as Fred Cornplow, George Babbitt and Lowell Schmaltz, American intellectuals continued their Parisian peregrinations, and otherwise betook themselves where they felt more comfortable writing their books and music, stretching their canvases. They had left American shores for other reasons. Randolph Bourne's *History of a Literary Radical* (1920), contends that America's aging generation had grown both conservative and stodgy; that it had refrained from considering some of life's more difficult questions; that it had disengaged itself from death (that frightened it), sex (that panicked it) and psychology (that mystified it)." Moreover, having lapsed into a comfortable routine of business, church and family life, it failed to address the current age's present needs and demands. "An excessive amiability," he wrote, "will... put a premium on conformity." Elsewhere, he warned, "folksiness evidently has its dark underlining in a tendency to be stampeded by herd emotion," and ominously, that "social conscience may become the duty to follow what the mob demands, and democracy may come to mean that the individual feels himself somehow expressed — his private tastes and intelligence — in whatever the crowd chooses to do." Mencken himself felt that the desire to rise socially was at the root of the American restlessness. Since the majority determines an individual's status, he individual assumes the protective coloration of the crowd and then wishes to be approved as one of its members.

As much as any fiction writer of that period and place. Francis Scott Key Fitzgerald movingly captured a sense of his own changing times, nostalgically remembered as the Jazz Age. As another young man from the provinces (Fitzgerald and Sinclair Lewis, were both Minnesotans), Fitzgerald was 28 when he published *The Great Gatsby* which even arrested the attention of T. S.

Eliot who claimed to have read it three times, concluding that "this remarkable book [that] seems to me the first step that American fiction has taken since Henry James." To express it, Fitzgerald had first to detach himself from American shores to find the necessary aesthetic distance. "In *The Great Gatsby*," Sergio Perosa wrote, "the motive of an impossible dream of love, which riches cannot fulfill after the right moment has passed over, finds it definitive consecration." Fitzgerald elsewhere in its pages struck upon some responsive chords, among them the failure of the American Dream and what Frederick J. Hoffman called "the vulgarization and venality of the privilege conferred by wealth." Neither the characters in the novel nor Scott and Zelda Fitzgerald sought the protective coloring that would cause them to blend with much of anything. Scott had been a loner since childhood. Biographer Scott Donaldson noticed that Fitzgerald in his ledgers had pointedly "recorded a series of childhood humiliations," such as the time when no one showed up at one of his birthday parties, when some boys at a potato roast told him to go away, and when he was (in his own words) "desperately unpopular" at a boys' camp. Donaldson cites Mencken's having said that "[l]iquor sends him [Fitzgerald] wild, and he is apt, when drunk, to knock over a dinner table, or run his automobile into a bank building." Donaldson also quotes Joseph Hergesheimer, the author of *Cytherea*, who recalled with implied disapproval that Fitzgerald caused a stir by rising from a dinner table, dropping his pantaloons and exposing himself. It was perhaps from having been on the outside looking in (he unobtrusively left Princeton in 1916 to avoid being dismissed for academic reasons) that he wistfully reflected upon his reckless youth. Whereas his intellectually-gifted classmate Edmund Wilson had Princeton to thank for a long and productive life in letters, Fitzgerald left it, the better to strike out on his own. He became, however, one of the important American literary voices of his time. Heywood Broun perhaps best captured the spirit of the Fitzgeraldian 20s through its published titles. "We begin," he said, "with the suggestion that Don Juan leads an interesting life (*Jurgen*, 1919); then we learn that there's a lot of sex around if we only knew it (*Winesburg, Ohio*, 1920), that adolescents lead very amorous lives (*This Side of Paradise*, 1920), that there are a lot of neglected Anglo-Saxon words (*Ulysses*, 1921 [*sic*]), that older people do not always resist sudden temptations (*Cytherea*, 1922), that girls are sometimes seduced without being ruined (*Flaming Youth*, 1922), that glamorous English ladies are often promiscuous (*The Green Hat*, 1924), that in fact they devote most of their time to it (*The Vortex*, 1926), that it's a damn good thing too (*Lady Chatterley's Lover*, 1928) and finally that there are abnormal variations (*The Well of Loneliness*, 1928, and *Sodom and Gomorrah*, 1929)."

For all their obvious faults and grievous imperfections, authors are fundamentally loners because writing is a deliciously solitary, sometimes civilizing activity. *The Great Gatsby*, most people will concede, could not have been written by a committee any more than a court case can be settled satisfactorily by a jury of dunces. Writers can, and do, behave in strange ways on strange occasions, which is why they would never have been acceptable fraternal candidates, obedient corporate citizens or spouses. Intellectually inclined loners are, if anything, worse, in that they not only have much to do with other people, but could not communicate with them successfully if they tried. As long as they have themselves in whom to confide, everyone else is both unnecessary and insufficient. Chances are that they're misanthropically inclined anyway, meaning that they don't hold the human race in particularly high esteem, but tend to view the world as composed mostly of dolts and jackasses around whom the banal world of television, for example, is expressly configured. Instead, they stay to themselves, and enjoy doing it. When they cast their chamber windows open, they may hear the distant sounds of nuptial bells, of raucous herds, of Christmas carolers, of tin horns touting someone's birthday, of Independence Day fireworks, or of corks popping on the eve of another year; but they remain profoundly grateful for being off the streets, alone and engaged instead in some intense activity of their own devising. They view society as consisting of herds and hermits. Since the single, independent life provides one with infinitely more options and opportunities, the individual is free to cast aside the things that others are obliged to acknowledge in one manner or another. "A man is rich," Thoreau wrote, "in proportion to the number of things which he can afford to let alone." Indeed, yes. Certain things can easily be, over time, altogether eliminated. Socializing, as we have seen, is all too convenient to forego because it is altogether pointless and free from any sort of reward for the time that one devotes to it. Those who embrace it tend to be excessively dependent upon the approval and endorsement of others whose approval and endorsement signifies nothing. The time that one might devote to social intercourse may better be put to other, better purposes such as sowing, reaping, sleeping, music, literature and exercise. Organized religion can profitably be eliminated by knowing God directly, without the manifest nuisances of preaching, appearing, supporting, witnessing, listening, singing, shouting, assembling, admonishing, handshaking, confessing, repeating, socializing, proselytizing, communing and (at last) disappearing. The independent person has no need for this and accordingly imposes a distance between himself and public displays of worship. Politics, as most people know, is disreputable and demeaning, as are the scoundrels who trade in it. To cast votes for politicians constitutes an endorsement of them that (as some have been heard to say) "only encourages them." Holidays, when observed, are wastes of time and money, and are therefore best ignored and devoted to other, more creative, possibly amusing activities. Although weddings are an occasion for grieving, and funerals for joyous celebration, the odds are strongly against inviting anyone who endorses this view. It is better, therefore, to stay innocent of them both — with or without an invitation. The ceremony that attends them has mainly been debased and trivialized, and is best not witnessed. Marriage, as almost anyone knows, or ought to know, doesn't work. It might be satisfactory for some people if it did work, but it doesn't. Anecdotal evidence supports this view, and so do statistics. If it were a hundred years ago when one married at 16, worked diligently at merely staying alive, then died at around 30, a marriage might have held together. But to marry at 18 and survive to 81, is quite another thing. It no longer works. Alas, it just doesn't work.

Now we know. In addition, speaking of knowing, many of the solitary figures to which we have referred show evidence of having known themselves — which is the point at which adult life begins. Self-understanding means that one can construct one's own life, by sifting the magnificent possibilities, the options, the choices, the commitments, the means, the ends and the rationale. Each person charts his own journey. It is the responsibility of every person to know where he wants to go — and then go there. It is everyone's obligation to himself, and the ultimate decision is one's own. The successes of certain people to whom we have referred are mainly the result of iron commitment and unflagging persistence. The individual is king. The mob is merely — the mob, the secret societies, the bureaucracies, the corporations, the political partied, the riff-raff, even (yes) the universities and what they've become. They like more than anything to discourage, undermine, derail and detract. They move in herds. They cannot survive without joining. Leaderless, they even resort to imitating each other. They destroy their own identity, if indeed they ever had one. The single, independent life is there for the claiming. In the end, it is the hermits who seize the confidence and the courage. In the end, the hermits prevail.

BIBLIOGRAPHY

Ackroyd, Peter. *T.S. Eliot: A Life*. New York: Simon and Schuster, 1974.

Aldridge, John W. *After the Lost Generation*. New York: Noonday, 1951.

Alexander, Paul. *Salinger: A Biography*. Los Angeles: Renaissance, 1999.

Allen, Frederick Lewis. *Only Yesterday: An Informal History of the 1920's*. New York: Harper & Row, 1931.

Allen, Gay Wilson. *Walt Whitman Handbook*. Chicago: Packard, 1946.

Arvin, Newton. *Herman Melville*. New York: Viking, 1950.

Bak, Hans. *Malcolm Cowley: The Formative Years*. Athens, GA: University of Georgia, 1993.

Bank, Stanley, (ed). *American Romanticism*. New York: Capricorn, 1979.

Barzun, Jacques. *Classic, Romantic and Modern*. New York: Anchor, 1961.

Beard, Charles A.and Mary R. *The Rise of American Civilization*. New York: Macmillan, 1930.

Becker, Carl L. *The Heavenly City of the Eighteenth Century Philosophers*. New Haven, CT: Yale University, 1932.

Beerbohm, Max. *Zuleka Dobson*. New York: Dodd, Mead and Company, 1911.Boswell, James. *Life of Johnson*. London: Oxford University, 1960.

Bourne, Randolph. *War and the Intellectuals*. Indianapolis: Hackett, 1999.

——. *The Radical Will*. New York: Urizen, 1977.

Boyd, Brian. *Vladimir Nabokov: The American Years*. Princeton, NJ: Princeton University, 1991.

Brooks, Van Wyck. *The Flowering of New England, 1815–1865*. New York: E. P. Dutton, 1937.

——. *New England: Indian Summer, 1865–1915*. New York: E. P. Dutton, 1940.

———. *The Times of Melville and Whitman*. New York: E. P. Dutton, 1947.

———. *The Ordeal of Mark Twain*. New York: Dutton, 1970.

Brown, Tamara L. *African American Fraternities and Sororities*. Lexington: University of Kentucky, 2005.

Brunvand, Jan H. *The Study of American Folklore*. New York: Norton, 1968.

Burton, Humphrey and Maureen Murray. *William Walton: The romantic Loner*. New York: Oxford, 2002.

Carpenter, Humphrey. *A Serious Character: The Life of Ezra Pound*. New York: Delta, 1988.

Cash, W. J. *The Mind of the South*. New York: Vintage, 1941.

Christie, John A. *Thoreau as World Traveler*. New York: Columbia University, 1965.

Cohen, Hennig (ed.) *The American Culture*. New York: Houghton Mifflin, 1968.

———. *The American Experience*. New York: Houghton Mifflin, 1968.

Cotterell, John. *Social Networks in Youth and Adolescence*. London: Routledge, 2007.

Cowley, Malcolm. *Exile's Return*. New York: Viking, 1934.

Davenport, Guy. *The Geography of the Imagination*. San Francisco: North Point. 1981.

DeVoto, Bernard. *Mark Twain's America*. Boston: Little, Brown, 1932.

Donaldson, Scott. *Hemingway vs. Fitzgerald*. Woodstock, NY: Overlook, 1999.

Dykstra, Robert C. *Losers, Loners and Rebels: The Spiritual Struggles of Boys*. Louisville, KY: Westminster-John Knox, 2007.

Edel, Leon. *Henry James* (5 vol). New York: Lippincott, 1953.

Ellmann, Richard. *James Joyce*. New York: Oxford, 1959.

———*Bloomsbury: A House of Lions*. New York: Avon, 1979.

Firchow, Peter (ed), *The Writer's Place*. Minneapolis: University of Minnesota, 1974.

Foot, Michael. *Loyalists and Loners*. London: Collins, 1986.

Frederickson, George and Joycelyn M. Johnson. *Public Management Reform and Innovation*. Tuscaloosa, AL: University of Alabama, 1999.

Fromm, Erich. *The Sane Society*. New York: Rinehart, 1955.

Gurvis, Sandra. *Careers for Non-Conformists*. New York: Marlowe, 2000.

Golden, Marissa M. *What Motivates Bureaucrats?* New York: Columbia University, 2000.

Goodwin, Donald W. *Alcohol and the Writer*. New York: Penguin, 1988.

Harding, Walter. *A Thoreau Handbook*. New York: New York University, 1976.

Herman, Stanley M. *A Force of Ones: Reclaiming Individual Power in a Time of Teams*. San Francisco: Jossey-Bass, 1994.

Hine, Thomas. *The Rise and Fall of the American Teenager*. New York: Bard, 1999.

Hofstadter, Richard. *Anti-intellectualism in American Life*. New York: Knopf, 1966.

———. *The Progressive Historians*. New York: Random House, 1970.

Jacoby, Russell. *The Last Intellectuals*. New York: Noonday, 1987.

Jones, Ricky L. *Black Haze*. Albany: State University of New York. 2004.

Kitto, H.D.F. *The Greeks*. New York: Penguin, 1951.

Lasch, Christopher. *The Culture of Narcissism*. New York: Norton, 1978.

Lawrence, D. H. *Studies in Classic American Literature*. New York: Viking, 1964.

Macionis, John J. *Sociology*. Upper Saddle River, NJ: Prentice Hall, 1987.

Martin, Ida Shaw. *The Sorority Handbook*. Boston: Roxburgh Press, 1909.

Mason, Eudo C. *Goethe's Faust*. Berkeley, CA: University of California, 1967.

Matthiessen, F.O. *American Renaissance*. New York: Oxford, 1941.

Maxwell, John C. *The 17 Essential Qualities of a Team Player*. Nashville: Thomas Nelson, 2004.

———. *The 17 Indisputable Laws of Teamwork*. Nashville: Thomas Nelson, 2004.

McBrien, William. *Cole Porter: A Biography*. New York: Knopf, 1999.

Mencken, Henry L. *The American Language*. New York: Knopf, 1919.

Mill, John Stuart. *On Liberty*. New York: Norton, 1975.

Miller, Perry. *The Raven and the Whale*. Baltimore: Johns Hopkins University, 1956.

Mommsen, Wolfgang. *The Age of Bureaucracy*. New York: Harper and Row, 1974.

Newer, Hank. *Broken Pledges*. Atlanta: Longstreet Press, 1990.

———. *High School Hazing*. New York: F. Watts, 2000.

———. *Wrongs of Passage*. Bloomington: Indiana University, 1999.

Parker, Glenn M. *Team Players and Teamwork*. San Francisco: Jossey-Bass, 1996.

Pippert, Timothy D. *Road Dogs and Loners*. Lanham, Md.: Lexington, 2007.

Posner, Richard A. *Public Intellectuals: A Study of Decline*. Cambridge, MA: Harvard University, 2001.

Putnam, Robert D. *Bowling Alone*. Baltimore: Johns Hopkins, 1996.

Ralph, Philip L. *The Story of Our Civilization*. New York: Dutton, 1954.

Reynolds, David S. *Beneath the American Renaissance*. Cambridge, MA: Harvard University 1989.

Riesman, David and Nathan Glazer. *The Lonely Crowd*. New Haven, CT: Yale University, 1950.

Robbins, Alexandra. *Pledged: The Secret Life of Sororities*. New York: Hyperion, 2004.

Rogers, Raymond. *Coming Into Existence: The Struggle to Become an Individual*. Cleveland: World Publishing, 1967.

Rousseau, Jean-Jacques. *Confessions*. London: Routledge, 2003.

Rufus, Anneli. *Party of One: The Loners' Manifesto*. New York: Marlowe, 2003.

Ruland, Richard. *The Rediscovery of American Literature*. Cambridge, MA: Harvard University, 1967.

Schaefer, Richard T. *Sociology Matters*. New York: McGraw-Hill, 2004.

Schlesinger, Arthur M. *The Crisis of the Old Order: 1919–1933*. New York: Houghton Mifflin, 1957.

Schwartz, Charles. *Cole Porter*. New York: Dial, 1977.

Sewall, Richard B. *The Life of Emily Dickinson*. New York: Farrar, Straus and Giroux, 1974.

Shirley, Mary M. *Bureaucrats in Business*. Washington: World Bank Group, 1995.

Shoemaker, Sidney. *Self-knowledge and Self-Identity*. Ithaca, NY: Cornell University, 1963.

Skotheim, Robert Allen, *American Intellectual Histories and Historians*. Princeton, NJ: Princeton University, 1966.

Stephens, Joyce. *Loners, Losers, and Lovers*. Seattle: University of Washington, 1976.

Sutherland, James, (ed.). *The Oxford Book of Literary Anecdotes*. New York: Oxford, 1975.

Tadie, Jean-Yves. *Marcel Proust: A Life*. New York: Penguin, 1996.

Tocqueville, Alexis de. *Democracy in America*. New York: Harper & Row, 1988.

Trawick, Leonard (ed). *Backgrounds of Romanticism*. Bloomington: Indiana University, 1967.

Turner, James. *The Liberal Education of Charles Eliot Norton*. Baltimore: Johns Hopkins University, 1999.

Vida, Vendela. *Girls on the Verge*. New York: St. Martin's Griffin, 2000.

Wallace, Ruth A. and Alison Wolf. *Contemporary Sociological Theory*. Englewood Cliffs, NY: Prentice Hall, 1980.

White, Michael. *C. S. Lewis: A Life*. New York: Carroll & Graf, 2004.

White, Theodore H. *In Search of History*. New York: Warner, 1978.

Wilson, Colin, *The Outsider*. Los Angeles: Tarcher, 1982.

Wolff, Sula. *Loners: The Life Path of Unusual Children*. London: Routledge, 1995.

Woodward, Robert H, and James J. Clark, eds. *The Social Rebel in American Literature*. New York: Odyssey 1968.

Whyte, William H. *The Organization Man*. New York: Simon and Schuster, 1956.

Young, Stanley Paul. *The Last of the Loners*. New York: Macmillan, 1970.

INDEX